MW00813241

Advance Praise for

How Crested Butte Became a Tourist Town:
Drugs, Sex, Sports, Arts, & Social Conflict

"Roger Kahn writes a love story to the small town of Crested Butte, Colorado that he discovered in the late 1960's when old miners, young ski bums, wandering hippies, and anonymous outlaws all convened in an idyllic high mountain nirvana that included cheap dope, copious sex and free roaming dogs....

"But that nirvana came with a clash of cultures not just between the old timers and the new pioneers but between the smart, young transplants who disagreed on how to grow the place. Kahn's love story probably describes a number of these wild, small town outposts in the mountains of America as the sport of skiing took hold of the general population in the 60s, 70s and 80s. Roger was fortunate to experience the early days of a special time that has been long abandoned in most of these places and he has the writing skill to bring those days back to life. He delves into the politics of growth and gentrification ...and while making clear the 'good time' can never be repeated, he explains how these communities that reflect the libertarian values of the 1960's continue to attract interesting, creative people looking for an alternative lifestyle."

—Mark Reaman, Editor, *Crested Butte News*

"Drawing on extensive interviews, archival research and personal experiences, Kahn vividly describes the social forces that defined the 1960s and 70s in Crested Butte. He deftly points his sociologist lens on this pivotal period of Crested Butte history, describing the various factions of people that lived in and moved to town, bringing with them different backgrounds, values, forms of expression and visions for the future. Kahn shows how the conflicts and collaborations, between these factions shaped Crested Butte's evolution into the tourist destination and recreation exurb that it is today. A must read for anyone interested in the history of Crested Butte, the US counterculture, and an engaging read about a wild time in a wild place."

—Shelley Popke, Executive Director,
Crested Butte Mountain Heritage Museum

"Towns and cities all have a 'birth' story but few have as a dramatic and different 'rebirth' story. After 72 years as a mining town and 10 years as an almost ghost town, *How Crested Butte Became A Tourist Town: Drugs, Sex, Sports, Arts, and Social Conflict* tells the story of a town emerging from its dormant cocoon, struggling to find its identity being pulled from divergent groups from old time miners to the counterculture radicals of the 60's. It reminded me of HBO's superb series "Deadwood" that showed how civilization is shaped by strong personalities and the need for some law and order."

—Jim Schmidt, Crested Butte mayor and
a town elected official for almost 30 years

"This is a detailed perspective on the transformation and evolution of community. The reader is treated to the spatial, cultural, economic and social elements that shape the places in which we live, work and play. This work reveals the political, personal, and familial challenges, that many have endured in their pursuit of 'life, liberty and happiness.' The book defines the journey that many communities like Crested Butte have taken, are taking, and *will* take resulting from the multiplicity of divergent lifestyles and societal norms occurring globally."

—Cedric D. Page, Professor Emeritus of Geography,
University of New Mexico at Los Alamos

How Crested Butte Became a Tourist Town

Drugs, Sex, Sports, Arts, and Social Conflict

a fun-filled social history

Roger Kahn

ISBN: 978-1-7339622-0-9 (Hardback)
ISBN: 978-1-7339622-1-6 (Paperback)
ISBN: 978-1-7339622-2-3 (e book)

Library of Congress Control Number: 2019904684

Cover images by Dusty Demerson
Book design by Lee Lewis Walsh, Words Plus Design

Printed in the United States of America

First edition 2019

Roger Kahn Publishing
2217 Forest Street
Denver, CO 80207
rogdikahn@aol.com

For my family, with love
Diane
Randy, Kelly, Eric, Jenifer
Taylor, Ashley, Daynan, Jackson, Reed

Contents

Acknowledgments

People interviewed: My heartfelt thanks to the following people who shared their memories and insights and granted me the time that was necessary for our formal interview/conversations. They made a great deal of this work possible: Noel Adam, Ed Benner, Nathan Bilow, Bob Brazell, Janet Carnes (nee Keyser), Steve Carson, Butch Clark, Kemp Coit, Mickey Cooper, Allen Cox, Bill Crank, Gloria "Glo" Cunningham, Brian Dale, Patricia Dawson, Ruth Esserman, Dan Gallagher, Denis Hall, Cotton Harris, Alan Hegeman, Dan McElroy, Lyn Faulkner, Susan Gardiner, Steve Glazer, Craig Hall, Linda Hall, Michael Helland, Lynda Jackson, Dan Jones, Walter Keith, David Lasky, Sandy Leinsdorf, Iris Levin, Wes Light, Nick Lypps, Dick Markwood, Gene Mason, Reggie Masters, Denny McNeil, Ceil Murray, Sue Navy, Mike Pilert, Myles Rademan, Henrietta Raines, Nick Rayder, Paul Roggenbuck, Eric Ross, Ron Rouse, Annie Rowitz, Richard Rozman, Barbara Segal, Candy Shepard, George Sibley, Cathy Sporcich, Randi Stroh, Tony Stroh, Ann Swanson, Roger Swanson, John Taylor, Terry Taylor, Jim Thomas, Tuck, Jim Wallace, Rob Wolf, Jay Wolcov, Trudy Yaklich, and John Zink.

Continuous conversations: The following people also contributed significantly to this project, through on-going but periodic conversations as this work evolved. I am grateful to them for their insights, critiques and patience: Susan Anderton, Cordley Coit, Kemp Coit, Dave Coney, Diane Kahn, Harold O'Connor, Ron Vaughan, and Alfredo Villanueva.

Archival assistance: For the cheerful assistance that was provided when they allowed me to access archives that helped document a lot of the written source material contained in this work, my thanks go to the Crested Butte Heritage Museum staff, especially Gloria 'Glo' Cunningham, Brooke Furimsky (nee, Murphy), Suzette Gainous, Barbara Mason, and Shelley Popke. The Denver Pubic Library and the Western State College Library micro-fish staff also provided important help.

Manuscript reviewers: Earlier versions of this work were generously, carefully, and critically read by Susan Anderton, Elizabeth Bruce, Bill Hynes, Diane Kahn, Bob Mahoney, Michael Oliver, Myles Rademan, George Sibley, Ron Vaughan, Bruce Watson and Erika Wentworth. Each of them challenged my thinking and their efforts made this work stronger. I am especially thankful to them, and assure them that they are not responsible for any of my errors of fact, descriptions, analyses, or conclusions.

Preface

A few days before Thanksgiving 1967, my wife, Diane, and I arrived for the first time in Crested Butte, Colorado. The tiny town had only five avenues that were intersected by six short streets. Modest, single family, wood frame houses were built right next to each other amidst an array of vacant lots scattered throughout the former mining town. We drove back and forth a few times along the wide, unpaved, and completely empty, pot-hole filled, dirt, main street before making a U-turn in the middle of it. We parked to look for the friend we were supposed to meet in one of the town's five bars.

Before we even got out of our rented Volkswagen, we were harassed by a surly, burly, twenty-something Crested Butte born and bred hardrock miner. He ran out of a bar across the street and stood on the driver's side of the car and leaned on top of it so I could not get out. He bellowed, "Do you make U-turns in the middle of the main street in the town where you come from?!" I later learned he was one of the town's elected councilmen. That incident was the first indication of the intense personal, social, and political conflicts that, along with the innumerable wildly good times, characterized the early development of Crested Butte in its latest iteration: a tourist town and recreation community.

That incident was the first indication of the intense personal, social, and political conflicts that, along with lots of wildly good times, characterized the birth and development of the contemporary version of Crested Butte: a tourist town and recreation community.

We slept on the couch of our counter-cultural ski patrolman friend, George Sibley. We hung out and partied with his friends, mostly new locals and one old-timer. We foot-packed snow at the ski area on Crested

1

Elk Avenue (main street) circa 1971.
Photo courtesy of Helen Wright

Butte Mountain for free skiing. We partook in a potluck dinner. We enjoyed meals and adult beverages in the local restaurants and taverns that, we came to understand, were where a lot of Crested Butte's overt cultural life was centered. The town's newest, The Fondue House, was on an alley behind a boarded-up former hotel on the town's main street. The restaurant opened by request for small parties. At a dinner there the evening before our week-long stay ended, one of our new acquaintances asked where I thought we should eat the following night. I said that he or someone else should make that decision because we had to leave to go back to school and work. Until that moment no one ever asked what degrees or pedigrees we had, or what kind of work we did.

Unlike our other young adult life experiences, where people's first question after learning one's name was typically, "What do you do?", that was unique, and heartwarming! When we left town the next morning, we were pensive. I found myself weeping silently as we drove down the poorly maintained, twisting highway. I thought we would never return again or bask in the "magic" we had just experienced. Despite our initial brusque encounter, our visit to Crested Butte turned into a love fest with the fun-loving people we met. Ultimately, it was a life-changing experience.

We returned to the Boston-Cambridge area to adopt our first son, Randy. If we had not been returning for him, we might have just remained in the little town that sat amidst the most majestic landscape we had ever seen. As had several other newcomers, we might have moved to Crested Butte right away.

In 1967 Crested Butte had fewer than 250 remaining mining-era residents; they stayed in town after the mines closed in the early 1950s. According to one of them, Leola Yaklich, they consisted of only about 15 interrelated extended families. There were sixty-nine abandoned, boarded up houses in town. A few years later the 1970 voting registration rolls included fewer than 35 separate mining-era family names, plus approximately 50 new people. The old town residents were resilient, resourceful, and strong, and the new ones were adventurous, creative, fun-loving, and they too were strong. Either by necessity or choice, each group lived a simple lifestyle.

We returned to Crested Butte for a short visit in the summer of 1968, this time with our eight-month-old son in tow, and we had another enchanting experience. We stayed in the rustic Cement Creek hunting cabin of one of the long-time native Serbian-American locals, Rudolph "Botsie" Spritzer, and we were welcomed back as long-lost friends by the newcomers and old-timers alike. We basked in the glorious summer days that made those who grew up in the area say, "Crested Butte is nine months of winter and three months of relatives." We lazed in the sunshine of Crested Butte's blue-like-nowhere-else skies, it's snowcapped mountain peaks, multi-colored wildflowers, and crystal-clear stream waters; and we took part in the constant revelry we found in the town's eating and drinking establishments. We hiked amid the huge rocks and fluttering aspens in Cement Creek and walked around Lake Irwin. We had an evening pot-luck campfire barbeque at Botsie's cabin with our unofficial welcoming committee.[1] We also went to our first back yard wild brook trout fish-fry and keg party at a house shared by three of the new people in town.[2] Then, within a week, we returned to our "real world": academia, arts, and activism.

During the following year, we returned to Crested Butte, sometimes spending more time on the road than we actually spent in the town. Given our deepening love affair with this welcoming wide-open community, it did not seem unusual to us to devote so much "windshield time," including driving through fierce lightning storms in the nation's flatlands, to spend only a few days in a rural mountain community that was unlike anything we had ever known. We did this to be with people who were mainly into the outdoors who had values and beliefs that differed significantly from ours, and those of our friends in the East and mid-West, who were all social activists in the civil rights and peace movements, academic intellectuals, and visual and performing artists.

During the summer of 1969, we returned for a longer stay. I had to study for doctoral exams, we had a young son to rear, and we were subsisting on a graduate student's meager research fellowship. Not only was rent cheaper in Crested Butte than it was where we lived on Long Island in New York but, above all else, it was Crested Butte!

We rented a small, sparsely furnished house for $40.00 per month. Our refrigerator was a wood-framed, wire rabbit hutch that we placed in the ice-cold water of a drainage ditch that was fed by melting snow; it ran immediately in front of the house. In the mornings, I studied at a desk in a corner of a newspaper office one short block from our place. In the afternoons, driving our new VW bug, I went to local scenic spots to study: Lake Irwin, Emerald Lake, Judd Falls, and Paradise Divide. Actually though, I sat, spaced out, and looked in awe at the incredible summer panoramas, or hiked in them. It was hard for me to study esoteric philosophers and social scientists and read books and scholarly journals when there was so much new beauty and a new culture to absorb. In the evenings, Diane, our young son Randy, and I visited and partied with our Crested Butte friends.

Near the end of that summer, following a tip about a family estate that had to be settled, the Evic's, we bought our first Crested Butte house. That lead came from a new local councilman, Don Bachman, who owned one of the old-timer's favorite drinking establishments, Tony's Tavern, (where a glass of beer cost ten cents.) Since we did not have an extra penny to our names or any credit, we borrowed $1,000.00 from each of four different friends and family members and paid cash for the house. It had not been lived in since 1952 when the last large operating coal mine in the area, the Colorado Fuel & Iron Company's "Big Mine" closed. The hardworking mining family of seven who lived in the house left to find work elsewhere. The house was a typical six hundred square foot, simple wood frame structure. It had one electric circuit with a light bulb hanging from the living room ceiling and a cold-water pipe running into the kitchen, sourced from our next-door neighbors' house (owned by Tony and Mary Gallowich.) It also had a pantry, a few small sleeping rooms, and an amazingly beautiful, big, old, coal-burning, Victorian pot belly parlor stove. Because of a recently enacted zoning ordinance, the house was located in the *"business"* district on the town's unpaved main street and sat on one-and-a-half 25' x 125' lots. Behind it there were some overgrown raspberry bushes, an outhouse, a smoke house, and a coal shed that backed up to an alley that separated two rows of similar houses.

Even though we left town shortly after purchasing our new "little old house," as property owners we then had a stake in Crested Butte. We opened a local bank account in Gunnison because Crested Butte had not had a bank since 1952. We also hired a highly respected Gunnison lawyer,

Marsh Seraphine, to represent us at the closing, because Crested Butte did not yet have any lawyers. Before we left, Diane took precise measurements of our new house. She was a stage set designer and had a great sense of space. Back East, she designed what eventually became our home, focusing first on getting a bathroom with functioning plumbing *inside*. Eventually, our house became the first complete modern renovation of an historic Crested Butte miner's simple wood frame home.

Once we had bought a house, people in town knew we would return. From more than two thousand miles away, we increasingly became *"locals,"* part of the community. I talked on the phone with our friends about the town's current events and wrote opinionated letters to the editor; Diane advertised in the local newspaper's tiny classified section that she would create and sell one-of-a-kind, tie-dyed, turtleneck shirts that were then in vogue among young people, promising "each one would be different in either Red, Blue, Green or Orange".

Diane and Randy returned to town in the summer of 1970. Diane installed our new bathroom with the help of a few Crested Butte old-timers and some early new town residents.[3] The local grocers, Tony and Eleanor Stefanic, and hardware store owner, Tony Mihelich, ran a tab for us, as they did for local residents, and even for the few "summer people" who only lived in Crested Butte one or two months a year.

That summer I was finishing a work commitment in one of our nation's national civil rights organizations. My job required me to travel nationally. I was able to arrange frequent stopovers in New Mexico and Colorado, especially around weekends, so I could visit my family and friends in Crested Butte. At the end of that summer we rented our little old house for $40.00 per month to a new friend, Jim "Gemini" Normandin, and returned East for the last time. We had decided to move to Crested Butte permanently, despite what appeared to be a promising career path for me as an executive in civil rights and social service organizations. We thought we would have more comfortable, enjoyable, and well-rounded personal lives compared to those we led as intellectuals, theater people, and especially as social activists; although we thought our lives would not be as socially meaningful, intellectually stimulating and challenging, or artistically engaging.

We were wrong.

We did not know how we would support ourselves, but when we left New York City I had a small consulting contract with the National Urban League. It covered our living expenses for a few months. I had almost no skills necessary for life in a rural environment. I did not know how to fish, hunt, or plant and tend a garden. I barely knew how to hold a hammer and certainly did not know how to build a house or use coal to heat one. More important than specific rural skills though, in our prior lives we had acquired the self-confidence to believe that, somehow, we would make it.

We made our final move in the beginning of the summer of 1971. Our main activity was gutting and renovating our house so that it would be habitable, especially during our first winter. During the course of that summer and early fall, we reconstructed the interior of our house, and added a 200-square-foot addition for a laundry room and sauna. By mid-fall, the original house had plumbing and electricity, and a complete kitchen with new appliances and beautiful custom-made wood cabinets that were built by a 19-year-old new resident, Bob "B.C." Vandervoort. There was a full bathroom, a living room and dining area with multi-toned artistic parquet ceilings, a separate small children's play room with a slightly sloping floor and lots of sunlight, a private office/study area, and three A-frame pup tent-like sleeping lofts that were 4 1/2 feet high at their apex. Except for electric baseboard heat in the bathroom and laundry, everything was heated by the beautiful coal-burning Victorian stove that came with the house. The new addition had a washing machine and dryer and open shelving for our clothes and a cedar lined sauna that was heated by a wood burning sheep herder's stove. Even though the inside walls of the original house were unfinished with the studs and insulation left uncovered, our partially renovated home was ready for winter. We survived the minus twenty-degree weather with "practical tutoring" from Tony and Mary Gallowich, especially about how to keep the house at an almost consistent temperature by "banking the coals" (placing the coals in the stove on a sharp angle and almost completely closing the air vents so they would burn slowly).

Renovating our house was made more complicated because there wasn't a right angle in it. I later learned it rested on a primitive stone foundation that sagged and shifted over the 18 or so years when it was unoccupied. Instead of being shoveled regularly, as it had been when the Evic family lived there, the approximately 250-inch annual snowfalls were left to accumulate on the roof, causing it to sag and the house to shift.

An almost identical, boarded up vacant building less than a block away was perfectly square. I wanted to know why. Being curious about the variation, I inserted my hand through an opening in its front door above the doorknob, unlocked it, and entered. It was owned by the local sawmill operator, Joe Rozman, and his wife Vonda. Shortly after entering, while I was standing inside looking at the structure, I heard a distinctive "click." It came from a newly cocked rifle, held by an irate Vonda Rozman. She did not like newcomers very much, especially those of us with long hair and beards. She demanded to know what I was doing and asked rhetorically who gave me permission to enter. When I explained, she clearly thought my answer was not good enough. At gunpoint, she told me to get out, and promptly called the town marshal, and had me arrested.

She first charged me with trespassing. On the town's main street, the lawman handcuffed me. At that precise moment, I received a phone call from my former boss. When Diane said I had a long-distance call from New York, I asked the arresting officer if I could take it before I was hauled off to jail in Gunnison. He said "yes." When I explained to my ex-boss what was happening, he laughed so hard he almost forgot why he called. It was inconceivable to him, (an African-American male who was raised in the Roxbury ghetto of Boston, that a policeman would release someone so he could go back into his house to answer a phone!) He did not understand that the marshal knew I could not run away because there was only one road out of town and that, even while in the process of arresting someone for a petty offense, small town civility prevailed. We finished our phone conversation and I went back outside where I was re-handcuffed and taken to jail. There, we discovered Vonda Rozman wanted to change the charge to breaking and entering, a felony.

The police blotter in the town newspaper noted, however, there was at least a little confusion about the matter: "Roger Kahn of Crested Butte [was] arrested for trespassing on a complaint signed by Vonda Rozman. Matter pending in Municipal *or* [emphasis added] County Court."

Fortunately, a young new lawyer in the area had been appointed the Gunnison County Deputy District Attorney. He was one of our earlier "welcoming committee" during a prior Crested Butte visit. He told the very angry Mrs. Rozman that he knew me, and that I certainly was not a felon. Most importantly, he said he would not prosecute me for breaking and entering. Eventually, all charges were dropped and I never was prosecuted. (Perhaps, though, I should have been for being "culturally ignorant, arrogant, and insensitive"). Three weeks later the *newspaper's* police blotter noted, "Roger Kahn of Crested Butte, charged with trespassing on complaint of Vonda Rozman. Case dismissed at request of prosecution."

In the mornings of that summer, before I began working on our house, I went to a small back room in Tony's Tavern, where I had set up an office. I intended to write two books for which I had taken many notes during the previous decade. Because I spent most of my twenties working primarily in African-American led organizations in the civil rights movement, I had many experiences that were unusual for a white person. I wanted to use them to speak to other white people to help them see what racism was doing to them, and especially to black people. It was tentatively called "White on White." I had also watched how other social movements emerged or intensified in America in the sixties, and how they were dealt with by America's establishment, and I also wanted to write about that.

Neither book ever came to fruition.

Like my earlier experiences in progressive social movements, I found my life in Crested Butte unusual, engrossing, intense and, once again, life-changing. Instead of writing those books or even articles about those issues, I kept a diary about what was happening around me and my personal reactions to that, (some of which now serves as data for this work). There were plenty of socially interesting things going on in Crested Butte. Moving into both a small town that had fewer people than the New York City apartment building in which I grew up, and a rural county that had one of the largest land masses in the continental United States but a smaller population than one side of the block where I was raised, was like moving to a foreign country. I also found it difficult to write those two books because I was

Moving into a small town that had fewer people than the New York City apartment building in which I grew up... was like moving to a foreign country.

becoming less angry about all the things I experienced personally during the sixties. As I moved further from those events, I realized that psychologically I had needed the immediacy and anger that I felt daily for a decade as mental fodder; now, in the jargon of those times, in Crested Butte, I was quickly "mellowing out."

I was in the midst of a community that was rapidly changing. Its economic base was transitioning from mining to recreation. Its social and cultural ways were also changing due to the different types of people associated with each industry. Ranching surrounded both the mining and early tourist-oriented communities and, albeit uneasily, over time co-existed with both. As also was the case in what would become other Colorado tourist towns and recreation communities, (like Breckenridge, Steamboat Springs and Telluride), there was both a generation gap and a class divide between the mining-era residents and the newcomers. The new people were almost all young, adventurous, reared in relative affluence in cities and suburbs; and were influenced by the progressive social movements of the sixties. The hard-working miners and ranchers were mostly middle-aged or older, and held traditional values influenced by surviving the Great Depression and World War II, and by living in a small, *isolated*, rural community that suffered extremely hard times when the area mines closed. Although both populations were white, their world views were vastly different. The old-timers had a hard work ethic; the new residents had a hard play ethic.

...their world views were vastly different. The old-timers had a hard work ethic; the new residents had a hard play ethic.

Historically, philosophers and social scientists have argued about social change and how it comes about, whether as a consequence of cooperation or conflict. In Crested Butte, (which I've now been a part of in different ways and watched closely for over fifty years), both collaboration and large and small confrontations have been part of the town's evolution into what today is a typical, 21st century "recreation exurb." One can imagine that the transition from a tight knit traditional mining town where few of the 600-1,000 square foot homes even had indoor plumbing, to today's mature, very comfortable, urbane, tourist town and recreation community where many of the new *smaller* homes are 3,000 square feet and have all the most up-to-date conveniences, was intense. It came about mainly through on-going discomfort, disruption, and social dislocation, especially when the old-timers clashed with what I think of as the early recreation community's first "ski area trailblazers," "tourist town pioneers," and "recreation community settlers."

... the transition from a tight-knit traditional mining town...to today's mature, very comfortable, urbane, tourist town and recreation community, was intense. It came about mainly through on-going discomfort, disruption, and social dislocation, especially, when the old-timers clashed with ... the ... early recreation community's first "ski area trailblazer," "tourist town pioneers," and "recreation community settlers."

In my effort to understand the cooperation/conflict paradigm that was happening in Crested Butte in the late 1960s and early 1970s, I looked for analogies. The social and political thrust of African-Americans in the Civil Rights and Black Power Movements from the mid-fifties through the early seventies, and the mostly hostile reactions of whites to them, were the best parallels upon which I could draw. The increasing influx of young people who were coming into Crested Butte, and the reactions to them from the long-time mining-era and ranching residents were like those of white people who were threatened by, and resented, the thrust of black people wanting personal respect, social justice, and political parity.

Through my life experiences as a social activist and my formal education, I knew that *major* societal change happens only through social upheaval and strife, although it can be softened sometimes by periods of collaboration. Significant transformations come through protracted periods of social dislocation. I clearly recognized that the town was going through a period of profound change, and the concomitant struggles were clear, but I did not sense or understand at that time, that Crested Butte was in its early stages of becoming a modern "recreation exurb" for America's affluent population.

Introduction

Crested Butte today is a sophisticated, well-off, tight-knit, town with many amenities. It caters mainly to affluent tourists and provides a good living for its residents. Like many other tourist towns in the mountains, at seashores and lakes, and even in deserts, it may be thought of as a new type of exurb, one that is based on outdoor recreation. It is not related to a particular municipality, as is the usual definition of the term; it is part of and related to the nation itself. Most of these "recreation exurbs," significantly, grew out of what were formerly rural, working-class, hamlets surrounded by vast, awe inspiring, land and seascapes.

Crested Butte, although it is unique in many ways, it is also typical of these new communities. Importantly, however, it was not always as it is today. In the process of becoming the mature community it is now, with its full array of cultural and athletic offerings and manicured lawns and paved streets, the town went through many stages. In its initial re-incarnation as a ski town in 1961, it arose from the remnants of a once thriving mining town. Then, it went through several growth phases as it became the bourgeoning year-round destination tourist town and recreation community which visitors often travel great distances to reach. Now, almost sixty years later and well into its maturity, Crested Butte is still evolving. This new type of rural area caters to both a growing number of permanent residents and tourists alike, as it becomes ever more polished and sophisticated.

Since the 1950s, most other contemporary recreation communities evolved in much the same way as Crested Butte, whether they too were in Colorado like Aspen, Telluride, Breckenridge and Steamboat Springs, or on seacoasts such as Cape Cod, Nantucket, St. Augustine or any of the beach towns in California. Notably, the east coast tourist towns began their evolution more than a half century earlier, when they began catering to the very rich in society. That said, even among those small towns, their evolution accelerated dramatically following WWII. All of them were set in beautiful natural environments where other industries already had existed;

...contemporary recreation communities ...were set in beautiful natural environments where other industries already had existed, typically mining, logging, ranching, farming or fishing.

typically mining, logging, ranching, farming, or fishing. Those small towns were populated by hard-working men and women, often from European ethnic backgrounds, who formed tight knit communities. By looking at Crested Butte as an example, one can understand the evolution of the other recreation-oriented communities, most of which also began as rough-hewn, small towns, and ended as the new culturally refined and urbane, well-groomed American recreation exurbs.

Beginning in the middle of the 19th century, after the industrial revolution was fully entrenched and its titans had amassed fortunes, there were mountain and seashore resorts in rural areas that catered to those very wealthy individuals who usually vacationed in grand hotels. It was a rich person's option. They and their families went to them for extended periods of time. When ocean liners and railroads made inter-and intracontinental travel more accessible for the ultra-rich in that Gilded Age, vacation resorts developed throughout North America and Europe. In an 1880's historical tract on St. Augustine, Florida, for instance, it was noted that the multi-millionaire associate of John D. Rockefeller, Henry Morrison Flagler, "… saw the possibility of a great tourist development. Soon thereafter … St. Augustine buzzed with well-to-do visitors. … visitors came from the North by steamer or, after completion of the railroad, by train. They came to stay the entire winter…"[1] (Notably, similar retreats also existed in Asia, especially for royalty. China's "Summer Palace" is a prime example). In the northeast the Rockefellers, Kennedys, and others owned their own mountains for skiing and also had seaside mansions. These became the initial precursors to today's tourist towns.

By the post-World War II period, as Western society moved from the industrial to the information age, the increasingly large, more affluent, mostly white, middle-class grew dramatically. They often vacationed yearly as had the industrial barons and their families before them, although they did so for shorter periods of time, usually one to three weeks. By the late nineteen fifties and early sixties, large numbers of people were, to paraphrase Henry David Thoreau, leading more pressurized lives of "not-such-quiet-desperation" in the cities and the newly forming suburbs, and taking time away from them to recharge and reinvigorate themselves. They relaxed and played in emerging regional and local resort areas, as the wealthy had earlier. They went to small existing towns in beautiful, natural areas. New communities based on tourism began to emerge on the seacoasts, at inland lakes, and in major mountain ranges.

By the post WW II period...the increasingly large, more affluent, mostly white, middle-class grew dramatically. ... people were ,.. leading more complicated lives of 'not-such-quiet-desperation"... and taking time to recharge and reinvigorate themselves ... by relaxing and playing in emerging regional and local resort areas, as the wealthy had earlier. New communities based on tourism began to emerge...

Those tourist towns with their recreation communities catered to the broader middle classes' need for individual and family re-creation even though they already had, in most cases, existing industries and small populations. Though at first tourist towns formed to cater to one sport or season, like skiing in winter or water centered activities in summer, most eventually evolved into year-round communities that provide a broad range of recreational options. Today, typically, they offer all types of outdoor sports, an abundance of parades and festivals, cultural offerings that include a variety of visual art forms and many types of performing arts including music, theater, and dance. Reflecting the increasing emphasis in society on life-long learning as a form of self-fulfillment, especially among those people who benefited from excellent formal educations, adult education is usually a part of these communities' offerings through a variety of forums, seminars and workshops on an array of subjects. These towns mainly contain upscale housing, and many high-end specialty sports

Today, ...they offer...all types of outdoor sports...joyous parades and festivals, cultural offerings that include ... music, theater, dance.... adult education ... upscale housing ... high-end specialty sports shops, clothing boutiques, art galleries, lodges, health food stores, spas, ... fine restaurants and bars ...local weekly newspapers and public radio.

shops, clothing boutiques, art galleries, lodges, health food stores, spas, and a wide range of fine restaurants and bars, as well as local weekly newspapers and public radio stations.

These communities are often characterized by a strong small 'd'-democratic and libertarian social and political ethic, especially in regard to sexual activity and preferences, drinking and drugs, civil liberties, and law enforcement. They are, perhaps, the only distinctly identifiable communities in America that, as they evolved, incorporated into their major institutions and structures the values of the sixties' and early seventies' progressive social movements: civil rights, peace and anti-war, women's equality, gay and lesbian rights, and personal growth and health. An ethos prevails that individuals' civil liberties and rights should be exercised freely and fully. That ethic encourages people to do what they want personally, as long as they are discrete and do not hurt others; and that law enforcement should not interfere with them as they do that. These communities also highly value children's and animals' rights and, appropriately, given the natural beauty of their locations, have very strong environmental sensibilities.

Tourists visit these communities to rejuvenate, either by relaxing or playing actively. For the same reasons, some remain or move to them later and become "locals." Others come to find new ways of living and existing that differ from the lives and lifestyles they lived previously. Significantly, with very few exceptions, virtually all tourist town and recreation community residents migrate to them voluntarily. These mostly young locals work at multiple low-paying jobs servicing the needs and wants of visiting tourists and they often excel at the very activities that attract visitors, especially sports and partying. Although some local residents choose rather conventional lifestyles, most usually play and party heartily, and work mainly to support their fun-filled way of life.

> ... "locals" ...often excel at the very activities that attract visitors, especially sports and partying.

There are exceptions, but like visiting tourists, most locals too are transient. They only live full-time in a recreation community for several years. This is true even among those who own businesses or are elected to local government offices. Housing, particularly, is expensive and wages are low. That suits these daring, fun-loving people when they are young and/or unattached. They can share housing with friends and work at multiple jobs to get by. That lifestyle, however, becomes more difficult as they grow older, take on family responsibilities, or want to pursue careers in fields outside the recreation and hospitality industries.

Another significant factor contributing to local residents' transience is that they are often going through personal life changes and, as they get to the new side of that transition, they move to more conventional communities. In big cities and suburbs, where most locals were reared, people play different roles in their various settings — a husband, wife or parent at home, an employee or employer at work, an amateur athlete in yet another location. In each place, they assume slightly different personas and interact differently with various people. By contrast, in these intimate, geographically remote, small communities, that type of role differentiation is not possible. People have to figure out basically who they really are, irrespective of their different roles. Essentially, role segmentation does not exist. That makes it difficult for local residents to put on airs or hide parts of their beings from others or, perhaps more importantly, from themselves. It is the same person, for example, who works as an elementary school teacher during the week, who plays softball on a local team after work, who parties hard at night and comes to breakfast at a local restaurant with a new friend the following morning, and who also volunteers with an environmental group on weekends.

Essentially, role segmentation, does not exist. That makes it difficult for local residents to put on airs or hide parts of their being from others or, perhaps more importantly, from themselves.

Consequently, individuals have to get it together and, as transactional psychologist Abe Wagner said, "Say it straight or show it crooked."[2] That causes locals to judge others not by their personal history or by what they profess, or even by the work they do while they are in town. Instead, people are evaluated by the way they actually relate to other community members on a daily basis, and what they actively contribute to the common good. They are not defined by how they "talk their talk'" but by the way they "walk their walk." In resort community settings, as the different segments of each new local's being come into intra-or interpersonal conflict, the parts confront each other. As that happens, individuals "grow," often emerging as somewhat different beings, or at least with a different sense of self, from who they were when they first entered the town. As that personal metamorphosis occurs, the mostly young adults begin to figure out who they are and who they want to be. Although some locals remain for decades and become community mainstays, passing on the town's traditions, lore and values to another set of newcomers, most individuals move to other places and continue on their own personal trajectories, incorporating their experiences and the values they held while they were town residents.

As tourist towns mature, an increasing number of second home-owners become part of the community. They are usually older and wealthier than the full-time residents and blend in with the local community, although they are less adventurous. Their personal processes and behavior patterns usually differ from those of the locals', although they complement them. Second homeowners patronize local events, restaurants, shops, galleries, etc., and they enjoy similar physical and cultural activities. Importantly, they also support and provide funding for many of them, either through personal donations or by channeling funds through local "community foundations." They too are judged in the community, not by what they say, but by what they do in and for it.

The epilogue in this work briefly discusses the more mature phases of Crested Butte's development and, by inference, other "recreation exurbs" like it, but this writing focuses on its earlier stages: the ones that were wild, raucous, conflict-ridden and, most significantly, were formative to the very nature of the on-going culture of Crested Butte and those other tourist towns and recreation communities that became our nation's newest exurbs.

For most of today's modern recreation exurbs, the most formative years of their development occurred during the 1960s and early '70s. That era was one of unusual economic opportunity in Western society, and also of social and political upheaval, idealism, and optimism. People who lived in Crested Butte and other similar *"Shangri-las"* during those years used their strengths, creative energies, and aspirations to forge a new kind of town, one that reflected and incorporated the sensibilities of the era. During their formative years, these emerging communities allowed and even encouraged a broad range of personal lifestyles and ways of being.

Over the years Crested Butte and other similar communities matured and became less experimental and more traditional. Today, while a token of the optimism and idealism of the sixties and early seventies is embedded in the institutions and culture of these towns, they have become more conservative, as has the rest of the country. As they do elsewhere, business priorities increasingly dominate the community culture. That said, however, in social and political terms, these communities are usually more progressive or liberal than the geographical political districts that surround them. These new towns are where people go for respite from the hectic daily lives they live in their year-round environs. Indeed, they are a new type of community set within inspiring natural rural settings and are separate and distinct from the urban centers that dot the national landscape.

Part I:
Culture

Chapter 1

Old-Timers and the New Recreationists

The Old-Timers

Before the ski area was created in Crested Butte in 1961, there were two major groups of people who the new town immigrants called, "the old-timers": resilient mining-era families that remained in town after the mines closed, and rugged cattle and hay ranching families that worked their ranches in the valleys surrounding it. There were also a few merchants, teachers, and loggers. Taken together, they

...before the ski area...there were two major groups... resilient mining-era families ... and rugged ... ranching families .... about 250 people.

amounted to about 250 people. Although there were some significant differences among them, they had a lot more in common.

Crested Butte was founded in the 1880s. It was originally a mining town, first hard rock and then coal. The upper Gunnison Valley, which surrounds it, consisted of ranches. Twenty-eight miles south of Crested Butte is the City of Gunnison, a ranching hub. Ranchers worked the land above ground in daylight; coal miners worked underground and, especially in winter, rarely saw much sunshine. With the exception of a few Catholic families, the ranchers were mostly white, Protestant, Anglo-Saxons. In the last few decades before the coal mines closed, when the new people began arriving, the coal miners were mainly Catholic of Serbian, Croatian, Italian, or Mexican decent. Ranchers owned their land and leased more of it from the federal government for grazing their cattle. They worked alone or with other family members and a few hired hands on large tracts of acreage. Miners worked underground in pitch-black tunnels, mainly in small groups. Ranchers worked for themselves; miners worked for the companies that hired them. Ranchers were mainly anti-union; most miners supported unions. Although there were a few miners north of Gunnison who sometimes worked on ranches and even fewer ranchers who occasionally worked in the mines during winter months, few men crossed that divide. In elections, Gunnison County ranch men and women mainly voted Republican, and the mine workers of Crested Butte supported Democrats.

Despite those differences, from the perspective of the new people who came to develop the ski area and a recreation industry, it was more significant that mining-era town residents and those who worked in the valley surrounding them both shared an old-Western way of life. Both groups held conservative social and political views and a life-style that encouraged self-reliance coupled with community cooperation and, especially, hard work. They were "proud people" who believed in "family values," with distinct traditional definitions of men's and women's roles, entrepreneurship, ethnic pride, religion, and patriotism. They shared a "macho" culture in which gun ownership was traditional, especially for hunting and "to protect one's castle;" alcohol was their drug of choice, and heavy drinking, drunk driving, and poaching game were regular occurrences. When talking about how they dealt with clashes, men like patriarch Charlie Veltri would lean forward and say, without a hint of irony, "My attorneys are 'Smith and Wesson'." Their rifles, clearly displayed in gun racks above the seats of their pickup trucks, bore witness to their words. Their outward physical appearances were also similar. They were mainly in their forties, fifties, or early sixties. They wore traditional, functional, 1950's style clothing. Even the few who were younger dressed alike. The women donned simple, traditional dresses or skirts and blouses, wore bras, used modest make-up, and sometimes sported a little jewelry. Their hairstyles were usually short and carefully tended. The men had short haircuts, were clean shaven, and wore blue denim jeans, heavy twill chinos, or bib overalls, and plain or

...both shared an Old-Western way of life. ... held conservative social and political views and a life-style that encouraged self-reliance coupled with community cooperation and, especially, hard work. ...They believed in "family values" ... traditional definitions of men's and women's roles, entrepreneurship, ethnic pride, religion and patriotism.

plaid functional work shirts. Town men wore baseball caps and ranchers wore wide-brimmed cowboy hats.

Before the ski area opened, for a decade or more, visitors came to the Crested Butte area in the summer. They came mainly from Oklahoma and Texas, to escape the blistering heat, and to hike, fish, jeep, and camp in the cool mountain outdoors. Instead of camping, some would rent a hotel room or a bedroom in a local family's home (temporarily evicting the children who then would camp outdoors). Another few came to conduct geological or biological research, or for continuing education classes. Since 1928, physical scientists conducted high altitude research at the Rocky Mountain Biological Laboratory in the abandoned mining town of Gothic, located six miles north of town. Beginning in 1958, Dr. Hubert Winston Smith, who held both medical and law degrees, founded the innovative Law-Science Academy in town, a post-graduate continuing education program that was affiliated with the University of Texas. It offered seminars and workshops that tried to span the chasm that then existed between the two professions so, essentially, they could better serve their clients or patients. The Academy educated practitioners in one field by teaching them about the other. A number of the doctors and lawyers who attended, bought "summer places": small houses in town that they got for a few hundred or a thousand dollars after the out-of-work miners moved *en masse* to find new jobs elsewhere.

As early as the late 1800s when mining was still a new regional industry, a few observers thought tourism could become a thriving second business in the area,[1] but that did not begin to take hold until more than a half-century later. When people started vacationing in Crested Butte during summers in the 1950s, they brought a little outside money into the community; however, they were not defined as a significant economic force in the town's well-being, and certainly not as the basis of a local economy. They were seen by residents as "summer visitors," not "tourists;" they were not yet identified as a vital part of the town, and certainly not as the mainstay of its economy or social and political life.

When the ski area opened in 1961, it was seen as a mixed bag by mining-era people. They hoped it could provide a little economic opportunity and a few jobs for the community members, both of which were badly needed after the mines closed. They also thought, as most people did in the early sixties, that skiing was not a real industry and was merely play. George Sibley wrote that miners and their families thought that for "real" work, "You gotta have the lunch bucket."[2] They certainly did not think skiing could bring substantial, long-term, viable employment to the area. They and the ranchers had little time for "playing;" prolonged down time was scarce. They did not understand that the new ski industry increasingly was supported by a growing affluent population that wanted and psychologically "needed" recreation and vacations. An often-repeated quotation, first attributed to either Tony Kapushion or Tony Verzuh, both highly respected old-timers, claimed *"You can't eat the scenery."* It was their way of saying that skiing, unlike mining, logging, or ranching, could not provide a meaningful living.

When the ski area opened in 1961, it was seen as a mixed bag by the mining-era people. They hoped it could provide ... economic opportunity and a few jobs.... They also thought... that skiing was not a real industry and was merely play.... An often-repeated quotation ... claimed, "You can't eat the scenery."

As the ski area developed some mining-era residents did, in fact, get jobs. Along with the earliest new immigrants into the area who came with the ski business, they cut trails, installed lift towers, and constructed the first buildings at the area – a warming house, a couple of lodges and restaurants, and a few private homes. Besides construction, they worked as ski lift operators and did maintenance and housekeeping work; as well as all the other jobs associated with bar and restaurant operations: cooking, table service, bartending, dishwashing, etc. Despite their skepticism and mixed emotions wrought from their historical relationship to what they considered "real" industries, lifelong Crested Butte residents generally welcomed the ski business.

■ ■ ■

The Ski Industry Trailblazers

A few new people moved into Crested Butte in the mid-to-late 1950s, such as Phil and Lil Hyslop. They had been in other mountain towns that were just beginning to attract tourists as their former thriving industries were folding. Aspen is an example. The Hyslops came from there and bought three separate commercial buildings in the middle of Crested Butte's main street for a total of $4,000.00 and created the Grubstake Restaurant and Saloon. They built a roof that rose above all three, and combined them into a single structure. Those individual establishments had served other purposes during the mining years but the Hyslops recognized they could fulfil a present need.

After the mines had been closed for almost a decade a first wave of new Crested Butte "immigrants" came to town, the *"ski area trailblazers."* Two of them, Dick Eflin and Fred Rice, were the original owners and developers of the area. They came from the plains of Kansas, as did several other key ski resort employees. As was the case with the initiators of many other American ski resorts, Eflin had skied in Europe when he was in the Air Force. Almost all the other trailblazers were from other flatland areas in Oklahoma and Colorado, many of whom were reared in tiny, old-west communities or the small cities or new suburbs in those states. These newest immigrants to Crested Butte grew up with, knew, and were comfortable with ranchers and miners and "Western ways" and, importantly, they shared many of the social and political values that Crested Butte area residents held.

... "ski industry trailblazers" shared many .... social and political values ... that mining-era Crested Butte residents and ranchers held.

It was relatively easy for this first group of new people to get to know and appreciate, even idolize, the old-timers, although it often seemed to them to be a long time before they were accepted. (Compared to the even newer people who followed later, however, it was easy). These ski area trailblazers worked closely with the long-time residents on the mountain and in town in the businesses associated with the embryonic resort. They also socialized with some of them in the town's bars and restaurants, and the few other existing retail establishments. In a few instances, they attended church with long-time residents. Dan McElroy, a Western State College student who came to town in the mid-sixties with his young family and worked first as a ski instructor and then opened a motorcycle shop in town and sold real estate, remembered, "We attended church for three years before we were accepted. I think that finally happened because three of the Sporcich sisters [young teenage girls native to Crested Butte] babysat for us, and that opened doors in town." The oldest of the Sporcich sisters, Cathy, referring to the old-timer females said many years later, "…by the time the area started up, they began working outside their homes with the new people. They cleaned lodges and homes, worked in restaurants, etc. So, some got to know newcomers that way."

These ski industry trailblazers wanted to become part of the existing community, and many assimilated into it. Although they were first seen as "outsiders" in the close-knit Crested Butte community of 15 or so extended families, trailblazers were ultimately accepted, because there were not very many of them and they were culturally similar. In fact, a few, mainly men, married into the local families.

These ski industry trailblazers wanted to become part of the existing community, and many assimilated into it.

In addition to working hard, the trailblazers played hard too. Many were motorized sports enthusiasts who liked and raced Jeeps, snowmobiles, and motorcycles. In the main, they co-existed as co-workers and neighbors; and in a few social settings, especially for the men, in the local bars and restaurants. One of the early new young craftsmen who attended Western State College and lived and worked in Crested Butte for over a decade said forty-plus years later, "I grew up in Cortez in western Colorado. In high school I spent a lot of time on my friends' ranches outside town riding horses, herding sheep or cattle. When ranchers came to town, they wore pistols on their hips and carried rifles. It was probably the most conservative place in the country. So, in Crested Butte I adopted a mountain-man persona and just fit in."

Many new young people, especially those who were reared locally, attended Western State College (WSC) in nearby Gunnison, as did some of the younger college-age town residents. It was widely regarded as a "party school," with a lot of drinking, the drug of choice of old-timers and ski area trailblazers alike. A man who has lived in the Gunnison Valley for over fifty years and who first came from Southern California to attend WSC in the mid-sixties remembered, "I was part of a student group that started the Luftseben Club that TKD'ed – 'tapped a keg a day'." When born and bred young Crested Butte mining-era residents and the new trailblazers went to college, whether at Western State or elsewhere, they typically attended public state institutions. The men often majored in industrial arts or business administration and the women majored mainly in education.

Several trailblazers originally came to Crested Butte because rents were cheaper than in Gunnison, under $60.00 per month for a small, run-down house that had been abandoned by a mining family when they left town. Or, depending on when they arrived, they could buy a place for less than two thousand dollars. Other WSC students moved to town because it was closer to the ski slopes which afforded job opportunities on the ski patrol or as ski instructors. Several of the new people, with little money and lots of energy, started or worked in tiny businesses that catered to skiers and the few summer visitors, as well as to the local residents. A significant additional number came because they could create art in a "low rent district." A few came because they could begin a family and raise children in a safe, small, town in a beautiful environment with plenty of opportunities for inexpensive, outdoor, recreation. A few others came because they could party in town in relative safety, even more so than at WSC, particularly if they wanted to experiment with recreational drugs. Each came, more than likely, for a combination of reasons.

All of the ski area trailblazers, except the few who had independent incomes from inheritances or were supported by their parents, made their living in one way or another from the new industry. They became the newest population of town locals. As they developed roots in the community, in spite of liking it as it had been and wanting to keep it that way, they needed to earn a living and were financially dependent on the skiing industry. Without being aware of it, they began a process similar to what occurred in major urban centers across the country beginning in the 1960s: gentrification. They, however, were not in urban areas; thus, it was "rural gentrification."

the ski area trailblazers ... began a process ... beginning in the 1960s: It was 'rural gentrification'.

■ ■ ■

The Tourist Town Pioneers

The second group of new immigrants in the Crested Butte area was the "tourist town pioneers." They began arriving in the last half of the 1960s with a large number coming in the summer of 1970. They continued migrating into the area until spring 1972. They were the mountain "variant" of the youth counter-culture of the 1960s and early 1970s that included activists in the civil rights, anti-war, free speech, women's, and "hippie" movements. In some ways, they were indistinguishable from those other young people. Crested Butte was one of the tiny towns or rural areas that attracted adventurous youth who were seeking new ways to live. They often lived communally in the small, frequently vacant, old mining-era houses, and some formed food cooperatives, and "alternate" schools.

They were roughly the same age as the trailblazers who came before them, in their late teens, twenties, and early thirties. Other than age, however, demographically and culturally the two populations were very different. Not only did the tourist town pioneers arrive later than the other newcomers, most had personal backgrounds that differed significantly from those who preceded them. And, importantly, they also had additional reasons for moving to Crested Butte, other than skiing and working in the ski industry.

These new pioneers were reared mainly on the East and West coasts. They came from upper-middle class professional and business families. Many went to private prep schools during their high school years and were educated in the nation's highest quality undergrad and graduate colleges and universities; and they had traveled widely. They participated in or were influenced by the various progressive and counter-cultural movements of that era, and held liberal and radical social, cultural and political views. Their values and adopted life styles that

These new pioneers were reared mainly on the East and West coasts. They came from upper-middle class professional and business families. Many went to private prep schools during their high school years and were educated in the nation's highest quality undergrad and graduate colleges and universities; and they had traveled widely. They participated in or were influenced by the various progressive and counter-cultural movements of that era, and held liberal and radical social, cultural and political views. They held values and adopted life-styles that differed...from both the recently arrived ski area trailblazers and the life-long Crested Butte area residents.

differed in fundamental ways from both the recently arrived ski area trail-blazers and the life-long Crested Butte area residents. Not surprisingly, intense conflicts between the latter two groups and the new pioneers began soon after these latest newcomers came to town. Further, within five years these new pioneers outnumbered the other two groups combined.

Outwardly, these pioneers looked different from those who came before them. They wore more revealing and colorful clothing that was often tie-dyed, which was popular in the youth culture of the era. Some wore leather pants, shirts and skirts. Most women had long flowing hair often held in place by a headband, wore lots of jewelry and little or no make-up, and many did not wear bras. In the summer, they wore maxi- or mini-skirts often with sheer muslin blouses, and outdoor casual tee-shirts. Most men sported beards or moustaches, long hair, and they too sometimes wore headbands. Many men wore plaid or embroidered cotton or wool shirts and torn or colorfully patched well-worn jeans, or casual, outdoor recreation clothing. In summer, many men also wore shorts.

Primitive Cabin (Brush Creek Cow Camp) behind Crested Butte Mountain.
Multimedia drawing courtesy of Diane Kahn.

Like the trailblazers, many tourist town pioneers came for skiing and other outdoor activities; a few came for jobs or ancillary business opportunities associated with the ski resort. A relatively large proportion came to ply the visual arts or crafts as had some of the trailblazers before them, or to participate in the performing arts, particularly theater. The Crested Butte Mountain Theater, for example, attracted a large contingent from Chicago. Several came seeking a simple "back to the earth" existence. They flocked to the relatively low cost of living in town, and also to the high mountain valleys within several miles of it, where they lived in teepees and primitive log cabins without plumbing or electricity. Many others came seeking freedom for individual or community experimentation and, concomitantly, because law enforcement was minimal. Many decades later, one of them, Larry Tanning, wrote of that "Shangri-La"-like era, "… it was an unprecedented time of frolic and fun. … things happened here in the early 70s [sic] that could never happen again."

Perhaps most importantly, in contrast to ski area trailblazers and the locally reared residents, many new pioneers came specifically because the town is geographically remote and isolated, and they were escaping authorities for one reason or another. A critical mass was evading the military draft that was then compulsory for men between the ages of 18 and 26. Some were

… many new pioneers came specifically because the town is geographically remote and isolated, and they were escaping authorities for one reason or another.

decompressing from military service and their experiences in it, or the negative reactions they got from Americans when they returned to the States after having served in Vietnam. Several tourist town pioneers were drug dealers. Others were either completely rejecting or taking a "moratorium" from something significant in their personal lives — marriage or a significant other, parental and family expectations, or a professional career path. Many saw themselves as "the black sheep of their families," as "outcasts," or even "outlaws." Often, in fact, they had been seen that way in their families or the communities from which they came. But they were accepted by the other new pioneers in Crested Butte just as they were, for this newest group of town immigrants rarely asked each other about their prior lives. They were what the broader society in that era called "dropouts" or "hippies."

A long-time local, who remained after she first came to Crested Butte as a tourist town pioneer, later became one of the town's most prominent citizens. She commented many years later about a good friend of hers, an "outlaw," remembering that he only had a single name. Shortly after they met, he told her, "I'm not who you think I am." That man was widely accepted in the community for years, and became a beloved "local" because he contributed his talents to the Crested Butte Mountain Theater, managed a health food store, and helped bring mountain biking to town. Many years later he was arrested by federal narcotics agents and brought to trial on tax-evasion charges. He had been "hiding in plain sight" under a fictitious name, one by which he was known by *all* the town residents. He also worked as a staff member at the local pre-school, and when he was brought to trial, one of the girls who had been in his care, now a mature woman, testified that he had molested her. Community members withdrew their personal adulation and the support they provided him earlier. Then, instead of being a local Crested Butte hero, he became a town pariah. In that context, the now prominent woman recalled, "Back then, we never asked people about their pasts. We accepted whatever they offered about themselves and didn't ask questions. We took them as they were."

Another woman remembered, "Especially among men, personal anonymity was widespread and personal histories were unknown. I remember that many men only had first names or nicknames, in contrast to women whose full names were usually known, because many of the men had earlier run-ins with authorities and didn't want anyone to know their real identities." She then illustrated her point by remembering, "After 'Pleasure' [Roy James] had been out of town for a while and then came back...I watched him shoot himself in his "foot" in the Grubstake, at the front round table near the window, and it freaked everyone out. Everyone knew he was an outlaw but nobody knew his foot was wooden." She added, "People accepted outlaws because it was the first time that most of us were truly free in our lives, and outlaws represented freedom."

She further noted the changes in Crested Butte's ambiance as it morphed from a "wild west" community into one that was, as she perceived it, more cultured and urbane, "Beginning in about 1975 people started coming to town who were part-time residents, especially during the summer, and they wanted this place to be like the ones they came from. This led to the end of the "outlaw" style and the beginning of development, making Crested Butte like a suburb."

Still another woman said, "'Outlaws' were mythologized around here because we all saw ourselves as outlaws, rebelling in one way or another from the values we were raised with, and the family expectations that were put on us. We wanted to create our own world. That's why people came here. We came to this place where we could make children who would function in the new world we were in and felt was coming."

"Outlaws were mythologized around here because we all saw ourselves as outlaws, rebelling in one way or another from the values we were raised with, and the family expectations that were put on us. We wanted to create our own world. That's why people came here. We came to this place where we could make children who would function in the new world we were in and felt was coming."

Many in this tourist town pioneer group were at least temporarily alienated from the dominant values of mainstream society. They did not care about upward mobility, a career and financial success, or having a family consisting of a husband, wife and "2.3 children" living in a suburban home with a well-tended grass lawn. Like many young people in the late sixties and early seventies, they were trying to find new ways of "being" and living in community. These were extraordinarily creative, adventurous, energetic and idealistic young people. Notably, while they were living differently from the way they were reared, their traditional, comfortable, families often provided them with a "safety net" while they chose to be "downwardly mobile" and experiment with alternative lifestyles.

Looking back and reflecting on that unique era forty-five years later, Joe Grabowski, a tourist town pioneer, wrote a letter to the editor in response to a contemporary editorial that said that the current townspeople should not be nostalgic about those "good old days" because they had been impoverished and tough. He remembered fondly that "[we] were able to work part-time, live in town, and spend the majority of [our] days hiking, fishing, skiing, hanging with friends in the bars…knowing everyone (and their dogs) on a first name basis …having your pick of wonderful places to eat and drink at reasonable prices with no wait … purchasing season passes…without taking out a loan…short lift lines, skiing with half the town on a powder day followed by cocktails on the Artichoke deck at the base area that didn't resemble a small city. Hanging with the Crested Butte Hot Shots to fight a forest fire in some corner of the West and coming back to a big party at the Grubstake … A fourth of July parade with crazy floats. … I could go on … but the point is, the 'old days' *were* as good as advertised…part of a hearty, unrestrained and joyful lifestyle."

Importantly, as was the case for the earlier ski area trailblazers who came to town, the pioneers' motivations for moving to Crested Butte involved a combination of reasons.

A few of them were, indeed, like the earlier ski area trailblazers: from working-class backgrounds in Colorado or neighboring states, but most were not. If some of them worked before coming to Crested Butte, except in a

As with youth in other social and political movements of that era, they were the children of … the "entitled affluent."

few instances, they'd never toiled at jobs requiring hard manual labor. They mainly held part-time white-collar jobs during their summer vacations, often in their parents' businesses. A lot of them had also traveled extensively and/or lived abroad and visited sophisticated European tourist towns. As with youth in other social and political movements of that era, they were the children of a new, broad, professional and independent business class that emerged in the United States and Western Europe after WW II, what one might call the "entitled affluent."[1]

Before coming to Crested Butte, many pioneers participated in the civil rights and anti-poverty movements; the anti-war, peace, and student "free-speech" movements. Several others also had been involved in or influenced by the women's movement; the gay and lesbian movement; the consumer movement; and the various personal "alternate" or "counter culture" New Age movements including the drug, personal growth, health and com-

…. many pioneers participated in the civil rights and anti-poverty movements; the anti-war, peace, and student "free-speech" movements;. Several others also had been involved in or influenced by the women's movement; the gay and lesbian movement; the consumer movement; and the various personal 'alternate' or 'counter culture' New Age movements…

mune movements. Over half a dozen such tourist town pioneers, for example, were lawyers at Colorado Rural Legal Services, an anti-poverty organization that worked with Native Americans and other impoverished people in the Southwest. A New York City reared, Ivy-League-educated lawyer who had worked for Ralph Nader in the consumer movement, and a Connecticut-raised, Ivy-League-schooled lawyer, volunteered on Bobby Kennedy's 1968 presidential campaign. (Significantly, a few years after they arrived, following the town election in which pioneers won all local public offices, those two lawyers were the finalists for the town attorney position. A year later, one was elected a Gunnison County Commissioner, and the other became the judge for the City of Gunnison.) There also were new people who worked as community organizers in major urban cities, including New York. Two pioneers were campus activists. One participated in the Free Speech Movement on the University of California's Berkeley campus in 1964, and later evaded the draft by declaring, falsely, that he was homosexual. The other was a draft resistor and self-declared anarchist who was among the original student protestors in 1968 who sat-in and occupied Columbia University in New York City. (Ironically, after serving five months in prison for evading military induction, he became a life-long career employee of the federal government who worked as an elite forest-fire fighter).

Indeed, a proportionately large number of these new pioneers came to Crested Butte specifically to evade the compulsory military draft and hide in town or the mountains surrounding it. They were often actively aided and abetted by others who opposed the Vietnam War, especially combat and non-combatant Vietnam veterans who themselves were using Crested Butte as a place to decompress and re-adjust before again entering mainstream civilian society. For them, Crested Butte served as a type of "halfway house". A few pioneers were conscientious objectors, or men who were in the military but for varying individual reasons of conscience refused orders to go to Vietnam. By 1970, in addition to the many new women who opposed the military and the War, there were over twenty-five men who in one way or another had taken a strong stance against the War in Vietnam or to "militarism" that had *personal* consequences for them. According to the official US census, at that time there were 372 people living in Crested Butte. If approximately 275 of them were old-timers and the more traditional ski area trailblazers, over 25% of the new tourist town pioneers actively demonstrated opposition to the Vietnam War or the military, a critical mass.

The new pioneers were against military means to settle international disputes. They were also opposed to fighting as a way to resolve personal issues. They thought differences should be resolved through diplomacy and dialogue. Unlike the mining-era residents and trailblazers, many even looked down on gun use for hunting. A handful were conservatives, but most pioneers were politically progressive both in the small "d" participatory democratic sense — favoring dialogue and active citizen engagement and "letting the people decide" — and in the capital "D" sense; they were voting Democrats who thought the federal government should use its power to enhance "the common good" by ending poverty, fostering racial and gender equality, protecting the environment, and ending the Vietnam War.

Among tourist town pioneer business owners there were traditional and non-traditional or "hippie entrepreneurs;" some of whom wanted the ski area to develop and economic growth to come to the area quickly while others did not. Those wanting growth had businesses like ski shops, lodges, or bars and restaurants that were directly related to the area's development and tourism. Among them, there were only a few exceptions, such as Barry Cornman who owned and operated the Forest Queen, a small hotel and restaurant in town that served as a morning gathering breakfast place for the new locals. For those business owners who were less concerned about development

Among tourist town pioneer business owners there were traditional and non-traditional or "hippie entrepreneurs;" some wanted ... economic growth ... quickly ... others did not. "Snow days when shops closed were possible because owners didn't have to operate ...to make a living. Many were 'trust funders' ...."

coming to the area rapidly, the town as it then existed was just fine as it was: remote and unpolished. They made their living mainly from outdoor recreation activities other than downhill alpine skiing, like fishing and mountaineering; or they had arts, crafts or jewelry shops, or other small, low-keyed businesses. They could close them to ski on a cherished mid-winter's "powder day," and many did. One of the early pioneer developers who initially bought, remodeled, and sold old houses in Crested Butte said four decades later, "Snow days when shops closed were possible because owners didn't have to operate them to make a living. Many were 'trust-funders'."

Many of these small business owners did not come to Crested Butte to earn a living primarily but, rather, to find new ways of living.

Many pioneers who did not own businesses also came to town to live differently than the way most affluent people did where they were born and raised. Thus, they just worked occasionally, often at part-time jobs. Some, in fact, did not work at all. They enjoyed a laid-back lifestyle with lots of time for all kinds of playing, as well as time for individual and group experimentation. Many were called "trust-funders" or "trustafarians" and lived on unearned income, monies they received regularly from their parents, trusts, or investments. One of the very few self-declared conservative pioneers, an eastern educated surveyor, who came to Crested Butte from Aspen because he saw a business opportunity in the area, said many years later that he dismissively called them "the check of the week club." They were in town because they enjoyed the easy "café society" or "country club" life styles lived by many new young people in Crested Butte.

One of the very few self-declared conservative pioneers, ... called them ... "the check of the week club"' .... because they enjoyed the easy "café society" or "country club" life styles lived by many new young people...

Other tourist town pioneers made their living selling recreational drugs, such as marijuana, LSD or cocaine, and they liked the town's isolation and its dearth of skilled law enforcement personnel. If one of them was arrested, more often than not, his case would be dismissed in court, because his lawyer would point out that illegal procedures were used during the arrest process by the poorly trained Gunnison County Sheriff's officers or the local town marshal. A few other pioneers worked as professionals outside town, where they made substantial incomes compared to local wages. Coupled with Crested Butte's low cost of living and land costs, that enabled them to stretch their incomes by living "on the cheap" in town. Meanwhile, they invested in real estate and built homes and businesses. Pioneer Eric Ross, for example, left town for a while and went to Chicago to work in the advertising industry for a few months so he could earn enough money to buy land and build a home in what was, in effect, the small town's first "suburb," "Wild Bird Estates". There was also a relatively large group of visual and performing artists, and a few social and physical scientists.

It was hard for most mining-era residents to figure out how many of these new pioneers got the money they lived on; to them they often seemed indolent, self-indulgent and entitled. While it was easier for the long-time residents to understand trail-blazers and the earliest pioneers, who made meager livings by working at the ski area or at multiple jobs in the bars, restaurants, or the emerging construction industry, it was hard for them to figure out how the newer young people who came in the early '70s, made a living, particularly since they seemed to live comfortably.

It was hard for most mining-era residents ... to figure out how many of these new pioneers ...lived; to them they often seemed indolent, self-indulgent and entitled.

Despite the dissimilarities, there was some contact between a few tourist town pioneers and old-timers. One early pioneer, Steve Carson, an anti-war veteran, remembered: "Tommy Sneller and Tony Lujan [retired miners] took me, Wally and Gil [early pioneers] hunting one spring. They called what they shot, "early lamb." All of them poached regularly. When we [pioneers] poached we called ourselves, 'The Crested Butte Shot, Gut and Run Club.'" A pioneer woman said forty-five years later about early contacts between the mining-era residents and newest immigrants, "I had a few old-timer women friends. They liked to share their stories. Several of them surrogate parented new people and helped us learn rural survival skills. A few helped me learn to plant a garden, go mushrooming, and fish."

While there was some social contact between the earliest pioneers and the old-timers, after a couple of years, the positive contacts diminished as more and more newcomers arrived. Reflecting many years later on that old-timer/newcomer social dynamic, ski-area trailblazer Sandra Cortner wrote, "...during the late 1960s and early 1970s, the first hippies and dropouts of my generation started trickling into Crested Butte. The old-timers were tolerant at first. Later they complained about their being 'trust funders,' subsisting on monthly checks sent from Mom and Dad, and doing drugs. ... Unshaven, uncut, unwashed, and often partially undressed—that's how the locals saw them."[2] Understanding between the groups was made even more difficult because, as George Sibley, the first tourist town pioneer newspaper editor, commented many years later, "The old timers liked you if you wanted to listen to their stories, but didn't if you wanted to tell them yours."[3] The old-timers' strongly held work ethic was based on hard manual labor; their readiness to stereotype the new pioneers as privileged, idle, "hippies" and their reluctance to get to know them individually, perhaps with the occasional exception of their immediate neighbors, contributed significantly to the intense community-wide cultural and social conflicts that became commonplace in the late sixties and first half of the nineteen seventies.

■　■　■

The Recreation Community Settlers

In spring 1972, after an intense voter registration drive among the new residents, tourist town pioneers won *all* publicly held offices in the town council election. As a result, Crested Butte became known as an emerging "counter-culture" community. Word spread nationally, particularly among the youth, that a small, growing town existed in a beautiful environment near a ski resort with a progressive, hip, population and local government. Following that election, a third group, began arriving *en masse*. They were the *"recreation community settlers."*

In spring 1972, ...tourist town pioneers won **all** *publicly held offices... Crested Butte became known as an emerging "counter-culture" community. Following that election, a third group began arriving en masse. They were the "recreation community settlers."*

Myles Rademan, was a city planner and non-practicing attorney. He was probably the most influential activist in Crested Butte's early "smart growth" development. Almost 45 years after he first came to town, Rademan said that other lawyers that he knew in Denver told him, "You should go up there and check it out because there's been this election and the hippies took over."

Demographically and in their personal life-style choices, recreation community settlers were similar to the tourist town pioneers. They too came from big cities and suburbs and were financially well-off, white, well-educated, and widely traveled, and influenced by the social movements of the era. They were the same ages and dressed and played like the pioneers.

Many were small business owners, and professionals. This wave of new people also included another influx of visual and performing artists. They, generally, also had a civil libertarian bent toward individual life-style choices and liked the range of personal options that were tolerated in town, especially in regard to recreational drug use and sex. They wanted personal civil liberties and rights respected.

...recreation community settlers were similar to the tourist town pioneers. ...from big cities and suburbs and, were financially well-off, white, well-educated and widely traveled, and influenced by the social movements of the era. ... They .... liked the range of personal options that were tolerated in town...

Significantly, even though they also left the lives they were living before coming to Crested Butte, most were *not* looking mainly for alternative ways of living. They came to what they saw as a burgeoning small town with opportunity for growth, and they wanted to prosper. A few newcomers who came in the trail-blazer and pioneer periods were actually the earliest settlers; they stayed in town and owned lodges, restaurants, small ski-oriented businesses, and real estate offices. They also wanted to succeed financially. Most settlers, however, did not come until after the 1972 spring election and continued arriving throughout the seventies; and they changed the dominant values in town among the new people. These newest town immigrants were not mainly "anti-growth" people; indeed, they wanted growth and development. Eventually, the settlers outnumbered the combined population of existing mining-era residents, trail-blazers, and pioneers.

Recreation community settlers bought old-timer businesses. "Tony's Tavern," for example, was sold and later renamed, "The Wooden Nickel." They also started new ones like "Le Bosquet" and "The Finishing Touch," a fine dining restaurant and an interior design retail shop, respectively. They diversified the resort-related offerings that townspeople and tourists alike could enjoy. Compared to the tourist town pioneers, among the settlers there were far fewer alternate life-style proponents and progressive social activists "escaping" mainstream American politics and culture, on "a shoestring and a prayer." The "cost of entry" into town was increasing rapidly, and laws were being enforced in more traditional ways than they were when the pioneer town council first took office. Nationally, moreover, the mood was beginning to change dramatically, as evidenced by the re-election of President Nixon.

Recreation community settlers came because they thought the emerging tourism industry would allow them to earn a good living, while at the same time permitting them to enjoy an increasingly high-quality, recreation based, life-style. Forty years after first arriving in town, one of the new settlers who grew up in a comfortable, Southern California family said, "We came to Crested Butte partly because of skiing but we could see — even through the buzz on the rumor mill — that Crested Butte was going to be the next Aspen. We saw financial opportunity here. There was a great potential for amassing wealth. Crested Butte was cheap then and you could buy almost anything with only 10% down." They wanted financial well-being above all else, and they also wanted the town to develop as fast as possible.

... settlers ... wanted financial well-being and security above all and... the town to develop as fast as possible.

Instead of starting retail businesses, others opened professional offices and became part of the town's growing new political and bureaucratic elite. One, who later became the town attorney, explained why he came to Crested Butte. "It was not to achieve 'commercial success.' It was for the lifestyle." He added pointedly, "However, I didn't go to Telluride, [another West Slope, small, former mining town surrounded by ranching, whose economic base turned to tourism] because after the '72 election Crested Butte was more 'organized' and I knew it would prosper."

The succession of owners of a popular bar among newcomers reflected the changes from one group of new immigrants to the next. The Grubstake Restaurant and Saloon served food and adult beverages and, especially for Crested Butte's new ski area trailblazers and early tourist town pioneers, was the main informal cultural and communication center during the late sixties and very early seventies. A March 1971 *Chronicle* editorial opined that, "... the Grubstake Restaurant, which back in the 'quiet days,' was the Town Message Center, Debating Forum and Politicking Headquarters...". Originally developed by Phil and Lil Hyslop they sold the business in 1965 to a Colorado born and bred ski area trailblazer couple, Jerry and Tina Sampson. In 1969, the Sampsons sold the Grubstake to an early tourist town pioneer couple from Wisconsin, Jeff and Cathy Hoehne. Fewer than two full years after the Hoehnes bought the restaurant and saloon, in early 1971, they sold it to a tourist town pioneer conglomerate from New York City that included people of inherited wealth and professional backgrounds: Tommy Jacobs and Corrine Barr, John and Iris Levin, Terry Stokes and Honeydew Murray. Many years later, Iris Levin spoke about her group's ambitions, compared to the way the Hoehnes had run the Grubstake, "We tried to keep the steak house atmosphere, but added fancy sauces and homemade poppy seed bread in an attempt to make it appeal to a more gourmet-oriented clientele." Two years later, they sold the Grubstake to another tourist town pioneer group. It included another Easterner of inherited wealth, Judy Naumberg, and mid-westerners Jack Faude and Fred "Derf" Lough. They liked the earlier wild-west ambiance of the Grubstake and, under their ownership, it reverted stylistically to its earlier ways. One pioneer woman who arrived in the early seventies, said of the Grubstake, "Maybe it was a little more 'Western' when Naumberg and Faude owned it than when Levin and the others did. They were a little more 'Mafia,' but basically the same shit went on." A ski area trailblazer, Cotton Harris, who came from Colorado Springs to be a ski patrolman, remembered the transitions a bit differently, "Jerry and Tina were great to the patrolman, and we met for early breakfasts and had dinners there too. When Levin and the others bought the Grubstake, they tried to make it into a 'fern bar' like Penelope's [a new, fine dining, restaurant developed by pioneers] when Eric Roemer built it to serve tourists, or later when he bought 'Tony's Tavern' and changed it to a 'pseudo-Victorian' place. The Grubstake went back to being a 'Western bar' after Naumberg and Faude bought it."

To accomplish their goals of financial success and developing a full-fledged tourist-based economy that appealed to a wide range of affluent tourists, the recreation community settlers, along with those development-oriented ski area trailblazers and tourist town pioneers, thought the town's wild western ways had to end. They thought Crested Butte needed to be tamed. Indeed, through a variety of social and political means, they began cleaning up, updating, and modernizing the town.

...recreation community settlers ...thought the town's wild western ways had to end. They thougt Crested Butte needed to be tamed.

Chapter 2

The New Wild West: Drugs, Sex, Sports and "Culture"

Most of the newcomers in Crested Butte were in their late teens, twenties and early thirties. They were adventurous, idealistic, creative, and physically fit. As was the case in earlier Western frontier towns, most were single. Besides drugs, drinking, music and outdoor recreation, there was sex. Unlike the period of the original frontier towns that developed during the late 1800s, the new feminism and the "pill" made an important part of this era possible. The sexual revolution of the late sixties and early seventies was in full swing throughout the western world. Crested Butte was no exception. Plus, the period was more than a decade away from the AIDS epidemic that would modify sexual behavior and encourage more caution. The overt, visible culture among those seemingly fearless, new immigrants was part of the national "singles scene." One female oil painter later insightfully said about that era, "Everyone was trying everything. Sex was widespread and women were becoming free."

... the new feminism and the "pill" made an important part of this era possible. The sexual revolution of the late sixties and early seventies was in full swing.... "Everyone was trying everything. Sex was widespread and women were becoming free."

There was nude bathing daily during the summer at Lake Nicholson, a small lake about a mile north of town, and in the hot tubs at the area lodges all year long. One of the first new public structures constructed in town after the new tourist town pioneers had become a large portion of the local populace, though not yet a majority, was a "bathing suit optional" bath house, although that option was rarely exercised. It was built by an

...a "bathing suit optional" bath house .... quickly became a center of the new pioneers' and settlers' communal life.

heir to the founder of the Law-Science Academy and a few early pioneers, two of whom were, incidentally, gay men and the other was a cross-dresser. It quickly became a center of the new pioneers' and settlers' communal life. As one man said of it many years later, "Back then, if someone wore a bathing suit in the bath house, someone else asked 'what are you ashamed of?' or 'what are you trying to hide?'" A young divorced single mother who was very active with the Crested Butte Mountain Theater, recalled, "I went to the bath house and to Nicholson Lake where we bathed nude." When asked if she ever had sex in it, she responded with mock indignation, "Well, certainly not with anyone I didn't know." When her response was repeated, without attribution, to a gay man from that era, he said, "Well I certainly did!" Identifying another part of the singles scene, the divorcee added, "We had the 2:00 a.m. shuffle in the bars. When they were closing, you had to decide if you were going home alone or not." Notably, several other early pioneer women said similarly, "Ten minutes before the bars closed, you knew if you were going to have sex and, if so, with whom, by 'looking at who was sitting on the bar stool to your left'." A prominent oil painter who also held staff positions in non-profit arts organizations remembered, "One night at closing I brought someone home when my kids weren't there. The next morning, I stripped the bed and changed the sheets. The guy said to me, 'You sure erased me pretty fast.' He's still in town and we're still friends. But we never talk about us having had sex that night."

Most of the new pioneers had a series of sexual partners, some had multiple sex partners and relationships simultaneously, and a few engaged in group sex. One woman said, "I dated a lot of guys for varying periods of time. If I was seeing one of them and someone else who I dated earlier came back to town, I might spend a night or two with him, instead of the guy I was currently seeing." A bachelor from that era who was instrumental in creating a summer event, Aerial Weekend, said, "Being single was great in those days. There was a lot of hanging around in the bars and having a good time. I was young, in my twenties; the bath house was a place where you could let go. There were times when it got sexual in there. There were no orgies, at least that I participated in, but couples had sex in different corners at the same time. One night I saw a ski instructor I knew

in there and we got it on."
Summarizing that era, he said succinctly, "Dope was never cheaper and sex
was never freer."

"Dope was never cheaper and sex was never freer."

Another pioneer from that era said about the bathhouse, "It was a
public bathing place; no one wore bathing suits." Yet another almost
echoed the previously quoted pilot, "I had sex in it, but never an orgy,
although people were in other corners screwing when I was." A ski patrolman said he watched a female ski instructor, "having sex with several guys
in there while I and others watched." He added that couples also had sex
in the enclosed gondola (ski lift) at the ski area during that era.

Several people mentioned that, in addition to the bars being a place
where they met partners with whom they went home for the night, they
actually had sex in them. One said, "There was a lot of sex in the
Grubstake in the small rooms in the
back. It was more edgy stuff than in the
bath house because of heavier drugs."
Another said, "I had sex with lots of
guys, including on the Pac Man

… people… had sex in [the bars] "…the Grubstake …. was more edgy stuff than in the bath house because of heavier drugs."

machine in the Eldo [another locals' bar], and in Kochevar's storage room
[yet another local watering hole]. It was only separated from the bar area
by a burlap curtain and I was afraid it would open and everyone at the bar
would see us." A recreation community settler woman recalled a sexual
escapade that clearly violated the new immigrants' cardinal rule regarding
drugs or sex: discretion. The woman said, "One New Year's Eve I watched
a married couple having sex on the pillows in front of the fireplace at the
Tailings." A man remembered that the couple were tourists and that a
local, whose parents had been visiting, became so incensed that "he started pounding on the guy's head and back while they were screwing." (That
incident was also described in the *Chronicle* shortly after the beginning of
the 1975 New Year. It said the bar then was 'The Jokerville," the Tailings'
successor, and that the sex act had been encouraged by the bar's management. As punishment the town council, which by then was growth-oriented, closed the bar for *two* days).

There was also small group sex, primarily threesomes, as well as
spouse swapping.

One female elementary school teacher who was in her mid-twenties remembered:

> I sought permanent relationships but the men I wanted, either weren't interested in me, or were not ready for a serious relationship. I learned a lot about sex when I was in Crested Butte. I had a number of casual encounters, one-night stands (and always felt guilty), and a couple of threesomes, which were pretty common then.

Another woman said, "I had a series of boyfriends but was monogamous with one exception: I had one three-way experience."

A prominent male elected official who was unmarried when he came to town remembered having sex in the bars and in a parking lot next to the post office. He said that one night when he and a female friend were leaving a bar to go to his house, they simply could not wait to get there; they stopped in the alley behind a main street book store, Heg's Place, and according to him, "Fucked right then and there." He later wed, and then he and his wife engaged in sex outside their marriage individually, as well as in spouse-swapping. He recalled, "There was sex in the bath house but mostly people just hooked up there and went home together. There was sex in the bars where the windows would fog up, and also in parking lots." He continued, "When I was married, I had sex with other women, and we swapped with other couples at our house." Smilingly, he added, "Back then we were 'flexible'." Part of another couple that included a high-level employee in the town government, said

"Back then, we were 'flexible'."

that she and her husband dated other people. She described their relationship simply: "We had an open marriage."

Drugs and sex did not only occur in town. The same activities also took place on "the hill." People at the ski area were mainly ski industry trailblazers, and they were culturally and politically conservative. They tried to put on "respectable" airs, and often disparaged tourist town pioneers calling them "freaks" or "hippies." But the singles scene was the dominant one there too. One early tourist town pioneer woman who originally worked in lodges and bars at the area as well as at those in town, was a "human bridge" between the counter-cultural people in town and the "hill-people." She said many years later, "The people on the hill hated the new people in town more than the old-timers did, but they did the same stuff."

One of the most respected long-time lodge owners and a founder of several of the resort community's most important new organizations explained:

> Most of the 'rock and roll' moved up to the hill and it was prevalent there too. There was a lot of nudity in those days. We used to jeep nude over Paradise Divide, and then jump in a lake up there and swim. I was at Nicholson Lake when Tom Mallardi parachuted nude into it. ... There was nudity at the Ski Crest [one of the early lodges], including a convention of nudists. The Matterhorn [another lodge] had a wet T-shirt contest and some women danced nude in front of a plate glass window. At the Nordic [another early ski area lodge] I watched _____ [a beloved older Crested Butte female pioneer who welcomed and mentored many young pioneers, especially women], wearing a bright yellow wrap and bathing suit, take them off, properly hang them on a towel and clothing rack near the hot tub, and then join a group of naked people in it .... Skiing nude at the end of the season got out of hand, with too many people doing it.

During that period there were also gay men, lesbians, bisexuals and a cross-dressing individual among the new pioneers and, with them, the embryonic beginnings of an openly gay and lesbian community. One gay man later said of the bath house: "Yes, I did have sex in there" and continued, "I knew of one threesome there that involved two guys and a woman." Another man who years later came out as gay said, "Macho is big in Crested Butte. As a hippie in the summer of love [1967] 'free love' was widespread. I was hetero and bi-sexual then, but not homo. My sexuality changed over time." He recalled, "Once I was in the Grubstake talking to a guy, fumbling around verbally, and he said to me, 'Are you saying you want to fuck me?' We went to a house on Sopris [a street a block away] and got it on." He also recalled that he and a prominent male pioneer had sex at a big party at Coney's cabin, one of the primitive cabins in Washington Gulch.

Pioneers who came to town as part of a monogamous married couple or with a young family had difficulty maintaining their relationships; only a few survived. With living in the "here and now," "having fun," "feeling good," and "going for it" being important values among new pioneers, and sexual innuendo and activity being overt, both married men and women had many temptations and opportunities to develop casual sexual relationships with partners other than their spouses or significant others, and they did. The dissolution of significant number of relationships among unwed couples, or divorces among those who were married was, indeed, very high.

Pioneers who came to town as part of a monogamous married couple or ...with a young family had difficulty maintaining their relationships; only a few survived. With... sexual innuendo and activity being overt, both married men and women had many temptations and opportunities to develop casual sexual relationships with partners other than their spouses or significant others, and they did.

The town's unrestrained sexual mores tempted married pioneers whose traditional post-WWII marriages were based on monogamy, like those that were modeled by most of their parents. A woman who came to town as part of a young family who yielded to that temptation and became part of the singles scene wrote to her husband before they separated, "I don't want to sleep with you ..." She added, "You may feel strange with ___ and ___. But it's with them that I learned... ___ taught me some things about myself and I'm grateful and very fond of him ... I need close relationships. I looked for them with ___ and ___ ... and I got them..."

The three New York City pioneer couples that bought The Grubstake Restaurant and Saloon, all ended their relationships. One couple was married; the other two were not. The two unmarried couples separated within a few months after arriving in town, and the married couple divorced a couple of years later. Another pioneer restauranteur with a young family had sex with women besides his wife; that marriage also ended in divorce. Years later, he commented in a way that summarized how many newcomers, especially men, saw the "new sexuality" of the era, "I never looked at having sex with other women as cheating; I saw it as a celebration of life."

"I never looked at having sex with other women as cheating; I saw it as a celebration of life."

By contrast, a large proportion of marriages among people who met and wed in Crested Butte endured, like those of Gene and Barbara Mason, Howie and Mary Beth Johns, Roger and Ann Swanson, and Tony and Randi Stroh. Perhaps that was because each partner knew the other's life style preferences and predilections before they wed; or because they had a lot of emotional and social support from others in the tourist town pioneer population during the formative stages of their marriages. These marriages typically began with spectacular afternoon, outdoor summer weddings that were held in beautiful awe-inspiring high mountain locales under brilliant blue skies amidst bountiful wildflowers and glistening streams. Often, hundreds of people would celebrate the couples' marriage with extravagant pot-luck feasts, ample supplies of alcohol and other drugs, as well as live, soft acoustic guitar music played during the ceremony by pioneer Eric Ross. Ross recollected, "I think I played at all the hippie weddings." Following the official ceremony loud amplified rock music was usually played by a live band to which the revelers danced during the long gala receptions that often lasted well into the night. Those weddings were spectacular joyous events from which to launch new marriages.

■　■　■

Recreational drug use among new townspeople clearly accompanied a lot of sexual activity, but it was hardly confined to that. It was a large part of the youthful immigrants' life style, and the town's emerging culture. The new Crested Butte locals, especially the tourist town pioneers and recreation community settlers, used them when they skied or otherwise pursued outdoor recreation activities, or partied

Recreational drug use ... was a large part of the youthful new immigrants' life style, and the town's emerging culture.

in the bars or their homes. One pioneer described their use as "endless." Even while working, especially on construction jobs, or in bars and restaurants, pioneers and settlers used alcohol, marijuana, hashish, ecstasy, cocaine and hallucinogens, including mushrooms, peyote, mescaline, LSD and DMT (dimethyltryptamine, another chemical psychedelic that produced a short intense high). Long after she stopped using them, one tourist town pioneer woman rhetorically asked, "Why wouldn't you expect recreational drug use in a recreation community?" While these illegal substances were almost never used openly on the town's streets, they were found in most pioneers' homes, in the mountain activities surrounding town, in the alleys behind the bars and, especially in the case of cocaine, in most restaurant kitchens and bathrooms.

Not only were recreational drugs part of the newcomers' chosen lifestyles, they were a substantial part of the town's economy. Quite a few new pioneers supplemented their incomes by selling relatively small amounts to their peers. One Crested Butte pioneer, who later became one of the town's long-time business owners, remembered:

> When I first came to town, people thought I was a narc because I looked so hippie and partied a lot. ... sometimes going on three-day benders after I left the house to get a pack of cigarettes. Because I did so much coke I was called 'Hoover nose'. I did coke when I was on the town fire department and when I waited tables at the Bistro [the Grubstake's restaurant]. It was practically free. On Faude's birthday [a Grubstake owner], his name was laid out in coke on a big mirrored serving tray and everyone partook... After hours I, ___, and ___ [a tourist town pioneer and a ski area trailblazer] would play pool through the night doing coke and drinking. ... It was just one big continuous party."

Regarding the role of drugs in Crested Butte's economic life, he continued:

> I could bring in an ounce of coke and sell some of it and use the rest; there was a lot of money transferred at the time with all kinds of different drugs. Crested Butte was a drug hub for other ski towns as well. Cops could live near big time dealers as was the case in the trailer court; as long as dealers were discreet, they could peacefully co-exist. It was the only community where you could have drug dealers and police living comfortably together.

A craftsman as well as a businessman, this tourist town pioneer remembered: "In the early days, a large portion of my sales were handmade coke spoons and hash pipes, especially at the early arts and crafts festivals."

Other entrepreneurial pioneers, however, formed national and international rings and made handsome livings selling large quantities of drugs outside the community, and they spent a lot of that money in town. "Phil" was the name used by each member of one such drug ring so that, for security purposes, each member would not know the true identity of the others. Forty years later one of them recalled: "'Phil' [the leader of the group] asked me to find and buy an isolated ranch in the Paonia, Hotchkiss, or Crawford area that could be used as a distribution center for our operation. I did. Later, I unloaded the first truckload of pot there, 35 tons. I got paid $15,000.00 and a pick-up truck for that work. 'Phil' was generous."

A young early trust-fund pioneer used to party heavily, and is now drug and alcohol free, and a long-settled, well-respected, community member. He described himself as a former follower of Timothy Leary, the counter-culture Harvard professor associated with proselytizing about LSD. He said of the two years he dropped out of Western State College and lived in town:

> Smoking dope, doing drugs and skiing is what I mostly did. … My generation, the hippies, didn't want law enforcement because we did drugs … I was a real druggie … I did LSD, pot, coke, mushrooms, and peyote in that era. I kept a record of my psychedelic "trips" in my copy of Leary's, "The Psychedelic Experience": at least 75 acid trips, 12 mescaline trips, 1 psilocybin trip. I didn't really keep track of my mushroom or peyote trips. All in all, I probably only kept track of half my psychedelic trips.

A ski patrolman who smoked dope and used psychedelics regularly described some of his favorite LSD trips:

> One of my best acid trips was with ___ and ___ [a prominent pioneer couple from New York City], when we dropped acid and tripped in the mountains above Gothic [a nearby mountain north of the ski area]. Another time was with ____ [an eastern, Ivy-League-educated bar owner] and ____ [a pioneer real estate broker]. We ate LSD on the Cumbres and Toltec Scenic Railroad narrow gauge train trip from Antonito, Colorado to Chama, New Mexico. Another great trip was

when a group of us went to Monarch [a nearby ski area], on the last day of the season before it closed.

One of the recreation community settler women who ultimately went through a drug-rehabilitation program said:

> I did lots of coke, although I never bought it, because a lot of my friends were coke dealers, and I was high all the time. ... When I worked at town hall, I did coke with a lot of the town employees. ... We used to play Trivial Pursuit. The games would go on for days. The only way a new person could get into the game was if they brought drugs or beer. ... I did coke later at the cable company with _____ and _____ when I first started working there. A few months later they took me to Le Bosquet [a settler owned French restaurant] for my birthday, and gave me coke as my present, which we did in the bathroom. ... Rather than just doing coke with one group, because I knew most people in town, I did it with everyone. That was my problem.

Many years later a prominent professional, who also went through a rehabilitation program, recalled:

> From 1974-1984 or so, in fact, there was never a conversation or activity where drugs were not a part of it. You could get peyote or mescaline or acid at any party ... I used almost all drugs – coke ('I put over $250,000.00 up my nose'), and Quaaludes, pot, hash, mescaline, magic mushrooms, etc. I did not use angel dust, ecstasy, meth, heroin or blue cheer (a combination of coke and valium) ... My favorite combination was coke, Quaaludes, black Afghani hash and red wine.

He added: "A month after I stopped using, I had a nervous breakdown and went into a rehab program in Denver."

Although recreational drugs seemed to be everywhere pioneers and settlers gathered, and almost everyone indulged, some did not perceive themselves as having used them much, at least in comparison to others they knew. One woman who wrote a local news column said:

> I never did much in the way of drugs but I drank a lot. I like the 'elegance' of wine and cocktails. In the Tailings once, ___ [a pioneer builder]

and I lined up about 30 shots of tequila on the bar, and each of us drank from one end going toward the middle to see who could do the most shots and last longest. ... I did do coke fairly often though. ... Coke was everywhere: in the streets, people would stop one and offer coke; coke was put on sandwiches in the Eldo [a local's bar and restaurant]; it was in all the bars, especially in the kitchens, bathrooms and even on the bars themselves. There was always a bunch of coke in the Tailings [a popular bar]. Once I went to the vapor caves in Glenwood Springs with _____ and did LSD. But all in all, I really didn't do lots of drugs.

Another woman, who was 10-20 years older than most of the tourist town pioneers and early recreation community settlers, who initially came to the area as a faculty member of a summer art institute, noted insightfully:

Locals were tolerant about and comfortable with recreational drugs, but were very clear that no hard drugs were tolerated, especially heroin. ... Everything was prevalent but not flagrant. Everyone was trying everything. At parties there was always a room with lines of coke laid out. The marshals didn't seem to care if people were discrete. I only smoked a bit and only did coke once or twice. Many Crested Butte people became alcoholics at a young age."

Notably, a chapter of Alcoholic Anonymous formed in Crested Butte in January 1972.

Still another woman said, "I smoked pot but that's about all because I had kids, responsibilities, little money, etc. Once or twice I tried coke, but never did the hallucinogens. ... I know my son tried different drugs and dealt for a while."

As prevalent as drug use was, not all kinds were acceptable. Clear distinctions existed. Demarking the limits of what was okay, an early heavy drug using pioneer who worked as a ski instructor said, "Heroin and speed were not acceptable. They weren't part of our culture of recreational drug use." A little later in the town's history, however, a small number of people did

...not all kinds were acceptable ... an early heavy drug using pioneer who worked as a ski instructor said, "Heroin and speed were not acceptable. They weren't part of our culture of recreational drug use."

experiment with heroin, but it was never widespread or considered "acceptable." One woman said she was pretty sure two people she knew used it; and another, who worked in several local bars and restaurants and did lots of LSD and cocaine recalled, "I tried heroin twice and then stopped. It was so incredibly good. I knew if I had more, I'd never stop."

■ ■ ■

Besides experimenting sexually and using recreational drugs, there were other ways town newcomers lived differently from mining-era residents. As contrasted to the ski area trailblazers, most of whom wanted to blend into the old-timer's ways, few tourist town pioneers wanted to assimilate into the existing community institutions or culture. Nor did the recreation community settlers. They did not go to church or polka parties or join existing ethnic or national fraternal or community organizations where old-timers socialized. To the extent there was contact between older mining-era men and the new people, it was in the town bars where they shared the most often abused drug: alcohol. Old-timers thought that, with a few exceptions, tourist town pioneers did not work and lived on inherited funds. They resented that. By fall 1972, recognizing the increasing polarization between the two groups, a *Chronicle* editorial called for the creation of a "real town park" as one way to bring people together so that those who went to lodge meetings, church services, and polka parties and those who went to the bars, weddings, ballgames, and house parties might meet on common grounds.

Most pioneers wanted to socialize with their counterparts who, by the late 1960s, were arriving in unprecedented numbers. The 1970 census showed that there had been an almost 50% population increase within the most recent five-year period. Pioneers created their own community culture, much of it by producing or reinventing new athletic events, festivals, and arts and cultural activities, many of which included hard partying. They also established businesses, and developed nonprofit organizations, like a food

Pioneers created their own community culture, much of it by producing or reinventing new athletic events, festivals, and arts and cultural activities, all based on partying hard. They also established businesses, and developed nonprofit organizations… institutions to support them.

56

cooperative, the Business and Professional Women of Crested Butte; the Crested Butte Business Association, a forerunner of the local Chamber of Commerce; and they reinvigorated and redirected the focus of other groups, like the venerable Snowshoe and Toboggan Club. While some of these new organizations were fleeting, like the food co-op, others endured and became vehicles for pioneer and settler communal voluntary efforts. Their memberships, moreover, often reflected their privileged, urbane, backgrounds and interests, which further separated them from the town's mining-era residents.

Many of those activities and organizations, in one form or another, became part of, and important to, the organizational, cultural, and economic base of the increasingly gentrified, tourist town and recreation community.

The Crested Butte Society, for example, was formed mainly by the first wave of tourist town pioneers, with a smattering of ski area trailblazers and mining-era residents. Its aim was to encourage the development of cultural and educational activities, and to preserve the town's mining history. In late 1967, the newspaper reported that ski area trailblazers Gene Martin and Carol Morganson, "asked for and received a 3-year lease on the Old Rock Schoolhouse that had been abandoned in 1966. The two represented an organization known as the Crested Butte Society, Inc., which sponsored such events as pottery and ceramics workshops in the summer months. Martin said they wanted the old school to enable them 'to expand their summer cultural programs'." Shortly thereafter, the Society developed a small museum next to the old abandoned school and exhibited historic household and mining artifacts: a coal cook stove, coal buckets, pots, pans, fancy dishes, lace doilies, china cabinets, framed individual and family portraits, kerosene lamps, mule harnesses, picks, shovels, head lamps, and the like.

Town visitors, many of whom had once lived in Crested Butte, often visited the museum. Although it originally was meant just to preserve the past and pay homage to mining history and the old-timer's way of life, it later expanded to include the recreation community's evolution, particularly in relation to skiing and mountain biking. Today, fewer former old-timers go to see it, partly because many have died since the museum first began. It is now located on Crested Butte's main street in what was formerly Tony's Conoco gas station and hardware store, and the museum remains a frequently visited tourist attraction, and a significant part of the town's on-going cultural offerings.

In 1968, the Crested Butte Lodge Association was formed. It was the forerunner of all forthcoming organizational efforts to promote the area, including the Crested Butte Resort Association and then the Crested Butte Chamber of Commerce. Its original Board of Directors included Rix Rixford of the Ski Crest Lodge, Gus Larkin, Vic Dennis, and Dick Eflin from the ski resort. The Lodge Association hired ski area trailblazer Nadine Israel as its full-time director, and a part-time assistant, pioneer Barbara Norris.

In 1968, the *Crested Butte Chronicle* was bought by a new "ownership group," each of whom anted $50.00 to buy it. They made George Sibley its "majority partner" for $1.00. Sibley became its editor and wrote optimistically about the formation of both the Crested Butte Society and the Lodge Association:

> ... these two organizations ... are made up entirely of people who have been here long enough to be called citizens. Not natives, not old-timers, but citizens; residents – Crested Butte is their home. The Rixfords, the Norrises, Pete and Cathy Collier, Gus Larkin, The Bachmans, Vic Dennis, Dick and Liz Eflin, Barbara Kotz, The Morgansons: they are not natives, but they are obviously not fast-buck and fly-by-night either – they are here to stay."

Only two of those named stayed permanently. In tourist towns and recreation communities even most of the "locals" move elsewhere after several years.

The Business and Professional Women of Crested Butte was initially a chapter of a national organization It began in 1968. It too was a non-profit organization whose members were almost exclusively early new pioneers.[1] By September 1970, the Crested Butte Chapter had disaffiliated from its national organization, and it became autonomous. It renamed itself the Crested Butte Women's Club and focused solely on *local* concerns. Their intended first project was to construct an ice-skating rink in the town park that could double as a volley ball court in summers. The rink was never built; but two posts were erected with a net strung between them, constituting the town's rock-laden, rough-and-tumble, first ever, volley ball court.

In October 1968, a group of artists and craftspeople got together at the Nordic Inn to encourage and advocate for the development of a formal summer arts program. That reflected the increasing number of new people in Crested Butte, who wanted to make cultural activities and art education a significant part of the town's attractions and economy. It was to be organized under the aegis of the Crested Butte Society and housed in the Old Rock Schoolhouse. The meeting was convened by silversmith Gene Martin who owned a main street gift shop, the Water Wheel.[2]

These organizations and others each had an overt purpose, but perhaps more importantly, collectively they provided vehicles for allowing the area's new immigrants to socialize with each other, and develop a communal identity that was based on Crested Butte becoming a tourist town and recreation community that, in addition to skiing, included a substantial educational and cultural component.

Chapter 3

Mining-Era Women, Mountain Mamas, and the New Feminism

To the new people who came to Crested Butte following the ski area opening, most mining-era women seemed practically invisible. As admiringly described by Myrtle M. and Michele Veltri in their cookbook and cultural history,[1] those hard-working women spent their time mainly at home, tending to their families' domestic needs. They cooked economical, nutritious, delicious meals even during the toughest times after the mines closed when money was even tighter than before. They also kept their homes immaculate, despite coal being their main heat source. When they socialized, they did so mostly with other mining-era women and their families. There were exceptions, however, particularly among women who co-owned or worked in the few local retail establishments, in addition to working at home.[2] These women generally had more contact with newcomers, and got to know some of them a little, irrespective of whether they were ski area trailblazers or tourist town pioneers. Mining-era business women for the most part were more open to, and friendly toward, the new arrivals than were their male counterparts.

> To the new people who came to Crested Butte following the ski area opening, most mining-era women seemed practically invisible. ...There were exceptions, however, particularly among women who co-owned or worked in the few local retail establishments, in addition to working at home.

The youngest generation of mining-era women, those who were teenagers and pre-teens when the ski area opened, had much more contact with new people. One of them, Cathy Sporcich, explained many years later, "Well there weren't very many of us. When you grew up in Crested Butte, the local boys were like family; they weren't for dating." Regarding new people she added, "We kind of liked them because they were new. We

61

were like a 'bridge' to new people. Trudy [Yaklich] was the leader of the pack in that way; she married Butch [Giddings, from Steamboat Springs, Colorado]. Henrietta [Raines] married Steve Smith [from Texas]; Nettie [Kapushion] married Jim [Sweeney]; Mary Ann [Gallowich] married Rix Rixford; my sister [Debbie] married [Ron] Barr." Trudy Yaklich remembered her early teen years and said, "We

"We really looked forward to the boys from Oklahoma coming to town in the summers." "...The Oklahoma girls taught us how to be sexy: to open the top button of our blouses and 'tease' our hair."

really looked forward to the boys from Oklahoma coming to town in the summers." Henrietta Raines, remembered, "The Oklahoma girls taught us how to be sexy: to open the top button of our blouses and 'tease' our hair."

There were a few older mining-era women who did not work in the town retail establishments who occasionally socialized with the new women, and helped them learn how to live in a rural, mountain environment. One early female pioneer, Sue Navy, remembered, "Annie Perko was very warm to me and I enjoyed hearing her stories. She helped me learn simple rural mountain survival skills, like gardening and gathering mushrooms." Implicitly alluding to the tensions between mining-era residents and town-newcomers, Navy added, "I never had problems with the old-timers but I heard some of the men were a little crusty. This was their town and we were coming in and changing it." Pioneer women seemed to have had fewer confrontations with old-timers than their male counterparts. A

"The old guys were like old men everywhere: they liked young women."

Crested Butte Mountain Theater female observed many years later, "The old guys were like old men everywhere: they liked young women." Also, woman-to-woman bonding was a factor.

Mining-era women, including the ranching women, were extraordinarily competent, strong and hard working. The new Crested Butte women were also strong, especially the ski area trailblazers and tourist town pioneers but, unlike their old-timer counterparts, they were mainly single and fiercely independent. For the most part, they were free-spirited, fun-loving, adventurous, creative, resourceful, and were living in a rural

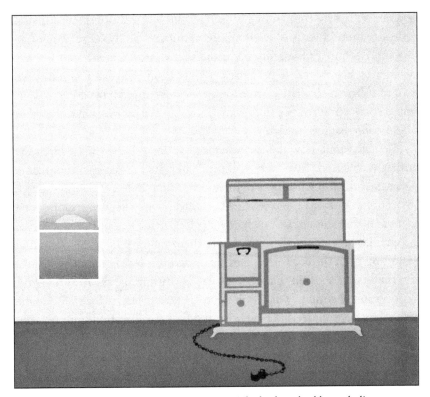

"Kolorado Kow Kulture # 4." Silk Screen print. The broken shackle symbolizes women breaking away from the stove and traditional female roles. Courtesy of Cordley Coit.

setting that differed dramatically from the communities in which most of them were reared. Further, many were influenced by the new feminist movement that emerged in the mid-1960s. One of them, Annie McElhinney, a Denver raised, tourist town pioneer and an influential early Crested Butte feminist said, "We were *modern* mountain women."

Nadine Israel was one of the earliest female ski area trailblazers. She moved to Crested Butte in 1962 from Pueblo, Colorado. She was among the earliest employees of the ski area. She worked there for several years until Howard "Bo" Callaway and his brother-in-law, Ralph Walton, bought it out of bankruptcy. A few years after that, she became the first paid director of the Crested Butte Resort Association, the original forerunner of what ultimately became the Crested Butte Chamber of Commerce.

At a farewell party thrown by her bridge club when she and her husband left town after 33 years, she reminisced about the family's first winter in a tiny, rented, miner's house in town, and the adjustments she had to make in order to live there. "If it hadn't been for Pauli Veltri and Annie Perko [two mining era residents] I don't know what I would have done.... One would come build the fire [in the coal stove] in the morning and the other would come bank it at night."

Remembering how the town water pipes froze in her first winter, she further recollected, "We were without water for at least two months.... We packed the tub with snow to melt to flush the toilet." Then she added, "They'd just finished the Ore Bucket [Lodge]. They kept one room open for us and after dinner we'd rush down [to the other end of town] with the three children to bathe them and clean them up for school the next day." Reflecting both the economic hard times and fun-loving nature of the ski area trailblazers she said that on a typical day during the ski area's first year of operation she might sell six or eight lift tickets after which, "I put the box [of money] under the bench [in the first small warming house] and went skiing."

Many trailblazing women who came with families were like mining-era women in important ways. They tended to their families and mostly socialized with other women and young couples, mainly at each other's homes or on mountain outings, and in "family-oriented bars and restaurants" like Frank and Gal's, where infants and toddlers could be found sleeping or playing under the tables while their parents visited with friends. Some worked, mostly in lodges and restaurants, and in a few cases, they attended church, where they met and occasionally mingled with some old-timers.

...many of the ... pioneer and... settler females came to town .... because they wanted to ski, party, and have outdoor mountain adventures, like many privileged Eastern women who had come west before them in earlier eras. Others came because they wanted to create art and the cost of living was low. Many came simply because they were seeking new ways of living.

For a variety of reasons, many of the tourist town pioneer and recreation community settler females came to town without families. Some came because they wanted to ski, party, and have outdoor mountain adventures, like many privileged Eastern women who had come west before them in earlier eras.[2] Others came because they wanted to create art and the cost of living was low. Many came simply because they were seeking new ways of living. They were rejecting, at least temporarily, the middle-class, upwardly mobile life-style in which they were raised. One of the early pioneer women said about arriving in Crested Butte:

> After graduating from ___ [an elite eastern] college, I came to Colorado to participate in an outdoor education program with Outward Bound. It was my first time in the West. After that, I needed 'personal time' to figure out what I wanted to do with my life. I was shopping for a mountain town because I wanted anonymity, a quiet place, and a friendly welcoming community.

She lived in a teepee in one of the surrounding high mountain valleys during that summer where she and her future husband met. (Like many who wed in Crested Butte, they are still married).

Importantly, early tourist town pioneer women, unlike many of their male "outlaw" peers, did not come to hide from authorities. However, they sympathized and identified with them.

Strong, independent mountain womanhood did not sit well with many men in the area, especially those trailblazers and early pioneers who had not been influenced by the new feminist movement, and who held traditional definitions of male and female roles, and how masculinity and femininity should be expressed. Many later pioneer and settler men also often had difficulty with aspects of the new "liberated" women, compared to what

Strong, independent mountain womanhood did not sit well with many men in the area, especially those trailblazers and earliest pioneers who ... held traditional definitions of male and female roles...

they were raised to expect in their homes and communities in the post WWII years, when monogamy was expected and extra-marital sex was covert. Male newcomers, however, clearly liked the increasingly open sexual freedom of the young women, even though they may have been less enamored with other aspects of their lifestyles and growing feminist consciousness. One young male pioneer remembered: "When I came to Crested Butte in 1967 there was an unwashed, unkempt, group of partiers....Girls were getting looser by the day and sex was easy."

That was fine for him since he usually had a female friend and was raised amid strong practical "can-do" ranching women. This independence and strength however, was not desirable to many other men, particularly those without girlfriends or spouses. One pioneer male who later became the town mayor remembered, "There were at least 3 or 4 men for every woman back then." Beginning in the late 1960s and continuing into the early '70s more pioneer women seeking alternate life-styles came to town. They were influenced by the growing national women's liberation movement and feminist consciousness. Many Crested Butte men reacted negatively. As an example, one early feminist recollected with amusement forty-five years later, that she had offered advice to a male pioneer who was helping her install a floor in the bathroom of the house she was renovating. She knew more about the task than he did. He responded to her suggestion, however, by saying, "Don't give me any of that liber-shit."

In the summer of 1970, *Chronicle* editor George Sibley, a seemingly "liberated" early pioneer who resisted military authority and rejected his Army officer's commission after having been influenced by the anti-war and civil rights movement, editorialized about the new feminism:

> There is something about the current drive for 'women's liberation' that I find disquieting. ... If women's usage had been as unpleasant and blatantly inhuman as the black man's field labor, you can bet that it would have ended long ago; the fact that women are still commodities in a man's world must have some relationship to the fact that the cage has been at least gold-plated and the objectification not without its aspects of deification .... I cannot see how the lib-ladies line of action is going to do very much for women at all. Provisions in the 'equal rights for women' amendment... seem bent on taking revenge against men...

He said further:

> So why do women, in seeking their desired liberation from those who have allegedly held them back, not sought it in establishing a separate identity from men, rather than trying to erase as many of the rather intriguing and wonderful things that make them different from men? ... Quite possibly, what we call the modern liberated woman is the first obvious product of what I choose to call the tragedy of Western

Civilization, a process we might tag dehumanization through utilization.

Finally, he wrote:

I know that nobody is going to be able to persuade WLF [Women's Liberation Feminists] that they would be happy if they would just go home and be good mothers. But whenever I see a woman who really knows what it means to be a woman – she doesn't have to tell, it just shows – I do not just hope, I know that WLF is looking in the wrong place, not for an equality that they never had, but for an identity that somewhere and somehow they lost...

That statement caused considerable consternation among the new young women. More than a few were enraged. Two weeks later, Susan Anderton, a married artist who co-owned Empire Tunnel Graphics, the local silk screen business, and who was a good friend of Sibley's, responded strongly. In a letter to the editor she wrote, "... I would like to point out that your remarks show a gross misunderstanding of the objectives of the movement, and that the hardest fight is not for legal and sexual equality per se, but against attitudes as those expressed in your article."

> *"... your remarks show a gross misunderstanding of the objectives of the movement, and that the hardest fight is not for legal and sexual equality per se, but against attitudes as those expressed in your article. .... an arrogant misinterpretation of the aims of the movement."*

She continued:

Has it occurred to you that women are not simply striving for a so-called equal position in a MAN's world but for an equal opportunity to realize themselves as human beings and so take a part in shaping OUR world? ... Women do not want to become omnipotent, nor do they want to deny their sex and everything it involves. The injustices they have suffered in the past as human beings are too numerous to mention here; suffice it to say that their potential for the future is unlimited, given the situation where they have an equal standing in the world as WOMEN.

The editor's convoluted, lengthy, response to her irate letter the following week contritely ended saying, "…I apologize to the women of the movement for being over presumptuous in suspecting the worst."

Significantly, Anderton did not self-identify primarily as a feminist, but as an art producer and shop owner. Her artistic and entrepreneurial endeavors underlaid and empowered her independence; and gave rise to her form of feminism. Several other tourist town pioneer and recreation community settler women, certainly a critical mass among the newcomers in Crested Butte, also owned their businesses. Many were based on the arts in one form or another. That made them, if not in doctrinaire ideology, financially independent and often feminists in practice.[3]

Other pioneer and settler women owned and operated restaurants.[4]

Still other pioneer women were entrepreneurial in other fields of work, using professional skills in Crested Butte that they had acquired before moving into the area. Jeanette "Sugar" Glass was a licensed preschool teacher in Connecticut who started a "progressive" nursery school in town. She sold it to female entrepreneur Honeydew Murray a few years later. Cece MacVittie was an accountant who developed a bookkeeping and accounting business and Miriam Zelenko was a nurse; they each worked regularly as independent contractors.

A few women designed and re-constructed their own houses. The first was Diane Kahn. She had been a stage set designer and technician before coming to Crested Butte. She designed and supervised a crew of unskilled volunteer workers that gutted and totally renovated her family home and installed the electrical and plumbing systems herself. Shortly after that, Joan Adams, who co-owned the Elk Mountain Lodge, was the second woman to design and oversee the renovation of her family's home. Other pioneer women, Tybel Edwards and Annie McEhlinney for example, worked as laborers on construction jobs both at the ski area and in town.

Men's consternation concerning the increasing independence of the "new feminist women" waxed and waned for several years. For instance, in November 1972, a not entirely satirical "Paid Political Advertisement by the Committee for a Better Looking Crested Butte" was signed by "Thirteen Local Bachelors." Along with 12 other men, Chuck Wirtz was a signatory. He was a popular, fun-loving, bartender who was widely considered a preeminent "ladies' man." He was also a socially significant human bridge between people on the hill and those in town. The ad was addressed to the local town women and was headlined, "Lost and Found":

> Just as we suspected, the Ladies Club Dinner Saturday night turned up quite a selection of … ladies. It was a pleasure to see several of the Town's lovelies looking their best. The evening also proved that women with some physical allure and grace are not, as rumored, an endangered species in the high country, nor the last of a dying breed known to us previously in our lost youth. There are still some potentially attractive women who persist in making local establishments look like they are hosting delegates to a truck-driver's convention, but we never intended to imply that all the local women are slovenly and uncaring about how they look. And we were very glad to see how many attractive females decorated the Matterhorn, Saturday. Thank you for making the evening so pleasant. If you can manage to keep up a little of those appearances, it should help provide a good deal of inspiration for the long winter ahead.

Annie McElhinney did not tolerate the sentiments expressed in that letter. She responded to the 'Thirteen Local Bachelors and Their Sympathizers':

> You post a want ad in the Chronicle in lament of the absence of a 'decent selection of ladies' gracing the street corners — ornamentation. Is femininity really so basic as having a slim figure, clean ultra-brite (sic)mouth, fancy clothes, and caring. To what are we indifferent — you? Those ideals of womanhood were put over on us by Madison Avenue needs; Barbie dolls, Revlon make-up (the 'natural look'), Playtex girdles, Lady Schick razors and Diet-rite and Metrecal. Some of us have gone beyond the 'type' while others have not. Many of us women in the Butte revel in feeling unfettered by the imposition of such models. You nearly shattered our illusion that there is no demand for us to copy such models to be regarded as attractive women. Has Madison Avenue detoured down Elk Ave? Perhaps the practical considerations would enlighten a few of you. To dress in an 'appealingly feminine way' (and I too can recall wanting to meet the rigid standards of fashion) entails some serious problems, such as frostbite, pneumonia or even hypother-

mia. ...the pattern people at Vogue don't design feminine apparel for sub-zero weather. Dainty boots ... don't make it when the snow squalls or you have to climb a hill. 'Lumberjack' clothes are not only well suited for comfortable exposure to our climate but also for the physical activities that attract us to this area. Are you suggesting that only men be suitable [sic] dressed for the life-style here and that women ... bare up ... trying to be appealing. On being overweight, that's a matter of taste. Reubens (sic) women kindled a fire ... Anyway, whatever shape a woman is, is womanly. About being 'foul-mouthed,' street talk is used by the people. Aren't women people too? (rhetorical) That women speak in vulgar and bodacious tongues reassures me that barriers between the sexes are falling, albeit slowly. But you would like to perpetuate select barriers. ... we associate closely enough to speak the same words. As for indifference, just living through a winter here requires caring and awareness. Priorities have changed ... largely because we are no longer comparing our departures from the ideal 'smilingforeversmilingpinklovelyfraildocilehelpless' wimp of a lady the mass media (and apparently you - sic) would have us emulate. In our reality it is more important to bank the coals properly than worry about keeping our hands pearly and lovely to touch. So that, I suppose, there is a sort of indifference – to the maintenance of that lovely creature we were taught so early to model ourselves after. Well, women in Crested Butte are already beautiful. If you 13 men are unable to see or appreciate that beauty then your awareness and sensibilities could stand some expansion. May I suggest getting together with some of your sisters and trying to discover a few of the alternatives to the code of beauty and femininity you have been trying to impose on us...

Four months later McElhinney wrote another letter to the editor denouncing the increasingly offensive and costly discrimination against women that she saw around her:

When I, or any woman, try to offer personal labor in hopes of gaining economically or experientially, we are most often refused on the premise that a woman does not possess enough strength or skill. ... Such notions appear early in one's experience. Say at Martha French's, age 10 years, when she reads in the town paper that she cannot attend a mountain 'backpacking camp for youth' because the camp is not for you at all, but really for boys.... And such notions plague one at every age thereafter. Terry Turner [one of the Chicago thespians who came to Crested Butte to work with the Mt. Theater] reads that an excellent summer job at 'a backpacking camp' for youth is restricted to MALES ONLY. ...opportunities are denied Terry solely because she is a woman. ...The cycle continues...as young boys partake and learn in segregated activities...they tend to correlate the absence of girls with a girl's inability or unsuitability... Further, the girls get no training or strengthening when they are denied such experiences. ...The attitudes develop firmly and penetrate most levels of our society; women are not strong enough to be on ski patrol; men are; women are not strong enough to serve as ambulance drivers; men are; women cannot be carpenters, men can; women are not mountain climbers; men are....

Shortly after her letter, an anti-discrimination lawsuit was filed against the area by Annie McElhinney who wanted to be hired as a ski patrol member but was denied employment because she was female. Top resort representatives met with her and some friends who wanted to be ski patrol members. The meeting was described in the *Chronicle* by staff writer Tybel Edwards under the headline, "One Step Forward for Womankind." It described the meeting between McElhinney, "one of Crested Butte's foremost advocates for women's rights," and area representatives Gus Larkin, General Manager; Terry Hamlin, Ski Patrol Director; Vic Dennis, Mountain Manager; and their lawyer Fritz Russell, as one that tried to settle the law suit that McElhinney initiated. Ultimately, the suit was dropped because the ski area agreed that the next three hires would be women, including Ariowitsch and Susie Fisher, both of whom attended the meeting. (McElhinney was not included because she intended to leave town). The report pointed out that the ski area questioned, but did not press, a point about McElhinney's morality, because she earlier had been a contestant in a wet t-shirt contest where, notably, many in the audience were ski patrolmen and town council members. Despite the negotiated agreement, as late as 1974, when the patrol roster was announced for the coming season, out of 17 patrollers, only one was a woman: Fran McIntyre, whose popular nickname then was "Fran 'The Man."

... an anti-discrimination lawsuit was filed against the area ...

Feminist sentiments of independence were expressed not only toward the ski resort, and work and sports activities. They were also directed toward the new "hip" pioneer council which was elected in the spring of 1972, and toward the new county judge. When a vacancy occurred on the newly created Board of Zoning and Architectural Review (BOZAR) in October 1973, for example, three people were appointed, two men and one woman. Two other female applicants also applied: Sandra Hickok, co-publisher and editor of the weekly newspaper, the *Crested Butte Pilot*, and Joy Rademan, wife of the town planner who had been one of the principals in BKR Associates, the town's planning firm. They were not appointed, according to the *Chronicle*, because of their perceived conflicts of interest. Joy Rademan was incensed. In a strongly worded letter to the editor she concluded:

> I must confirm that I see no Joy in BKR! Nor do I see any Joy Rademan in Myles Rademan or James Kuziak. I am my own person with my own mind and opinions, eyes, ears, etc! I do not feel oppressed in my marriage, at least not until this incident, nor am I bound legally, by choice or any other method to concede my own view in favor of Myles or Jim.

Similarly, early feminist Diane Kahn was the wife of a newly elected pioneer council member. He had often opined publicly that dogs were not a problem in town, and that they did not have to be leashed if they were under "voice control." She recalled that during a contested traffic ticket hearing she had in County Court, Judge John Levin berated her about her views on dog issues, although that was totally beside the point of the traffic case before him. Looking down from his elevated seat, he lectured her beginning with, "I know what you think about dog control!" He assumed, quite incorrectly and in a sexist manner, that her thoughts reflected those of her husband's.

There were constant examples where men used their privilege to make sexist statements or slights to demean women in one way or another. In addition to Sibley's outright editorial assault cited extensively earlier, editor Myles Arber used satiric commentary to exploit female beauty. When a fire total-

There were constant examples where men used their privilege to make sexist statements or slights to demean women in one way or another.

ly destroyed the ski patrol shack at the area, for example, its manager, Gus Larkin, reported the damage. Arber, alluding to the nude pin-ups that were on the shack's walls added, "In itemizing the property destroyed by the fire, Larkin omitted Tommy Glass' [ski patrolman and a council member] and Ed Costie's [fellow patrol member] priceless collection of erotic art which adorned the walls ... Glass said that he intends to make immediate efforts to reassemble his collection ..." While such satire might have amused the editor and his friends, he not so subtly regularly defined women as sex objects in his newspaper.

Other instances reflected the increasing awareness and articulation of women's issues and concerns, especially regarding personal life-style choices and politics. For example, in May 1973 Judy Naumberg, a new owner of the Grubstake, wrote a letter to the editor warning women about the dangers of the intra-uterine device, and urged them instead to use birth control pills to prevent pregnancy, despite possible discomfort and weight gain. Significantly, two months later, Kathleen Ross, the only female elected to the new 1972 town council, resigned. Naumberg applied to fill the vacancy, "Because I find myself representing the views of a majority of the people with whom I associate who are not otherwise close to anyone presently on the Council ..." She added, "... and because I am a female having a point of view which may be different from those of the male members ... and which would go mainly unrepresented except by a female member ..." She was *unanimously* appointed by the councilmen, irrespective of their stand on any individual issue or the faction to which they belonged. Indeed, in most cases, the individual consciousness of most councilmen and of the town collectively had been raised somewhat by the new feminism that was increasingly being articulated and exhibited by women. Crested Butte wanted a woman's perspective represented on its deliberative body. Significantly, on every succeeding town council there have always been councilwomen, and women also have been mayors.

By the summer of 1974, as feminist consciousness and activities were intensifying and widening, a unique work group was formed, "The Crested Butte Hot Shot Women." It was a female forest fire fighting crew closely associated with the Crested Butte Hot

By the summer of 1974 ... a unique work group was formed, 'The Crested Butte Hot Shot Women' ... a female forest fire fighting crew ...

Shots, an all-male brigade that fought fires throughout the Rocky Mountain West. A front-page *Chronicle* newspaper article was written about them, with a picture that depicted one of the top male crew leaders, Denny McNeil, orienting the women and teaching them how to fight forest fires with tools that were commonly used in that work. The caption beneath the picture said, "Hot Shot Ladies to Get Job Training." The piece noted that the female crew was being trained for "mop-up" operations. (The men's crew had begun as a mop-up team and later specialized in the more dangerous "initial attack" phase of fires). Forty years later during a panel discussion about the Hot Shots, several former crew members noted that it became harder to field a full men's crew because other employment opportunities were easier to find, and women filled what were formerly men's slots. Instead of fighting fires on separate crews, women fought them right alongside men on mixed-gender crews.

Despite having proven their mettle on construction sites, the ski patrol, and the Hot Shots, by January, 1975, women were still not considered suitable for Crested Butte law enforcement positions. Rob McClung, who by then was the new town marshal, announced that applications were being taken for a deputy, but he stated he would not hire a woman. He said, "I just couldn't see sending a woman in to break up a barroom brawl." Eight

> *Despite having proven their mettle...by January, 1975, women were still not considered suitable for Crested Butte law enforcement positions .... the new town marshal, announced ... he would not hire a woman.... "I just couldn't see sending a woman in to break up a barroom brawl."*

months later, however, he did hire Fran McIntyre as his deputy. At first, she had dog catcher responsibilities, but later was assigned substantially broader duties which were, in essence, the same as those male deputies shouldered.

Following Deputy McIntyre's advancement, other females began to make similar inroads into the town government bureaucracy; soon that trickle became a stream of women who were employed by the town. Together, these women strengthened what often was described years later as "the sisterhood." Terry Vaughan, for example, initially served as the town recreation director on a temporary contract basis. She then became the first permanent town recreation director and, after that, the town manager. Vaughan started a popular ski program for the town's one-and-a half to six-year olds, saying, "I feel skiing should be a way of life." All the instructors in that program were women.[5]

Not all of the expressions of independence and feminism were angry or even serious: some were satirical and playful. One letter to the editor in spring 1974, tried to clarify a popular misconception among townspeople about two in-laws, Pat and Patsy Reycraft. The two women wrote:

We no longer want to be (dis)credited with each others (sic) statements and activities. One of us, Mrs. Patricia Ann Reycraft (Patsy) is a respectable mother of four, wife of the postmaster, and free-lance stenographer. The other, Ms. Patricia Jean Reycraft (Pat) is a spaced-out, lazy, radical feminist, passive activist, conservative anarchist and ecological humanist. ... Thank you. ... Pat and Patsy.

There was a great deal of mutual support among pioneer women. Very close personal relationships emerged and a sense of sisterhood. Barbara Segal, a single mother, remarked years later about the bonding that occurred among them in the late sixties and early seventies. She said, "My twenties were here. I feel I grew up here. Plus, the deepest friendships of my life are from here. ... For my women friends, the relationships we had, the heartbreaks we had, the way we shared and supported each other when we were broke; women bonded here, in our searching time. We were always there for each other." She added insightfully, "I don't think that was true for men."

There was a great deal of mutual support among pioneer women. ... a single mother remarked years later about the bonding that occurred among them in the late sixties and early seventies. She said, "My twenties were here. ... the deepest friendships of my life are from here. ... For my women friends, the relationships we had, the heartbreaks we had, the way we shared and supported each other when we were broke; women bonded here, in our searching time. We were always there for each other."

Another woman who, importantly, is still a good friend of Segal's, echoed her remarks. "You had to want to be here." Segal's friend continued:

I cut my wood [for heating] for 18 years. Independent women stayed. Women who 'wanted a man' left after a few seasons. When I wanted sex, if there wasn't someone I was into in the bar, I called a male friend who was probably working in one of the restaurants, and told him, 'There's some good music going on here. Why don't you come over after work, hang out for a while, and then let's go back to my place.' Independent women didn't care if they had a long-term relationship. We wanted to climb a mountain, ski the steeps, etc. Women could be themselves here. If you were a character, that was okay; if you were into sports, and most women were, that was also okay. Women's softball was big in building female relationships, as was mountain biking.

As Segal did, she also noted the differences between men's and women's relationships:

Women were more in touch with each other and thought about the implications of their relationships with other women. Women took extended road trips together and that was bonding." Regarding those trips she added with a smile, "What happened in Vegas, stayed in Vegas.

A woman who was once between marriages remembered years later, "___ [a prominent public official with whom she worked] and I were sitting at the bar drinking late one night and we just looked at each other, and then went to his place to get it on."

Another woman who grew up, in her words, "as part of the country club set in northern Indiana," came to Crested Butte in the mid-1970s with her husband. After being in town for a year or two, they divorced. She then remarried for a short time to a newly divorced local man. Reflecting the post-WWII values with which she was raised, she said of her second marriage, "I guess I remarried because I always thought I was supposed to be married." A few months after their wedding she had the marriage annulled. She also talked about her drinking and drug use, and the sexual scene when she came to town in 1975. "I came to Crested Butte on New Year's Eve. ... I was told to go to the bath house where 'the whole town' would be. It was very crowded, everyone was nude, and I was uncomfortable taking my clothes off, so I left. I never went back." She added, "I used to go to bars a lot and played scrabble, bridge, etc. and drank." Illustrating how, compared to other pioneers and settlers she did not see herself as much of a drug user, she continued, "I never did much in the way of drugs but ... I did pot and coke fairly often ... and did LSD once ..."

As the pioneer women in Crested Butte were increasingly developing their modern feminist sensibilities, they, like their counterparts across the country, began a small "consciousness raising group." Tybel Edwards, wrote a March 1973 *Crested Butte Chronicle* piece about one of them under the headline, "Women's Group Gets Together." She wrote that a loosely knit small group of four (Diane Appleby, Diane Kahn, Margaret Bridgeford and an unnamed woman from Gunnison), met to offer "a confidential meeting ground for personal problems to be aired and mutual support and friendship to be given among the women. There is also the possibility that it could develop as a women's resource center."

By contrast, a small men's group also formed, but it broke up within two months when it became clear that the wife of one of the participants was having affairs with two other members of the group. A second attempt was made in February 1974 when a "men's consciousness" course was offered at the "Free Access University" (but it is not clear if anyone signed up for it or, if so, how long it lasted). Illustrating how female pioneers in town at that time saw the main difference between the sexes,

Illustrating how female pioneers in town at that time saw the main difference between the sexes, one... recalled it was common among women then to sum up the contrast by saying, "Men were boys; and women were men."

one of them recalled it was common among women then to sum up the contrast by saying, "Men were boys; and women were men."

Despite employment breakthroughs, sustained written and verbal protestations, sexual freedom, increasing women's solidarity, and male social sensitivity, male chauvinism and sexism continued to dominate the local tourist town pioneer and recreation community settler culture for many years. In December 1976, for example, a letter to the editor from a disappointed mother repeated the essence of Annie McElhinney's letters years earlier in which she decried men's traditional definitions of femininity and their practices of discrimination. The mom wrote that although her daughter wanted to play on the local school basketball team, she was not allowed to because she was a girl; and that was discriminatory, unfair and damaging.

Chapter 4

The Never-Ending Party

The strong-willed and creative ski area trailblazers and tourist town pioneers "went for it" as a way of life. They continuously looked for new challenges, and found innovative ways to play and party. "If you're not living on the edge, you're just taking up space" declared a piece of scrawled graffiti on top of a urinal in one of the town's bars, the Wooden Nickel. These adventurers were at the forefront of developing new outdoor sports including jeep, motorcycle and snowmobile racing, rock climbing, kayaking, etc.; and they reinvigorated others: softball, volleyball, horseshoes, cross-country and telemark skiing (a skiing technique that combines elements of Nordic and Alpine skiing), Gelande jumping (a form of ski jumping that uses conventional alpine ski equipment), and fly fishing. A few years later, they were at the forefront of developing mountain biking and snowboarding as popular sports. As the different athletic activities evolved and novices became experts, townspeople invented unique competitions. Many of them became endurance events, such as snowmobile "Safaris," or a grueling cross-country ski race, the "Al Johnson Uphill and Downhill Memorial Race." (That race was named after a hearty postal worker who skied between Aspen and Crested Butte and other late 1800's mountain mining towns to deliver mail on 9-foot long skis using only a single, long, heavy wooden pole for balance). A similarly strenuous "Pearl Pass Bike Tour" traversed the mountains between the two mountain towns on old, heavy, single gear, fat-tire bicycles.

The ...ski area trailblazers and tourist town pioneers "went for it" as a way of life. They... looked for new challenges, and found innovative ways to play and party. "If you're not living on the edge, you're just taking up space" declared a piece of scrawled graffiti on top of a urinal in one of the town's bars...

These strenuous sports were not enough for the new Crested Butte locals. They also created cultural activities like an arts festival, a community theater, and a dance company. Additionally, they fabricated an array of homegrown celebratory events such as "Flauschink" and, later, "Vinotok" which were multi-day festivals based on completely made-up legends, not unlike "the Easter Bunny" myth or the one about Santa coming down the chimney on Christmas eve.

The old-timers' five main holiday celebrations – New Years, Easter, Memorial Day, July 4th and Christmas – were just not enough for the fun loving, partying newcomers with vibrant imaginations and plenty of time on their hands. Their new creations were sometimes based in part on the town's ethnic history while others were totally devoid of it. A three-day madcap festival celebrating the end of winter, for example, was derived from the Serbian-Croatian heritage of many mining-era residents and their partying preference for heavy drinking and polka dancing.

In the late 1960s and early 1970s, other lasting community cultural institutions were launched by the tourist town pioneers that had nothing to do with the community's historical roots. Many still endure. The birth of the Crested Butte Mountain Theater, now the longest running community theater in Colorado, as well as the Crested Butte Arts and Crafts Festival that now, 50 years later, is the event that attracts the largest number of visitors to town each year serve as examples. Importantly, all of these activities were created originally by locals for their own amusement. Many of them included lavish float-filled parades, outlandish costumes and, of course, large quantities of drugs and alcohol. Later, many events also attracted thousands of tourists to Crested Butte, and became major attractions.

...all of these activities were created originally by locals for their own amusement. Many of them included lavish float-filled parades, outlandish costumes and, of course, large quantities of drugs and alcohol. Later, many events also attracted thousands of tourists to Crested Butte, and became major attractions.

Most ski area trailblazers and a few early tourist town pioneers enjoyed alpine skiing at the area and motorized outdoor sports: snowmobiling, jeeping, and motorcycling. As early as 1964, local snowmobile races were held, with trailblazer Jerry Sampson, proprietor of the Grubstake, winning the first one. In 1965 Ski-Doo snowmobiles were introduced as work machines at the ski area. A new Ski-Doo association was immediately formed; Chuck Wirtz was its first president. A picture in the first 1966 issue of the *Chronicle* caught a Ski-Doo racer in mid-air going over a jump at the ski area. The two following weeks' newspapers described a 60-mile Ski-Doo race from Crested Butte to Aspen that was won by western-Colorado reared trailblazer, Dave Watson. The newspaper reported that the race was the first-time motorized winter vehicles had *ever* gone from one town to the other, a feat that was featured in the *Denver Post*, generating much sought-after state-wide publicity for the town. (Ironically, the race had been sponsored by Columbia Pictures to publicize a new film about a ski chase in Norway, "The Heroes of Telemark.") Shortly after that, Crested Butte publicized that it would host Snow Mobile Championship races for the first time.

Motorcycle and Jeep races were summer sports events during the period when Crested Butte was first consciously becoming a tourist town. In late summer 1968, the local newspaper featured a front-page piece about a four-wheeler rally held in town. Dan McElroy, an early tourist town pioneer, was a ski instructor who moved to town with his young family. His first business, begun in the summer of 1969, was Mountain Cycles Shop. Years later he recalled:

> As part of that year's Labor Day celebration weekend, there were a bunch of motorized events, including a 100-yard horse vs. motorcycle race, between Trip Wheeler [an early tourist town pioneer] riding a Czech-made CZ bike, and Bobby Niccoli, [a son of a long-time upper Gunnison Valley ranching family], who rode a horse. It was held on slag piles from Colorado Fuel & Iron's closed coal mine, [known locally as the Big Mine], immediately south of Whiterock Avenue. After getting off to a slow start, Wheeler finally won. A lot of money was bet on that race.

By September 1970, McElroy announced that the area's first motocross, a dirt-bike motorcycle race, "is finally coming to Crested Butte…and it will be held on a track being constructed in [nearby] Washington Gulch, on land that Bill Lacy [a local rancher] owned."

By the tail end of the 1960s, a budding interest in "quiet" summer and winter sports was growing among some early pioneers. Roy Smith and Tom Morrell, both British adventurers, and an American, Leonard Ossario, were each part of an experimental outdoor education program at the small Arizona liberal arts Prescott College. These three men moved their base of operations to Crested Butte and introduced technical rock climbing, kayaking, and multiple day backpacking trips and, according to early pioneer Harold O'Connor, "lots of fun and humor." In the winter, similar non-motorized activities were being pursued, especially cross-country skiing in the relatively flat areas surrounding town, and in the mountains of the "back-country," where pioneers made long, sweeping, downhill turns on cross-county skis, a maneuver called "telemarking."

There were a number of reasons that this new winter sport developed: some obvious, others not. The natural beauty of the untrammeled winter back-county is clear to everyone who goes into it, and many skiers took up the sport for just that reason. Others took to it simply because they tired of alpine skiing, and it was a challenging "new" snow sport. Yet others were attracted to it because it was part of their personal rebellion. Denny McNeil, a draft resistor, a Western State College student, and one of the first pioneer woodworking craftsmen in town, said many years later, "I quit downhill skiing because it was 'corporate' and supported the system. I took up cross-country skiing." Some enjoyed it because for them it was part of the heavy partying scene. At "Coney's place," one of the cabins in Washington Gulch, parties often lasted for weeks. To get there, revelers trekked on cross-country skis. There they telemarked on what became popularly known as "Coney's Ridge." These activities, along with shooting guns off and blasting dynamite, became regular features of those now legendary winter parties.

Several of the original practitioners described the formative period of "cross-country" skiing. They described skiing around the nearby hills, sometimes climbing on skis to the tops of local mountains and then descending, tenuously at first and, later, as they became more proficient at carving turns in the snow, as fast as possible. These wild, partying, "devil-may-care," telemarkers used only 50-100-foot long, thin, red, nylon "avalanche" cords that they tied around their waists in case they fell, or they triggered a massive snow slide or avalanche on the steep terrain. Brian

Dale, a young pioneer from the mid-west remembered, "I was one of the early cross-country skiers. One sunny day Carol [his wife] and I went skiing up at Coney's. We left our baby daughter with Coney to babysit while we skied the Ridge. We told him to shoot a gun off if she cried; she did and he fired his rifle. Carol went to get her and then we raced home." Sue Navy, who had grown up in lower Manhattan, was another young pioneer who partied at Coney's. She later recalled, "People would eat, drink, do lots of drugs, and then go out and ski the Ridge." Denis Hall, a Colorado born and bred pioneer who went to WSC so he could ski, recollected many years later, "We would go out to Coney's on cross-country skis, and haul in huge quantities of Jack Daniels, beer, food – including wild game, explosives and drugs of all kinds. I learned to telemark up there and a group of us got really good at it: Rick Borkovec, who gave up drugs and found God, Buzzell, Kathy Crips, Susie Fisher, Baggins, Rudy, Walt Keith, Coney, and others." Walt Keith also remembered the scene at the cabin, and its participants:

> We learned to telemark in the backcountry. We climbed the Ridge without 'skins' [a Velcro-like material that is strapped to the bottom of cross-country skis to make uphill climbing easier] and skied down to Coney's cabin. We used thin nylon cords that were about 50 feet long that we tied around ourselves, hoping that if someone got caught in an avalanche, the rope would float to the top of the snow and others would be able to find him. After a while we used fishing reels to wind the cord around to make it easier.

He added playfully:

> Buzzell used to ski naked all the time, with only "gators" on. One time he had a bad fall on Gothic and nearly skinned himself to death. It was one of the ugliest injuries I ever saw."[1]

He continued:

> At Coney's, parties would go on for days. People would come, go back to town — usually for work, and come back with new supplies of food, drink and drugs. One day at Coney's, Doug Buzzell was falling asleep,

which wasn't allowed. So Crazy Dave poured ever-clear [alcohol] on him and lit him on fire. Sue Navy threw a bucket of water on Buzzell to put the fire out but he still got burned.

As many of the new tourist town pioneers increasingly took up "quiet" sports — cross-country skiing, hiking, backpacking and the like — they clashed with some younger mining-era men and ski area trailblazers, who favored jeeps, motorcycles and snowmobiles. Pioneers did not like what they thought of as the noisy, polluting machines. Besides, the cultural differences between the two groups

As many of the new tourist town pioneers increasingly took up 'quiet' sports – cross-country skiing, hiking, backpacking and the like – they clashed with some younger mining-era men and ski area trailblazers who favored jeeps, motorcycles and snowmobiles.

accentuated those confrontations. It was only many years later that a half-hearted on-going co-existence was established, although animosities between motorized and quiet back country users still continues to arise periodically. In early spring, 1968, beneath a newspaper headline "Big Game, Snowmobilers Don't Mix" an article said that deer and elk herds and other wildlife were threatened by the loud snowmobiles; but that snowmobiles were a new form of recreation and had to be recognized as such realistically. In commentary at the time the editor combined his awareness of the clash of the two sports themselves, as well as the inter-cultural conflict, "If the tranquility of the open space [enjoyed by the cross-country skier] is broken with the noise of a line of snowmobilers, and they comment on your hair length or style of dress [cross-county skiers will be intimidated by snowmobilers] …"

In late January 1969, the Second Annual Blue Mesa Snowmobile Rally was to have been held. In an editorial on the winter machines and the turmoil surrounding them, especially whether they could be used on the town streets, George Sibley, who had recently taken up cross-country skiing, called for an accommodation between the two sports and the people who enjoyed each. He opined, "Crested Butte is a winter sports area now. Snowmobiling is a winter sport. So, it only makes sense that Crested Butte must adapt her laws to 1) provide for the use of snowmobiles while 2) preventing the misuse of snowmobiles." Reflecting the tensions among new immigrants to Crested Butte in that era, motorcycle enthusiast Dan

McElroy recalled, "Many of the new people opposed the noise levels and the motorized use of the public lands. We favored their 'multiple-use'. I distanced myself from many new people who opposed the whole motorized thing."

■　■　■

Crested Butte mining-era residents proudly celebrated the Fourth of July. Like most first-generation immigrants, they were proud to be Americans, and were fiercely patriotic. Their celebration during the mining days clearly reflected the work men did. They set off dynamite blasts at the crack of dawn and, later in the day, held hard rock drilling, mucking, and log cutting contests; there were separate nail driving and log sawing contests for the women. Some observers thought the Fourth also had a distinctly European aspect to it as well, although others might have questioned how it differed from other July 4th celebrations.

In a 1968 newspaper piece Sibley noted:

> The Fourth of July is Crested Butte's biggest celebration of the year, but no one should mistake it for a typical American celebration. It is Old Country Slovenian all the way, consisting of three basic and necessary elements: large numbers of people in large rooms, much liquid refreshment, and unlimited music and dancing. For a proper celebration not one of the three can be missing…

To a few ski area trailblazers and some early tourist town pioneers, the annual celebration was seen as quaint or "camp," with its few mining and logging oriented events and its scant three or four floats mounted on old pick-up trucks crawling down the pot-hole pitted dirt main street, cheered on by local residents and a few Gunnisonites. To other pioneers, especially those who were anti-establishment, it seemed overly patriotic at a time when they were questioning the American political system and government itself. They thought America created and fostered racism, poverty, and promoted policies that harmed the natural environment. Internationally, they thought the Government perpetuated colonialism, and they used the Vietnam War as evidence. As old-timers became more isolated from the newcomers, mainly because they disliked their life-style choices and values, the July 4th celebration almost ended. Mining-era residents and trailblazers became less involved in mounting the annual event. In 1969, the volunteer fire department, which mostly consisted of the few younger mining-era men and a few trailblazers, announced that it would no longer organize the Fourth of July.

...the annual July 4th celebration was seen as quaint or "camp".... To other pioneers, especially those who were anti-establishment, it seemed overly patriotic at a time when they were questioning the American political system and government itself. ...the July 4th celebration almost ended.

The new pioneers, always up for a party and not wanting to give up a good excuse for one, took over the organizing activities. In the process, they transformed it into an event that appealed more to the new locals and to the increasing number of people visiting town who were part of the still embryonic but clearly emerging tourist economy. At first, they maintained some of the mining-era traditions. In 1969, for example, according to pioneer John Benjamin, he and Steve Glazer bought a 40-pound box of dynamite, "right off the shelf at Tony's Conoco," (the town's hardware store), and divided it. From the east and west sides of town, at precisely 7 A.M., they set off the dynamite in perfect unison, awakening and shaking up the entire town.

In that same year, the first July 4th Gothic to Crested Butte 1/3 marathon race was organized, complete with a $20.00 prize for the winner. Three free beers were provided to anyone who finished the race at Tony's Tavern. Virtually all the runners were young town newcomers or students at the research-oriented Rocky Mountain Biological Laboratory in Gothic, another former tiny mining town eight miles away. Thereafter, that 1/3 marathon, along with a pancake breakfast fundraiser for the town fire department, became the opening staple for the days' festivities.

Anticipating a wild multi-day July 4th party, newspaper editor George Sibley wrote an open "Message to Our Visitors." He apologized in advance for what he expected would be the raucous and perhaps irreverent behavior of some locals. He explained that Crested Butte people work and play hard, and sometimes get rowdy. After the celebration, he wrote that it was hard to make the planned events work. He declared that arrangements for the following year had to be made early if the Festival was to keep growing and attract tourists. He added that, alternatively, nothing had to be done, and July 4th could revert back to being solely an activity for local residents. He also acknowledged the many early tourist town pioneers who worked to put the weekend's activities together.[2] Indeed, the annual celebration did continue in succeeding years, albeit modestly. But by the 1976 bi-Centennial year, the July 4th transformation from a small mining town celebration to a major event that attracted many tourists was complete, as evidenced by a makeshift "float" of naked women who painted their entire

... by the 1976 bi-Centennial year, the July 4th transformation from a small mining town celebration to a major event that attracted many tourists was complete, as evidenced by a 'float' of naked women who painted their entire bodies in red, white and blue, and slowly paraded smilingly with the other floats on the town's newly paved main street...

bodies in red, white and blue, and slowly paraded smilingly with the other floats on the town's newly paved main street, along with approximately twenty-five other official floats. Ultimately, the July 4th celebration became one of the town's largest summer tourist attractions, annually bringing ten to fifteen thousand people to town to view the parade and enjoy the day long revelry and evening fireworks.

■   ■   ■

Continuing the Independence Day celebration was simply updating a traditional national holiday and modernizing it to reflect recreation community lifestyles while appealing to late 20th century visitors. However, for a town with an ethos that increasingly valued playing and partying heartily, the Fourth, along with Easter, Memorial Day, Christmas, and New Year's, was necessary but hardly sufficient, as it had been for the hardworking mining-era residents. So, tourist town pioneers created new celebratory events and festivals.

As mentioned briefly above, "Flauschink!" was the first. It was unique and became the most enduring. It was conceived by a few early newcomers in a bar in 1969, following a massive January snow storm that dumped 95 inches of snow in town. It was meant to coincide with the end of the ski season and to be an event for solely for locals, to celebrate the end of what they perceived as Crested Butte's interminable, snowy, cold, winters, and to welcome spring. From its inception, all publicity indicated that the founders intended Flauschink! to be an annual affair. The Festival's origin and mythological history was a product of the creative energies of a few of those party-loving, early pioneers who were starving for new activities, cultural events, and interesting, fun things to do in the isolated, tiny mountain town. After more than just a few beers, popular bartender Chuck Wirtz, Gunnison college business professor Art Norris, and *Chronicle* editor George Sibley originated the idea. Sibley, who created

... "Flauschink!" was the first. It was unique and became the most enduring. It was conceived by a few early newcomers....to coincide with the end of the ski season... It was meant ... solely for locals, to celebrate what the perceived as Crested Butte's interminable, snowy, cold, winters, and to welcome spring. From its inception, ... the founders intended Flauschink! to be an annual affair.

the mythology surrounding Flauschink! and some of the activities in the multi-day celebration, later told Gary Ferguson, author of *The Great Divide*, "If I was just going to report the news, it would've been a pretty freakin' boring newspaper. It dawned on me at the time that one of the best things about having a newspaper was the opportunity to invent things."[3]

Sibley's mythical creation was based on a fictitious, long-lost, legendary Eastern European people, the "Ugra-Sorbians." Through the years the tale has been retold annually in Crested Butte in much the same way that Jewish families pass on lore about their passage out of Egypt at the Passover Seder and Christians tell their story about the birth of Christ at Christmas. The Flauschink myth has become part of the community's lore and its continuity. It was introduced via the newspaper through a banner headline simply stating, "Flauschink!"; above that, it teasingly asked, "Did you hear the one about the two Ugra-Sorbians who were walking down the street? One said to the other:"

Five weeks later, another piece promoted the forthcoming events, and explained that buttons costing $1.00 were available that would allow participants entry into all Flauschink! activities. Signaling that from its inception the activities were meant to be merely the first of many succeeding ones, .41 cents of the $1.00 fee was designated to promote next year's bigger and better Flauschink. Then, on April 2nd above the *Chronicle* masthead in big, bold, letters, the paper grandly announced:

BY ROYAL PROCLAMATION: Flauschink is upon us – The first recorded Flauschink, the Year One. So being, it is our Royal Wish that all these attending unto us here, whether they be strangers today, old friends returning, or natural and life-long citizens of this place, join us this week in setting our Precedents for all Flauschinks-to-Come. Let the Passing of the Winter be never more warmly commemorated: let the Advent of Spring be never more joyously marked. So be it.

The first planning committee had included competitive and non-competitive snowmobile and ski races. The latter, in itself, was a race along the town's main street with snowmobiles pulling skiers. That event intentionally bridged a gap between two conflicting town factions: snowmobilers and those who did not like them. A king and queen of Ugra-Sorbians in exile were crowned, and a grand meal was held with lots of drinking and dancing (which Sibley had defined earlier as *essential* ingredients for the old-timer's July 4th festivities).

Flauschink! was a success! Everyone had a good time. The following week's paper was almost entirely devoted to the festivities, documenting them with both reports and photographs. One picture was of the first Flauschink! "royalty": mining-era resident Whitey Sporcich and early tourist town pioneer Cathy Wertz, king and queen respectively. The planning committee had painstakingly selected each one. They knew, importantly, that each person was well liked by *both* major factions in the community, and the original organizers were acutely aware of and sensitive to that schism and wanted to breach the divide. Not incidentally, as Flauschink! became embedded into the community's new culture over the years, to be named a "royal" became a prestigious sign of local acceptance, of being a man or woman of the people, a great honor. In a video-taped collective interview of the Flauschink "Has-Beens," those who had already been named as "royals," now archived in the Crested Butte Heritage Museum, recreation community settler and long-time local resident Mac Bailey perceptively said about the significance of being so named, "Being selected is a great honor, and everyone here who has been, knows just what I mean."

Another photo, this one of a torch-lit parade of skiers traversing one of the lower ski runs, included a peace symbol in its midst with an accompanying statement. It said that officially it was not known who created the peace sign but interested readers might want to speak to two anti-war pioneers, Doug Jenks and Eric Buzzell. The week's editorial commended Flauschink! activities, its joyous spirit, and the widespread community involvement. It noted the increasing rarity of collaboration between factions and alluded to the continuous tensions that were arising between them. "An on-the-corner and over-the-bar consensus of attitudes in Crested Butte these past several years has been that cooperation on community projects is not this town's strong suit, to put it very mildly. But…we of the Flauschink committee feel that we have evidence to the contrary."

At the end of January 1970, in preparation for the next year's event, a meeting was held at Chuck Wirtz' house. As seems appropriate for a town economy and social life that increasingly was based on partying, the paper reported "amidst a great deal of liquid refreshments, a tentative plan for this year's Flauschink festival was devised." The chair people and their committees were all trailblazers and pioneers.[3] A month later a *Chronicle* headline announced, "Hot Dog Race Set for Flauschink" and the piece following it described the forthcoming weekend as "Mardi Gras, Fourth of July, and New Year's Eve all in one."

That spring, in an elaboration of the Flauschink mythology, the paper included a (fictional) lengthy letter to the editor from a "Dr. Alan Smedhurst" of Budapest, Hungry entitled, "A Few Notes on the Elusive and Rarely Encountered Ugra-Sorbians." Sibley continued developing his fictional creation about the ancient people Flauschink celebrated. In the same issue a promotional piece pronounced, "…Crested Butte's second annual revival of the ancient Ugra-Sorbian end-of-winter, return of spring festival will take the town over in a storm of merry-making, rejoicing, and general carrying on." Accompanying that story was a separate supplement listing the schedule of the ensuing week-end events. The new king and queen of Flauschink were crowned: well liked mining-era resident Rudy Sedmack and equally favored early tourist town pioneer Barbara Sibley. They, again, reflected sensitivity to the town's two main factions. After the weekend was over, the newspaper reported, "…Flauschink '70' roared on through town with three days and two nights of general and highly varied celebration." Added to the old-timers' earlier traditional holiday celebrations, another weekend event was appreciated by the entire town. By 1970, both old-timers and new people almost universally accepted and enjoyed the new locals-oriented town event. The Flauschink! seed, with its intentionally and totally fabricated tongue-in-cheek mythology, that of the Ugra-Sorbians, had been successfully sown,

The Flauschink! seed ... had been successfully sown; and was now ensconced in the community's new playful party culture and would remain forever after as part of the town's repertoire of celebratory festivals.

and was now ensconced in the community's new playful party culture and would remain forever after as part of the town's repertoire of celebratory festivals.

■ ■ ■

Crested Butte's economy was increasingly dependent on attracting tourists. Its proportionately large population of artists and craftspeople wanted to encourage cultural activities as a mainstay of that development. They thought a mid-summer activity might provide a viable vehicle for town residents to show and sell their work, while also bringing visitors to town. Thus, in 1971 the first "Summer Festival of the Arts and Crafts" was born.

Crested Butte's economy was increasingly dependent on attracting tourists. Its proportionately large population of artists and craftspeople wanted to encourage cultural activities...They thought a mid-summer activity might provide a viable vehicle for town residents ..., while also bringing visitors to town. Thus, in 1971 the first "Summer Festival of the Arts and Crafts" was born.

The *Chronicle* announced the forthcoming event with an article and photos of two artists. Nina De Montmollin of Albuquerque worked in watercolors, oils, and acrylics and spent summers in Crested Butte. Painter Mike Berry was originally from Minnesota, where he studied at Alfred University and then attended the School of the Americas in Mexico City. By that summer he had been living in Crested Butte for about a year and was "one of the prime movers of the Summer Festival."

Second Annual Festival of the Arts and Crafts Poster. Courtesy of Susan Anderton.

The first Arts and Crafts Festival anticipated that about twenty local exhibitors would show their work, providing broader exposure for them. By the time it actually began there were over thirty, not all of them from Crested Butte or Gunnison, including watercolor, oil, acrylic, silkscreen, and ink drawing artists, a calligrapher, ceramicists, photographers, woodcarvers, leather workers, weavers, jewelers, candle makers, a bead worker, an iron sculptor, and a silversmith.[4]

Berry and Jim "Zoo" Cazier, a woodworker, designed the layout for the exhibit area and display booths. They erected it on an 80' by 40' wooden platform constructed of old railroad ties that were placed on three of the vacant lots in the center of the town's main street. Ironically, they could not show their own work; they spent too much time designing and creating that unique foundation and erecting the wood structure that housed the exhibits. The newspaper described the setting as having a "Mercado" ambiance. Besides the central area where people displayed their work in a traditional way, there were "artist-at-work" exhibits where spectators could watch people producing their work. Gene Martin, a silver worker, was an example. In addition, performing artists played folk music, actors gave short theatrical presentations, and the Western State College band presented a concert.

Prior to that first Festival, there were a few objections voiced by local residents who were concerned that too many people might inundate the town, especially counter-culture youth. A few exhibitors wanted only locals showing their work. They did not want, "people…to just drive up and start selling stuff out of their car trunks." After the Festival ended, despite a few nagging criticisms, it was deemed a success! More artists and craftspeople displayed their work than were originally anticipated, and more tourists came into town than were expected. Everyone and everything was "mellow." The *Chronicle's* banner headline summarized the general feeling, at least among the town's tourist town pioneers, "1st Summer Festival Surpasses All Expectations," and a long piece highlighted the weekend's activities. A separate feature reported that the Festival was filmed by poet/artist Cordley Coit with help from its producers, Tom Morrell and Tim Reed. Additionally, "all of the music and some of the dialogue generated by the fair for use in the soundtrack" was put together by impromptu soundmen Jim Cloud and Kemp Coit.

Despite the Festival's positive overall evaluation, however, there were several strongly made suggestions about how future art festivals could be improved. The second pioneer Crested Butte *Chronicle* Editor, Morgan Queal, who only had a six-week tenure in that position, opined that if organizers wanted succeeding festivals to be considered important to Colorado, a jury system needed to be put in place to screen submitted work, so only high-quality arts and crafts were displayed. Over the next few years, that became a recurring critique.

In the middle of the following summer, in 1972, the second annual summer Festival of the Arts and Crafts displayed the work of even more exhibitors from an even wider geographical area. Word-of-mouth praise spread about the first Festival, so in addition to locals from Crested Butte and Gunnison, even more people registered from other Colorado and New Mexico towns, and new states including Illinois, Arkansas, and

California were represented. For the first time, the event had a separate display area for the culinary arts and locally made foods, a forerunner of modern farmers' markets. In the evenings, the new Crested Butte Mountain Theater presented its first theatrical production, "Dark of the Moon." Set outdoors against the backdrop of Crested Butte Mountain, on opening night it was performed, ironically, under a full moon. Presumably due to word-of-mouth conversations about the success of the inaugural festival, and better and more widespread formal publicity, more visitors were expected and welcomed to the second one. Significantly, that year the Festival received funding for the first time from Crested Butte and Gunnison local businesses and personal donations, as well as from the Council on the Arts and Humanities in the form of a matching grant. Large tents, loaned by the US Army and National Guard, housed many of the exhibits.

Well over 60 exhibitors displayed their work that year. Many of the same Crested Butte people showed their work as they had the year before, but the majority were first timers. In addition to the crafts shown before, two separate exhibits displayed mineral specimens, two others erected teepees for visitors to go into, and another showed afghans, quilts, and bedspreads.

The second annual Festival was also deemed successful, mostly by those involved in organizing it and those who sold their wares. However, criticism about how "open" it was and the quality of some exhibits intensified, especially among the newest recreation community settlers who wanted to "clean up the town" and rid it of its hippie image; those who, in fact, wanted the town to develop in a way that appealed to more affluent tourists.

The third Festival committee tried to address those concerns. Tony Monaco, a commercial graphic artist who was the manager of the Water Wheel gift shop with his wife, Jill, became part of the planning committee. He was a new settler who arrived in town shortly before he joined the committee. He asserted that the 1973 Festival would be different from the first two. In an open letter to the *Chronicle* he wrote:

> Of course, the goal of the crafts council is to encourage the craftsmen of the Crested Butte and Gunnison area .... the 1973 Crafts Festival will

be held throughout the town of Crested Butte under the roofs of sponsors who would like to encourage the town to grow in the area of arts and crafts. Businesses and individuals will provide set up space for the artists they wish to represent and all displays therefore will be on private property. We hope this will eliminate the last-minute crashers who take advantage of us all and contribute little …. The Fair will be conducted as a walking tour.

That viewpoint was not shared widely among many townspeople, especially those who enjoyed the openness and spontaneity of the earlier two Festivals. The following week, another letter to the editor was written by David Leinsdorf, the first pioneer town attorney. Although Leinsdorf was one of the leading proponents of "smart" or "controlled" development, and part of the faction that favored it, he broke with some of the other pro-growth advocates. In response to Monoco's letter he wrote:

> … 'last minute crashers' should be welcomed not excluded by the Arts Council. The purpose of the festival should be to encourage as many people as possible – both artists and public – to attend. If some artists lack the funds, foresight or fairness to pay and sign up for the space in advance, so be it …. An open festival, not private exhibits with cash awards for contest winners will achieve that result.

By late April, following the public disputes and criticisms, and the "burnout" and absence of the earlier Festival organizers, George Sibley, who by then was the "former" newspaper editor, agreed to chair the coming summer's planning committee. Sibley was the earliest and most persistent proponent of bringing educational and cultural endeavors to town to enhance the quality of life for local residents, while providing a vehicle for economic growth. He also believed in "art for art's sake." The town's paper proclaimed, "Sibley to Head Art Festival Committee." After describing how this third annual event would be structured and where the exhibits would be located, Sibley indicated he understood some of the prior criticisms, and said that in his view one of the more attractive features of the earlier Festivals was that exhibitors had an "open forum" which encouraged them "to see and be seen" by others in the arts. Sibley wrote

This kind of atmosphere has to be healthy for the arts and deserves a more coherent implementation than it has had so far. But at the same time it is fairly easy for an open atmosphere to take on the negative connotations of 'wide open' for the marketplace of ideas to disappear under a 'carnie aspect'. It is neither in the best interests of the town nor the serious artists and craftsmen who come to town to not establish some sort of coherent criteria for the Festival.

Under Sibley's leadership, the Festival was not "closed" as Monoco had proposed. It was open to all who wanted to exhibit and attend. That year, in addition to the traditional exhibits, for the first time there was a cooperative effort among the exhibitors in one of the crafts. Five wood-carvers[5] created a 40-foot totem pole that was erected in a rubble-strewn vacant lot beside Coal Creek, a small stream that runs through the town. Over the following decade it became the centerpiece of a public, open "green-space" in town: Totem Pole Park. Notably, by mid-June, Sibley and his committee raised *public* monies for that year's arts fair based, at least partially, on the successes of the prior two years' festivals. The Festival of the Arts and Crafts received grants from local government entities and the State art council, indicating growing and broader support for it.

Although it seemed odd to some, in 1973, in addition to the arts, crafts and culinary offerings, a booth was sponsored by a local environmental organization that collected signatures on a petition calling for limiting growth in the upper Gunnison Valley. A new local newspaper, *The Crested Butte Pilot*, noted that "'The Crested Butte Environmental Action Committee' had a booth at the Festival and collected 375 signatures…to halt unplanned, uncontrolled, unneeded growth …. we do demand that the voice of the environment be heeded …. we are soliciting your support…"

For the second time the Festival included a Crested Butte Mountain Theater production, another grand outdoor evening production: Peter Weiss', *"The Persecution and Assassination of Jean-Paul Marat as Performed by the Inmates of the Asylum of Charenton Under the Direction of the Marquis de Sade."* It was staged in a spectacular outdoor setting, one half-mile past the base of the ski area, and it involved many new locals as actors and behind-the-scenes workers. As contrasted to the criticisms expressed

Poster for the The Crested Butte Mountain Theater's second major production, presented during the Second Annual Festival of the Arts and Crafts. Artwork by Ken Hall or Grower City Council of the Arts. Courtesy of Susan Anderton.

about some exhibitions, *"Marat/Sade"* universally received rave reviews in the local community and press.

Following this third annual summer Festival, however, there was more widely articulated criticism about it, especially from newcomers who wanted the town to develop in a way that appealed to upscale tourists. Councilman Tom Glass, the most pro-development member of the pioneer town council, wrote a letter to the editor stating explicitly and simply that the Festival should be discontinued because it brought in too many undesirable people and, in his view, there were other,

> *Following this third annual summer Festival ... there was more ...criticism ... especially from newcomers who wanted the town to develop in a way that appealed to upscale tourists. Councilman ... wrote a letter to the editor stating...that the Festival should be discontinued because it bought in too many undesirable people...*

better, ways to support local artists and craftsmen. Iris Levin, who worked on the committee that promoted the Festival and who was present for the previous two, asked publicly, "Before the planning of next year's Festival begins, perhaps we should stop and ask ourselves whether another festival is what we want. Do the residents and the town really benefit from the festival?" With a broad-brush, tourist town pioneer Gary "The Professor" Gorbett wrote critically in a letter to the editor of *The Crested Butte Pilot:*

> The recent pseudo arts festival reminds me of a roving gypsy parade. Lots of artistic items like roach clips, love beads, coke spoons and the like tell how artistic the arts fair was. A paradoxical view point made me laugh at the Crested Butte Valley Environmental Action Committee booth. They were saying, 'Hey, all you Hips that have arrived for the festival, help us keep this place from growing'.

Ironically and not incidentally, a few months later, Levin and two other women received a grant from the Crested Butte Council and the Businessman's Association, to attract summer tourists by emphasizing local arts and crafts, despite the fact that none of the three had any education or experience in the arts, advertising or public relations. However, Levin was a co-owner of the Grubstake; and a "smart growth" proponent as were the two other women. They were all part of the emerging local power structure. Many years later, Levin said, naively, that in her view they got the grant because, "We were cheap and there was really no other competition."

In a scathing editorial following that Festival, the third pioneer *Chronicle* editor, development-oriented Myles Arber wrote:

> ... we would like to mention the negative aspects of the festival. ... More transients drifting through, more traffic, law enforcement problems, more dogs, crowds, noise, invasions of peace and privacy, ... No list of the drawbacks of the week-end would be complete without giving ... credit to 'Jelly', the (ha-ha—sic) rock music group ... There weren't too many people who were able to avoid hearing them.... Most of what you saw were unwashed and unkempt strangers sitting around in the dust of the unpaved streets in loincloths and headbands. ... many of the people who come don't appear to be capable of buying and do appear to be keeping away many ... who are. ... it is hurting the craftsmen every bit as much as the townspeople to have a raggle-taggle manner characterize the people the Festival seems to attract.

Sibley responded pointedly. In an open letter, he implicitly illustrated some of the significant differences between Crested Butte's tourist town pioneers who were anti-growth or very slow growth-oriented artists and craftspeople, and the pro-development pioneers and recreation community settlers who wanted a more elite art festival. He said that by narrowly focusing on the elk horn hash pipes, coke spoons, and dirty feet of some exhibitors and tourists, and the loud music by one of the groups, the Festival critics missed the event's highpoints — the really good art and craft work of local and guest exhibitors, fine music, including performances by Bonnie Raitt and Michael Martin Murphy, as well as some classical music, the excellent theater production, dance, etc. The letter acknowledged that while critics had some valid points, they missed most of the positive energy from many people who were focused on producing the Festival. "...the Festival Committee is not oblivious to the problems and complaints generated by the Summer Festival.... At the same time, I do not think it unfair to hope that that the *Chronicle* will be a little less oblivious to the real achievement represented by pulling together of so much diverse but focused creative energy from so many people, both local and from other areas."

Twenty years later, Sibley perceptively reflected on those early years in the tourist town and recreation community's development. He wrote

> There is a misconception ... that the founders [of the Crested Butte Mountain Theater and the Arts Festival] were brave aesthetic pioneers, bringing culture in, down, to the unwashed. ... We ... realized [by contrast] that this was where the creativity was, just needing a little capital organization ... we wanted people to come see something home grown but unique and good, something ... that could only have happened ... through us.

He continued:

> There were ... other more conventional ideas around town. ... In 1973 ... we began to move into the new era of capitalism locally. The Community-as-Art people should have seen it coming ... a schism emerged. Some of us wanted to move on even deeper into the celebration of the Community-as-Art. ... But there were other people ... who thought it should be more about 'quality.'... *they wanted a juried art show,* with recognized artists selling their wares to a clientele lured ... by the promise of quality, to spend on quality. ... these people were interested in ... something that might lure people with money to town. ... It was the end of the Community-as-Art Festival. ...We were basically in transition... [from a time] when we had a lot of idea capital operating ... to a more conventional situation where the money capital was increasing, but wanting to work (as money tends to-sic) by money's relatively conservative proven formulae.[6]

Due to the criticisms, the Crested Butte Festival of the Arts and Crafts ended in 1973 and lay dormant for three years. In 1976, it was resurrected by the town's decidedly dominant pro-growth and development-oriented tourist town pioneer and recreation community settler faction. Wanting to appeal and increasingly cater to well-off people, the Festival was quite different than it was in its earlier

Due to the criticisms, the Crested Butte Festival of the Arts and Crafts ended in 1973 and laid dormant for three years. In 1976, it was resurrected by the town's then decidedly dominant pro-growth ...

iterations. Only juried entry exhibits were allowed; mainly out-of-town exhibitors showed their work, and increasingly affluent, well coifed, fashionable, visitors patronized it. That reflected the desires of most pro-development townspeople who by then dominated the town's politics, and that Festival became the forerunner of the annual, increasingly sophisticated, mid-summer "Festival of the Arts" that now attracts tens of thousands of tourists who spend increasingly larger amounts of money each year.

■ ■ ■

Beginning in the late 1960s, flat-track cross-country skiing and telemarking (a combination of cross-country and alpine skiing that entails making long, sweeping turns on steep untrammeled snowy mountain terrain) was slowly becoming a popular sport. After initially being rediscovered by Western State College students and early tourist town pioneers, these aficionados were becoming proficient. One of them, Jim "Beach" Thomas, originally a Western State College student, recalled many years later, "In 1970, I pioneered telemark with Rick Borkovec, Steve Smith (from Gunnison), and Michael Burns on Monarch Pass. In Crested Butte, "BC" [Bob Vandervort], Bill Frame, Doug Buzzell, Dave Coney, Craig Hall, and Borkovec too, also began telemarking in Washington Gulch."

After several years, a critical mass of these "telemarkers" became experts. They adopted cross-country as their preferred way to play in winter. As a reason for parties and celebrations, new athletic competitions were always welcomed by the adventurous pioneers and recreation community settlers. The first Al Johnson Memorial Telemark Ski Race was held in the spring of 1975. The new winter sports enthusiasts replaced the historical long, heavy, wood skis Johnson used with much shorter, thinner skis, and the single long ski pole he used for balance was replaced by two, much shorter, relatively lightweight, bamboo poles.

After several years, a critical mass of these "telemarkers" became experts. …The first Al Johnson Memorial Telemark Ski Race was held in the spring of 1975.

Rick Borkovec was a Western State College ski racer who later became a ski patrolman at the Mt. Crested Butte ski area. He organized the first telemark ski race. It was held south of town on an old avalanche path on nearby Mt. Axtel. About 40 people entered. Unlike later telemark ski races, it was only downhill. As an indication of the event's intimacy and informality, and that it was intended "just for fun", the first prize winner received only a hand-carved wooden troll. The following year the race was held at Mt. Crested Butte. Starting at the bottom of an intermediate hill serviced by a T-Bar, men and women raced together as the annual spring snow event became yet another reason for locals to celebrate and party.

Beginning in 1977, the ski race became bigger and more formal. A Rocky Mountain Telemark Series had started in Colorado and the Al Johnson Memorial Race became part of it, hosting about 200 racers from throughout the state. The starting point for the race was moved to a much more difficult expert run on the North Face of Crested Butte Mountain, and an uphill component was added according to Borkovec, "as a true test of strength and fitness." The competition with out-of-town racers was fierce, and substantial prize money was awarded to winners. For a decade or so after that, men and women raced separately and competed for increasingly large cash awards. Then, for a few years the race was discontinued but, like the Arts and Crafts Festival, it was resurrected and reappeared. The second time around, it reverted to a true Crested Butte party mode, with entrants wearing outlandish costumes and caring less about the prize money, and more about just having fun on the mountain.

■　■　■

In the mid-seventies, Denver-reared Crested Butte tourist town pioneers Steve Baker and Albert Maunz drove back to their hometown, and they returned with a truck-load of old bicycles they bought at a junk yard. They took parts from the different bikes and put them together to make rough, often-rusted, old-fashioned, one speed, simple bicycles with wide tires, handlebars, pedals, and chains, much like those used by newspaper delivery boys in earlier decades. They called them "klunkers." They sold them to other locals for $15.00. Young pioneers began riding these beat-up bikes on the pot-holed streets to get around town as a means of local transportation. Shortly thereafter, in the true spirit of adventure, innovation and "going for it," Baker and Maunz began hauling the old bikes in the back of a pick-up truck to the tops of nearby mountain passes, where pioneers then wildly peddled, or rode them "chainless," as fast as possible down the rocky, also pot-hole filled, dirt mountain roads.

(Klunkers) .... were one speed, simple bicycles with wide tires, handlebars, pedals and chains, much ... like those used by news-paper delivery boys in earlier decades .... Shortly thereafter, (pioneers) began hauling the Klunkers in the back of pick-up trucks to the tops of nearby mountain passes where pioneers then wildly pedaled, or rode them 'chainless," as fast as possible down the rocky, ... dirt mountain roads.

One summer afternoon in 1976, some klunker riders were sitting around their favorite watering hole, the Grubstake, when a group of motorcyclists from Aspen rode into Crested Butte via Pearl Pass, one of the mountain passes between the two towns. The Aspenites had the temerity to park their "bikes" right in front of the Grubstake's large plate glass windows, where they ceremoniously lined them up. Right then and there the afternoon revelers, following an idea hatched by pioneer Rick Verplank, decided they were going to spoof them, and show who was more *macho*, by riding their non-motorized beat-up Klunker bicycles over Pearl Pass into Aspen, and park them in a line in front of the Jerome Hotel's tavern, the Aspenites hip local's bar.

According to one widely publicized version of the infamous bicycle trek, fifteen Crested Butte locals, 13 men and 2 women, sometimes rode and oftentimes pushed or carried their heavy old bicycles, as they traversed the mountains between the two towns. They also had a large "support staff" that drove assorted vehicles carrying spare bike parts, tents, sleeping bags, food, alcohol, and various other drugs. One pickup truck even carried a fun-loving partier with a broken leg in a bathtub in the back of a pickup truck, Richard "Rat" Ullery. Crested Butte lore has it that only Bob Starr, the oldest participant, and Rick Verplank, who first conceptualized the spoofing, were the only ones to complete the arduous journey from the Grubstake without the assistance of essential support vehicles. In reality, however, everyone who started out, made it. Forty years later, Starr said:

everyone reached the top and completed the ride. There were no firsts, seconds, or thirds. A bunch of guys who were fighting a fire somewhere [with the Hot Shots] got back and joined us at camp that night, and we all raced into Aspen.

Indeed, everyone got to the base camp near the top of the Pass, some with help from the well-fueled support crew that hauled their gear, goodies, and them to the high point. After setting up camp and eating steak dinners and, purportedly, drinking a keg of beer, three bottles of Schnapps, 2 gallons of wine, and 3 bottles of champagne, and then getting a few hours sleep, *all* the riders, (according to Starr), remounted their bikes and rode into Aspen, yelling all the way down until they reached the Jerome. (Another often repeated version differs only slightly, saying that about 30 Klunker bike riders left the Grubstake and 4 reached the top without assistance. Perhaps the inclusion of those who joined near the top after fighting the forest fire accounts for the difference).

That early, fun-filled first Pearl Pass Bike Tour and Race was the forerunner of annual mountain bike races between the two towns thereafter. Two years later, for instance, in early fall 1978, after word of the feat and the wild partying got out in mountain biking circles, five mountain bike riders came from Marin County, California. They had much fancier mountain biking equipment with, for example, 12-speed thumb-change gearing and fore and aft center pull brakes, that made it much easier to climb the pass.

That early, fun-filled first Klunker Pearl Pass Bike Tour and Race was the forerunner of annual mountain bike races between the two towns thereafter. ... it would ultimately become another joyous, hearty, Crested Butte fall annual event.

Significantly, that year's race and revelry included the Associate Editor of the nationally circulated *"Bicycling Magazine"* who wrote about the event, assuring it global coverage in the biking community. That featured piece insured greater attendance at future Pearl Pass Tours and Races, and that it would ultimately become another joyous, hearty, annual Crested Butte fall event. Those future bike tours were tamer than the original two, because both the bikes and clothing were more high-tech (and notably, many of the bike modifications and clothing innovations were developed by the cyclists who made the first treks). Each year the Tour attracted more and more riders. Even though, or perhaps because of, the ruggedness and wildness of the first ones, other traverses even though they were never again matched, increasingly more mountain bicyclists wanted to test their mettle against the high mountain altitude and tough topography of the Elk Mountain Range, as mountain biking became a widespread, popular, national outdoor-recreation sport.

■　■　■

"Aerial Weekend" was another innovative reason for playing and partying that was created by tourist town pioneers. Initially, they wanted an event that celebrated and made competitive activities in which they were already engaged. Skydiving instructor and pilot, Mike Pilert, was the original mover behind the Weekend, along with his restaurateur girlfriend, Cathy Durham, and local thespian and tile setter, Tom Mallardi. Forty plus years later, Pilert recollected:

"Aerial Weekend" was another innovative reason for playing and partying .... "We had balloons ... skydivers, hang gliders. ... and even a kite flying contest for kids. Over the years other activities were added, like raptors, gliders, biplanes and several other ways to fly."

> In the summer of 1972 or 1973, we began 'Aerial Weekend.' In earlier years there were a few hot air balloonists who were coming to town, but that was nothing like what we put together. We had balloons; but we also had skydivers, hang gliders, and even a kite flying contest for kids. Over the years other activities were added, like raptors, gliders, bi-planes and several other ways to fly.

He said further, "I was an accomplished skydiver when I came to town. I started teaching sky diving. My first students were Cathy and Mallardi. Ron Rouse used to take us up in his plane, [in which Pilert later learned to fly], and we would jump out and skydive." Other local parachutists began skydiving shortly thereafter.[7] Illustrating the "going for it" ethos, he continued:

> We were chasing life to the max. After a while we started thinking about creating something. I talked to Jay O'Neal, who was then head of the

Chamber of Commerce, or something like it, who liked the idea. He thought it would bring in tourists. He was really good at promotion and had a lot of contacts.

Pilert, describing how the fun-filled event began, characterized it in much the same way other locals who created other activities remembered their beginnings, "Every-one just put their heads together and made things happen. It was fun."

Aerial Weekend lasted for over 20 years. It attracted increasing numbers of participants and spectators and was relatively safe, given the high-risk endeavors in which the participants engaged. In the Weekend's later years, however, there were two deaths. The first occurred when a professional Continental Airlines pilot flew a glider plane. Ron Rouse towed it from a local air strip a few miles away to a point near the top of Crested Butte Mountain. According to Rouse many years later, after he released the plane, inexplicably, the pilot turned right into the mountain instead of turning toward the open-air space; he crashed and died instantly. Several people associated with organizing the weekend speculated that accident might have been caused intentionally by the glider pilot. The second death occurred a few years later when a stunt plane crashed to the ground. It was attributed to unintentional "pilot error." It was flown by a relative of two prominent locals, Sharon and Tom Cox. (Tom later became the town mayor and president of the local bank.)

Forty-five years later another local small plane pilot who took sky-divers for jumps, Gene Mason, remembered:

> Aerial Weekend developed from the hot air balloon festivals. At first there were only skydivers and hang gliders that took off from a small, flat, surface near the top of the mountain. Para-gliders then started appearing. Vintage airplanes also came, like the P-51 Mustang, a low-wing single engine WWII American airplane that was the first to fly long-distances defending American bombers' airspace. This plane was like the one that crashed. Corsairs, another single wing WWII plane; Super-Cubs, a 1930's airplane; and various 'kit' airplanes that people made themselves, also came to Aerial Weekend. There were also 'ultra-lights' and para-gliders that came into town for the weekend and flew.

Pilert recollected that after he left town in search of other adventures, Cathy Durham continued organizing Aerial Weekend. Pilert thought that eventually the Weekend was discontinued because insurance costs rose drastically and, more importantly, there were too many other summer activities that attracted visitors, like July 4th, The Arts and Crafts Festival, mountain biking, summer music concerts, dance programs, etc. Crested Butte no longer needed the increasingly costly high-risk weekend; and stopped supporting it. Pilert concluded, "The town just got too big."

A newspaper piece many years later essentially affirmed his perspective. According to it, a financial shortfall in the by then very evolved local tourism promotion group, the Crested/Mt.Crested Butte Chamber of Commerce, had forced it to make budget cuts because their expenses exceeded their income for the year by about $30,000. In the words of the Chamber president, that weekend had become "an expensive proposition...and a money loser." At that point the Chamber decided to eliminate all the events except the hot air balloon events. Aerial Weekend devolved once again into a less risky and costly Hot Air Balloon festival.

■ ■ ■

The Crested Butte Mountain Theater was created by and for locals; but, unlike many of the other innovative pioneer organizational undertakings, it never became a major tourist attraction. It remained mainly a "locals" activity, another way for the community's residents to express themselves. Today, with hundreds of productions already completed, a great number of townspeople have participated in it in one way or another. That said, however, there have always been tourists and "summer people" who attend and support the theater, but the productions have involved almost exclusively local residents as actors, directors, technicians, and producers.

The Crested Butte Mountain Theater was another creation by and for locals; but, unlike many of the other innovative pioneer ... undertakings, it never became a major tourist attraction.

Originally, the theater was conceived in the spring of 1972 by two local counter-culture men, Tom Towler and George Sibley. They were working construction during the day and drinking at night, a common routine for single men during the summers at that time. Towler was a Vietnam veteran who was decompressing in Crested Butte. Sibley opted out of the military before his term of service was completed and edited the *Chronicle*. At first, they wanted to offer the community, and themselves, an option to the nightly bar activity. A little later Towler's vision broadened considerably: he wanted to create a professional company based in Crested Butte that toured throughout the region. He earlier had been active in the Goodman School of Theater in Chicago; Sibley had been involved with college theater at the University of Pittsburg and at Tufts University, just outside Boston, MA. Attempting to create a local theater by and for the people living in town was probably a natural outcome of their late-night, alcohol-fueled, bar conversations. In 1974, a few years after the theater group was first conceived, and after having put on a dozen or so plays, the theater was formally incorporated as a non-profit organization by Sibley and Diane Kahn, both of whom had been involved with each production since the theater's inception. Sibley produced most of the early plays, and Kahn designed the sets.

The Mountain Theater's first offering was Howard Richardson's, "*Dark of the Moon.*" Adele Bachman described the play as a "combination of fantasy, witchery, and song and dance."[8] It was directed by Towler, who energized and transformed a disparate group of individualistic locals to perform harmoniously and captivatingly on an outdoor open stage-set designed by Kahn. For the most part, "*Dark*" involved a large company of completely untrained actors and supporting personnel that included lighting designers, set builders, costumers, prop people, musicians and the like. That first theater production was universally well received by all the new townspeople.

The following fall and winter, in the barren, unheated, top floor of the "Old Town Hall" several other productions with considerably smaller casts were mounted. These involved already existing and new tourist town pioneers. The latter came to Crested Butte specifically to work with the theater or with Towler because they had worked with him at the Goodman School. Each of the succeeding plays — including, "*A Cry of Players,*" "*Krapp's Last Tape,*" "*Alice in Wonderland,*" and "*The Effect of Gamma Rays on Man-in-the-Moon Marigolds,*" — were also well received by locals. In the summer of 1973, another wild and ambitious, large scale, outdoor production again was produced, *"The Persecution and Assassination of Jean-Paul Marat as Performed by the Inmates of the Asylum of Charenton Under the Direction of the Marquis de Sade."* Popularly known as *"Marat/Sade,"* it again delighted practically everyone in town.

The theater space in the former town hall was later insulated, heated, and slightly upgraded in other ways so audiences no longer had to wear outer winter clothing to enjoy performances. In 2002, the space was renamed, "The Mallardi Cabaret Theatre," as a tribute to one of the theater stalwarts who had passed away.

Importantly, the new pioneers who came to town for theater rather than for outdoor recreation or the environment were the first group of newcomers who came specifically for the performing arts. Collectively, they comprised the newest town clique.[9] Paul Roggenbuck was a carpenter and stage set builder, who came to town with his actress and playwright wife, Peggy. They came specifically because they heard about the new community theater while they were working with a college theater group in Oklahoma. He spoke about the theater forty years later

> For us, the ski area was not what it was about. It was the young people and creating community. Just being here was great. The community was an 'alternative community,' and we were 'alternative people.' ... Theater people had a major influence on town. We were the new 'clique' and referred to as 'the theater people.' ... Many knew each other from before, especially the Chicagoans. We were cliquish, not because consciously we wanted to be, but because the other groups were closed, like the Penelope or Grubstake group, and we couldn't get into them."

As in the year before, prior to the spectacular second summer production, a number of smaller efforts were mounted in the Old Town Hall. They included, *"Hot L Baltimore," "Tiny Alice,"* and others. Eventually, Tom Towler left town to teach and pursue other professional theater and film work. He left behind a cadre of dedicated, competent, theater people who continued producing high quality *community* theater, by and for locals. As that cadre left town, and almost all did, other locals picked up the theatrical baton.

The Crested Butte Mountain Theater still continues to produce well attended and appreciated productions. Although it never became a major tourist attraction, it regularly sells out its annual array of musicals, dramas, improvisational works, youth productions, and 10-minute plays to town residents, summer people, and occasional visitors. The Theater became a major, on-going local organization and is still a core component of the recreation community's collective soul.

Chapter 5

Culture Conflict in Crested Butte

With the opening of the ski area and the influx of new people, the Crested Butte mining-era residents and Gunnison County ranchers stopped quarreling with each other; they had a new common enemy: the young outsiders and an embryonic tourism industry they did not understand. Their discomfort intensified and became especially pronounced in the late sixties and very early seventies when the much larger population of tourist town pioneers began arriving.

... the Crested Butte mining-era residents and Gunnison County ranchers ... had a new common enemy: the young outsiders and an embryonic tourism industry they did not understand.

Given the decade-long increasing diversity among community members, and that they all lived in a remote and isolated small town, it is not surprising that intense conflicts arose between the long-time residents and the new immigrants. Confrontations between mining-era residents and the ski area trailblazers were mitigated somewhat because most newcomers, as noted earlier, came from similar backgrounds. There were also relatively few clashes between the mining-era residents and the earliest pioneers, (although they did begin to surface in the later 1960s), because there were only a few who came to work at the area, and they were seen as *individuals* by the old-timers; and, importantly, because the earliest pioneers tried to assimilate into their community. That initial relative lack of inter-personal tensions contrasted sharply with the *social* conflict that prevailed beginning in the late '60s and early '70s, as the numbers of tourist town pioneers and the recreation community settlers poured into town, and were seen by old-timers as "hippies."

Those who were part of the established mining town and its surrounding ranching culture and the critical mass of tourist town pioneers

111

who came into Crested Butte understandably had issues with each other, given their very different backgrounds and values. Myles Rademan, an early settler who moved to town in the last half of 1972 and soon thereafter became Crested Butte's town planner, remembered forty-five years later, "... Tony Verzuh ... threatened to kill me all the time because I was a 'socialist, hippie, planner'. For seven years I had to sleep with a gun under my bed ..."

More surprisingly however, and perhaps less predictably at first, following the population explosion that began in the summer of 1970 and continued through the historic 1972 town election when pioneers won *all* the local town public offices, intense personal and political conflicts emerged within the pioneer's own ranks, as well as between them and the new settlers. These confrontations, for instance, over whether to enforce the newly enacted dog-leash law, architectural ordinances or paving the town streets, together with shifting coalitions and alliances from the beginning of the ski area through the mid-seventies, indeed, laid the economic and cultural foundation for Crested Butte's now mature, yet still evolving, cosmopolitan tourist town and recreation community: the one that offers a wide range of recreational and cultural activities and high-quality amenities throughout the year for visitors and residents alike.

... perhaps less predictably ... following the population explosion that began in the summer of 1970 and continued ..., intense personal and political conflicts emerged within the pioneer's own ranks, as well as between them and the new settlers.

Significantly, on the national level many other full-blown *destination* resorts, including those on the east and west coasts and in other mountain towns like Aspen, Telluride, Breckenridge, and Steamboat Springs, had parallel developmental paths with comparable social and political conflicts as their economies evolved into tourism. In Colorado, for example, Aspen began its evolution and the concomitant social struggles ten years or so before Crested Butte's, and Steamboat Springs' began about a decade later.

Conflicts in Crested Butte, notably, did not begin with the entry of people associated with the emerging tourism industry. As pointed out by philosophers and social scientists from Plato on,[1] conflict in society is endemic. Before Crested Butte even had the beginnings of a destination ski mecca in 1961, while it was still a mining town, there were intense identity-based struggles between local residents, usually based on ethnicity, religion, and class, between those who escaped working in the mines and started small businesses in town, and those who still toiled underground and were the shops' customers. Those confrontations were often intermixed. The English, Scottish and Irish mine

Conflicts in Crested Butte, notably, did not begin with the entry of people associated with the emerging tourism industry.

workers came first, and some worked their way out of the mines and moved up the socio-economic ladder. The Eastern Europeans, Italians and Mexicans came later, and were distinctly working-class miners. The fact that there were also fights with other Gunnison County residents, mainly ranchers, only complicated an already complex social milieu.

Referring to that period, Kelsey Wirth wrote:

> Tensions arose. … Crested Butte became a town made up of multiple and competing ethnic groups. … Prejudice among the first settlers of British background against the new Italian and Slavic peoples prevailed in many aspects of town life…" She then quoted retired miner Joe Saya who recalled, "There was all kinds of nationalities … Italians, Slovenians, Germans, and Irish and Welshman … Some thought they were better."[2]

In the 1920s the Ku Klux Klan came into town, and became active. Although there were no African-Americans in Crested Butte, who nationally were the focus of their most nefarious activities, the Klan was also anti-Catholic, those they called "Papists." They held rallies, marched, and burned crosses on top of the nearby hill on the west side of town, then popularly known as "Chocolate Hill." Wirth quotes former miner John Somrak:

> You know, the Protestants and the Catholics never did get along. That was one fight that was going on up there all the time. … You had to be a white person, you had to be no foreigner, and you had to be Protestant.

Sandra Cortner, in *"Crested Butte Stories… Through My Lens"* quotes mining era resident Rudy Sedmak:

The KKK called themselves 100 percent American, and they wore white robes and carried flags. They used to march down Elk Avenue. But everyone knew who they were. ... There were twenty or thirty of them, and their headquarters was at the Masonic Hall, which was called the Knights of Phythias then.

Wirth also quoted another old-timer, Fred Yaklich, who said:

... in the twenties ... they'd be burning crosses and circles up there [on Chocolate Hill]. ... they all had their robes. Nobody would admit ... that they belonged to the Ku Klux Klan, but our (school) janitor was just a little short fellow, and we always knew he was there ... I'd say maybe about four years they were pretty strong ... It got to where they were firing shots ... and then it kind of died down.

Rudy Sedmak, in a videotaped interview recollected that the Klan was active, that people would not admit to their membership and wore hooded robes, but that everyone in town knew who they were, and, confirming Yaklich's memory, he laughingly cited as an example a man with a diminutive stature who could not hide his identity because of it. Over time, however, the different elements in Crested Butte's community, for example, the Italians and the Slovenians, learned to get along. Sedmak recalled, "They didn't get along until later years when everybody started mellowing a little bit and softening up and decided we should just all work together..."

Not only were there tensions among those who lived within town, they also existed between the townspeople and ranchers. As noted, Crested Butte originally was a mining town. People lived and worked intimately with each other in close quarters in strong, extended, clan like families, with strong ethnic "we-feelings." In her book, Cortner identified only about 50 family names in town and among the surrounding ranching families. The 1970 small-sized 3 ½ page local phone book listed about the same number of residents. Gunnison County, which consisted mainly of ranches and its ranching hub, the "big" City of Gunnison (with approximately 5,000 people). Old-timers defined Gunnisonites as outsiders, "others," especially on the rare occasions when Gunnison people came to

Crested Butte. Conversely, when Crested Butte residents traveled to "the city," it was an excursion, an all-day affair, in which all kinds of errands and activities were conducted. They were defined by Gunnison people as the outsiders. Though the journey was only twenty-eight miles, over a rough, sharply twisting, poorly paved road, culturally the divide was vast.

The feeling of being "outsiders" was felt strongly by Crested Butte young people in the Gunnison public schools, particularly in junior and senior high. Some mining-era families and early ski area trailblazers opted to bus their children to Gunnison where they thought they would get a better education. After the mines closed, when most coal mining families moved to find work elsewhere, the Crested Butte school population dwindled drastically. Eventually, in April 1967, with a governing board dominated by Gunnisonites and the board's stated rationale of cost containment driving their decision, the board voted to close the local Crested Butte high school. Beginning the following fall, *all* Crested Butte junior and senior high students were bused to Gunnison. Many of them felt picked on and discriminated against, not only by classmates but also by teachers and the school administration. Indeed, that was a reflection of how they were viewed by many administrators and faculty.

Candy Shepard, a Crested Butte recreation community settler who taught in Gunnison for a few years before transferring to Crested Butte, recollected many years later that she was "bad vibed" in the faculty lunch room because she lived in Crested Butte and was seen as "one of them." She also remembered that faculty there categorized students as either "ropers, dopers or beaners [cowboys, hippies, and Mexicans or Mexican-Americans]." That categorization and stereotyping continued for many years. Long after Crested Butte was firmly established as a viable recreation community, the daughter of an early tourist town pioneer family, now a mature woman, recalled that most Crested Butte high school students in the 1980s and 90s were seen and treated as outsiders, as hippie kids.

The old-timers knew the new pioneers who came to Crested Butte differed from them! Wirth quoted them to illustrate their views. Ex-miner, John Krizmanich, described the newcomers simply as, "a different kind of people"; reflecting another family's view, Josephine Stadjuhar said, "...that was really bad...when all the filthy, you know, hippies came in. ... They were so dirty … their hair was long and matted… it just turned my stomach. Because we were used to being clean, everything nice … And all their dogs they brought in? Uh!" June Krizmanich agreed with Stadjuhar, "Some of them were really obnoxious, and cussing and everything …. they just didn't care what they said in front of you or anything – where an old-timer would never do that." Henrietta Raines, who moved to Crested Butte with her hard rock miner father and family when she was four years old, remembered 45 years later that June "used to say that the hippies were physically and morally dirty."

Some other old-timers felt differently. Some individual mining-era residents also held views about the new people that were not always disdainful or hostile. Botsie Spritzer, for example, perhaps the first outdoor summer guide, would take anyone fishing who would buy him a six-pack of beer, or talk to anyone who would buy him drinks in one of the local bars. Individually, he liked anyone but, collectively, he disliked and demeaned hippies. Mining-era men who lined the barstools in the afternoons would talk to new people and, if they would listen, would tell stories about the "old-days." But it was usually a one-way conversation. They liked telling newcomers their tales but did not want to hear the newcomers' stories. Others, like Frank Orazem, Fritz Yaklich and Willard Ruggera, were friendly without alcohol. Leola Yaklich, an open-minded, older, mining-era woman was quoted by Wirth: "So many of them were nice to the older people. They were so accommodating …. To me, they just weren't that bad …. The hippies were different, admittedly. I don't quite understand some people's reactions. Maybe it was just because it was something different. They didn't keep their houses as clean as the ladies here were used to." A few mining-era women besides Yaklich were also open to and friendly with newcomers, especially women. For the most part, however, these "open" old-timers were the exception to the general rule of most of their mining-era peers.

Perceptively, they saw the new people, especially pioneers and settlers, as a different *class* of people, living differently. John Krizmanich told Wirth, "We were just poor people … who worked in the mines … and we stayed poor. [It was] a good hard honest living." Matt Malensek opined, "Everybody's looking for something for nothing, see if you can get a job that you don't have to work…that's the attitude they got nowadays. There ain't nobody thinking about how much am I going to do. It's how little can I get by with." Josephine Stadjuhar observed, "…their life is different than ours. …they don't believe in sitting home and trying to save and do what's right. They just want to go for good times." Fritz Yaklich succinctly summarized his views about newcomers as a *group*, "…in those days…it was all

"…in those days…it was all work and no play. Now its play and no work."

work and no play. Now its play and no work." Forty-five years later, long time upper-Gunnison Valley family rancher, Richard Rozman, disdainfully said of the pioneers and settlers, "Most of them didn't even earn the breath they breathe."

Pioneer's liberal values and attitudes, especially about opposing the Vietnam War, and their chosen life-style, particularly using recreational drugs, contrasted sharply with the beliefs and behavior of mining-era residents and many of the ski area trailblazers. That gave rise to intense tensions between the two groups beginning in the summer of 1967 and continuing through the mid-seventies.

In fall 1967, the *Crested Butte Chronicle*, while Gunnison businessman and newspaper publisher Fred Budy had been editor, began writing articles and editorials that reflected long time Crested Butte and Gunnison residents' feelings about hippies and recreational drug use coming to Gunnison County, and the perceived evils they presented. In the November 11, 1967 issue, a front-page headline said "Addictive Drugs Uncovered in Police Raids." A front-page photo showed several pills, some of which were thought to have contained peyote, a hash pipe, and other drug paraphernalia. An accompanying piece said that Gunnison had caught up with the national scene and described the pitfalls of illicit drug use. It named two residences where narcotics were found, a Western State College dorm room and an off-campus college apartment. The report quoted from the Food and Drug Administration's Bureau of Drug Abuse Control, "there is today widespread abuse and illegal trafficking in the depressant, stimulant, and hallucinogenic drugs.… Users can become physically and emotionally dependent upon the drugs, but they do not yet have the same social stigma that is associated with narcotic drugs."

The following week, on the newspaper's front page, a banner headline blared, "Student Panel Says Drinking Is Big Problem in High School." The report quoted four high school students at a panel who addressed the issue. They said 90% of their Gunnison classmates drank and also had a strong interest in narcotics. (One of the four, Barbara Norris, was the teenage daughter of early tourist town pioneers. Shortly after graduating she moved from her parent's home and became a young adult member of the Crested Butte community). Three weeks later the *Chronicle* published another report about a band leader at a 3.2 bar in Gunnison, "The Last Chance," who had been picked up and held on a narcotics charge. A month after that it ran yet another front-page piece headlined, "Drugs ... Police Officer Says 'Nothing Worse for Kids.'" The story said that Gunnison County assistant police chief Boxley had been involved recently in drug cases and believed drug abuse was involved not only with the hippie movement, but with practically every element of society. He added, "The dangerous aspects of the 'mind expanding' drugs cannot be overestimated ... Nothing fouls up young people more." The account stated that Boxley thought the use of narcotics had spread to colleges, high schools, servicemen, and that it was even used by college instructors whom, he thought, "... unfortunately, had a great influence over their students."

Fred Budy, in his first ever *Chronicle* editorial, although he already had edited the paper for the previous three years, opined in mid-February, 1968, that recreational drug users and hippies were one and the same, reflecting a widely held view among Gunnison townspeople and long-time Crested Butte residents. The headline asked, "What's this 'Hippie' Business?" He wrote that hippies were dirty, disrespectful, and had no focused message or philosophy; that they used vague terms like "love" and "flowers" and were dedicated to social resistance, non-conformity, and the many other

In his first... Chronicle editorial Fred Budy... opined ...that recreational drug users and "hippies" were one ...reflecting a widely held view among Gunnison townspeople and long time Crested Butte residents. ... He wrote that hippies were dirty, disrespectful, and had no focused message...that they used vague terms like "love" and "flowers" and were dedicated to social resistance, non-conformity, and ...other avenues "that provide the easy way out." He added, "...we are all born with certain responsibilities –among which cleanliness and decency are paramount – and if our society is to survive, we must all realize and accept these responsibilities."

avenues "that provide the easy way out." He added, "...we are all born with certain responsibilities – among which cleanliness and decency are paramount – and if our society is to survive, we must all realize and accept these responsibilities."

A week later, his second opinion piece praised the County Republican Club. It was gearing up for, and actively participating in, the coming elections. However, he continued pillorying those he did not like:

> ... We are pleased to see that in these days of 'non-conformist groups' that there remain persons dedicated to the advancement of the American way. ... We have far too many 'rights' groups whose only purpose is to exercise the 'right' to get something for nothing. ... How many ...will actually take it upon themselves to be as outspoken for their political beliefs as they are in their criticism of the administration, Viet Nam, housing, civil rights, and a myriad of other 'causes' which they choose to champion.

In yet a third commentary a week later, meant to contrast hippies with other newcomers, Budy praised what he considered the constructive work and people of the recently formed Crested Butte Society, naming ski area trailblazers, early tourist town pioneers, and long-time Crested Butte residents alike.[3] He then cited what he considered the Society's laudable goals:

> To encourage, promote, and foster cultural endeavor in all fields of the arts and humanities ...; ... to promote the welfare of the Crested Butte, Colorado area and citizens therein; .... to discover, procure, preserve, display and protect whatever may relate to the natural, civil, literary and historical development of the Crested Butte area.

In the late spring of 1968, to great heraldry among the early tourist town pioneers, there was a major change in the ownership group and editor of the newspaper, which reflected the significant transitions that occurred in Crested Butte during the prior three years while Budy owned and edited it. More importantly, it forecast even greater social, cultural and political transformations, that later came to the

... to great heraldry among the early tourist town pioneers, there was a major change in the ... newspaper. It forecast even greater social, cultural and political transformations, that later came to the town and surrounding area.

town and surrounding area. The *Chronicle* continued writing about local people and issues, but it began focusing mainly on the new early pioneers and, on occasion, included national and international issues about which the newcomers were interested.

The newspaper's new owners and editor were formally announced:

> Starting June 5, the Crested Butte *Chronicle* will once again be written and edited in Crested Butte by citizens of Crested Butte. ... None of the members of the editorial board of the new *Chronicle* are natives of Crested Butte, or even of the State of Colorado, but it becomes more evident every day that they are here to stay .... Dr. Art Norris ... a Philadelphian by birth and background. ... Don Bachman ... comes from the opposite coast, being native to the San Francisco area .... And George Sibley, the new editor of the paper who was born and raised in Western Pennsylvania ...

Reflecting that change, the blatant negative stereotyping of hippies and recreational drug users was toned down considerably. However, following the 1967 "Summer of Love," the social phenomena known as "the counter culture" was already in full bloom among America's youth. Gunnison County and Crested Butte were not excluded. The new editor, George Sibley, was a university-educated, Eastern, liberal arts major, who had resigned his military commission in the Army. After spending a little time in Aspen, he came to Crested Butte in 1966 to work on the ski patrol. He and his mostly counter-cultural editorial board tried to diffuse the stereotyping of, and hostility toward, the new people. They walked the fence between the new pioneers, including the hippies, and those who disliked them.

Reflecting that change, the blatant negative stereotyping ... was toned down considerably. The new editor ... tried to diffuse the hostility and stereotyping of newcomers. .... (He) walked the fence between the new pioneers, including the hippies, and those who disliked them.

In one of his earliest opinion pieces in the middle of the 1968 summer, he wrote that many people were "asking in hushed tones" if Crested Butte had a "hippie problem." Titled, "All Quiet on the Flower Front" it opined, "...No, we are not having any trouble with hippies in Crested Butte."

Then he said it was difficult to respond because everyone seemed to have a different definition of hippie. He wrote, "Some people... think 'long-haired, bathless, greasy kook'. Others associate the hippie with marijuana and therefore dope fiends and the international narcotics traffic..." Then he parsed his words:

> Chances are a hippie will have long hair, but not everyone with long hair is a hippie; marijuana is an integral part of the hip cult, but that does not mean every pothead is a hippy, and some people believe seriously that one can be hip without having to smoke.... the most distinguishing feature about a hippie ... has to do with his personal philosophy.... But then anybody who raises a voice of logical rebellion in the face of heroic irrationality and patriotic stupidity is asking for social ostracism .... Like the hobo of the thirties and forties and the beats of the fifties, the hippie of the sixties might derive a measure of his identity from his persecution.

He continued:

> ... In Crested Butte there are maybe a dozen people who might qualify under the above criterion as hippies; there are some hangers-on that are as phony as can be, and there are friends passing through from time to time... Some have steady jobs...others are odd-jobbing and part-timing...and some are not doing much at all.... they enjoy their own company to the extent that they do not actively seek to become totally integrated into the community, yet they are a non-troublesome and contributing fraction of the town ... So that is the latest on the hippie situation in Crested Butte. Rest assured: no problem—except when people come around who irrationally and with no sound basis resent them.

This broadmindedness waxed and waned over the next few years. In early June 1970, to the consternation of old-timers, trailblazers, and even some of the earliest pioneers, a large influx of both counter-cultural young people and real estate speculators was expected. Instead of writing an opinion piece about the anticipated local population explosion himself, Sibley asked for existing residents to write them. Two people from the paper's new board were selected, one of whom was a little older and "more respectable" and presumed to be a member of the town establishment; the other was supposed to be a relatively new town resident and culturally more like those who were expected to arrive. The guest writers were asked to address their counter-parts in the community. Western State College business professor Dr. Art Norris was selected to address the long-time resident Crested Butte population and trailblazers. Although he was a generation older than many of the trailblazers and had a '50s rather than a '60s consciousness, he was quite different from both the long-time town residents, (many of whom were living on fixed incomes from disability insurance or social security and, in most cases, whose only fixed asset was their rapidly appreciating house); and from the early ski area trailblazers. Norris said that to protect what the town had and its way of life, both zoning and architectural controls needed to be enacted and enforced (as the Crested Butte Society, of which he was president, had been championing). Instead of relating and appealing to his targeted audience, his op-ed seemed to limit how much someone might get for his house and, at least of equal importance, contradicted the basic Old-West value that anyone should be able to do whatever he or she wanted with his or her property. Additionally, old-timers believed that zoning and architectural restrictions not only limited their ability to sell their property, but that they were tantamount to "socialism."

The second op-ed piece was written by Don Bachman. Although Bachman was not as different from the anticipated influx of young people as Norris was from his targeted audience, he too was a little older and, more importantly, already had established roots in the community. He was an early pioneer who wanted to assimilate into the existing local community. He addressed the anticipated new counter-culture arrivals saying they would have to respect the values and ways of life of the people who already lived in town, especially the long-term residents. He said that long hair, beards, dope, etc. were an affront to them, and that if one did not also actively contribute to the town, appearances were all old-timers saw and how the newcomers would be seen:

> There are three ways we are judged in this town: by your license plates (if you drive in), by appearance and by what you do (work, morals, language, conduct, etc). All societies judge; this is not utopian up here – so accept the fact of judgment. ... Regarding the first point of judgment –

'YD' Colorado plates [Gunnison County resident vehicle license plates] are in. If you live here or intend to stay, get a set.... Now...examine motives for being here. We all have some reason for coming to CB. To drop out is in fashion right now. ...we can get away from the 'establishment' that has created the society that is to be rejected. ... Well, baby, you just now dropped-out into a society: that of the Northern Gunnison County, Town of CB that you cannot disrespect if you are going to feel comfortable here. ... Appearance – people in this town are turned off by long hair, beards, beads, breach cloths, stash bags, maxi-dresses, band uniforms and robes and knives. ... However, if your bag is not to hassle people with your appearance, if you are into something you can share with the town, then come as you are. ... If you want to identify with the town (maybe you do not), figure out some compromise in appearance ... What you do is what you are. ... we, the long hairs have supposedly rejected the power society; and we are quick to judge the snowmobilers and the jeep racers, yet the long-haired motorcycle noise is constant this spring. ... if you are going to live the non-violent peace and tranquility flower-child scene then get off and walk. ... We, the young people, do have a chance to make this a beautiful place. Thirty percent of the property owners in this town are under thirty. They are not all groovy maybe, but they grew up with the same problems you did. Do not blow it by forcing a totally new culture into this town. ... I believe there is hope for this place. It is as much your place as mine. It belongs to the world – but it has its terms too."

Those views regarding the anticipated influx of newcomers were ironic. For several years the paper's editorial board members, and their early pioneer counterparts, wanted to see more new people come to town, particularly those with educational and cultural interests and talents. In August 1969, George Sibley wrote:

Looking at last summer and the summer in progress...there is one thing that really seems to stand out: how great it is to have people around who are connected with such organizations as RMBL (the Rocky Mountain Biological Laboratory), the University of Kansas Workshop, the University of Kentucky Geological Field Camp, and the California Players. ... they are here long enough for us to get to know them. ....There is much discussion in and around town these days pertinent to the future of this town. The central question...: How do we make earning a living in Crested Butte less of a marginal operation, without changing what is so unique and attractive about the place? What is it that is so 'unique and attractive'? ... there are not many places so openly friendly and communicative. If ...most of us are here because Crested Butte is just basically a really friendly community, then a direction for 'growth-without-loss' is made manifest: work to enlarge the community of friends.

Almost directly mirroring these sentiments, Ruth Esserman, one of the earliest regular summer residents who originally came to town with the Art Institute of Chicago, and who then built a unique house on land she bought close to town, recollected forty years later:

> We came to Crested Butte because of its amazing environment, its edginess, and the welcome the community extended to us. There were no financial enticements but we were encouraged to use the old rock school-house for our workshops and seminars and our students were able to use the town, including the main street, to make films. Bill and Sally Crank, owners of the Ore Bucket Lodge in town, and Susan Anderton, who owned a silk screen business, and the wonderful community of artists were very open to us.

She added, reflecting the subtle transition that already had begun to occur from a town that mainly attracted young skiers to one that appealed to a wider range of people and interests:

> I was not an outdoor person, skier, etc. but I responded to the beauty of the outdoors. It wasn't just friends or the environment; *it was the whole package*. It was also a plus that the town was growing. I stayed because of the people, the environment, my house which we built in '72 & '73, and 'the dream'.

Part II:
Politics

Chapter 6

Town Politics and Elections: 1966-1971

For the approximately five years after the ski area began, the political issues within and around town were mainly like those that existed before it opened. The town population consisted of mining families who were mainly working-class conservative Democrats, much like their white southern counterparts. The area surrounding the town was made up of ranchers, most of whom were western "libertarian" Republicans. In the 1966

For the approximately five years after the ski area began, the political issues within and around town were mainly like those that existed before it opened.

"off-year" election, for example, all the winning candidates at the county level were Republicans, even though a large proportion of the ballots in Crested Butte were cast for Democratic candidates. By the 1968 national election the same overall pattern held, although a greater number of Democratic votes were cast in town as the small but growing number of tourist town pioneers began trickling in. Following the '68 election the *Chronicle's* front-page headline announced, "Election Returns: Crested Butte Counters the County" and the account below it began:

> Crested Butte, to the surprise of no one, went strongly Democratic this recent election, although only by a 2-1 majority. ... Crested Butte and Somerset [another small, coal mining town in Gunnison County] together went contrariwise to the rest of Gunnison County, the State, and the rest of the country in every contested election except for the reelection of Rep. Wayne Aspinall [a popular Democratic Colorado Congressman from the Western Slope] ....

Although ski area trailblazers were more like ranchers than miners in their voting preferences, i.e. Republican, they all wanted the economic revitalization of the area and that transcended any differences that existed between them. The political tensions that existed were between Crested Butte area residents and the people in Gunnison, about whether to keep the public schools in Crested Butte open or to bus students to Gunnison, twenty-eight miles away.

The political tensions that existed were between Crested Butte area residents and the people in Gunnison, about whether to keep the public schools in Crested Butte open or to bus students to Gunnison ...

Through the 1960s and during the first two years of the '70s, almost all the Crested Butte town council people were long-time born and bred residents. In the late sixties a couple of ski area trailblazers were elected and during those years, when vacancies occurred on the council, three early pioneers were *appointed* to it. The deliberations and decisions of all the councils during that period reflected the values, attitudes and priorities of mining-era residents, and those who wanted to assimilate into their community. With the increasing influx of tourist town pioneers in the later 1960s, that perspective was challenged.

At first, as discussed earlier, old-timers tried to understand individual newcomers and they, in turn, tried to become part of the existing community. Allen Cox, for example, first came to Crested Butte as a visitor in 1966 for a jeep race. He returned in 1969 and bought the Nordic Inn at the base of the ski area. He was an early tourist town pioneer who liked the mining-era people. He recalled in a videotaped 2005 interview, "[The mining-era residents] were like fathers and brothers and sisters. I had a wonderful relationship with them." Some of the earliest pioneers went further: they idolized and even deified the born and bred Crested Butte residents. Former town attorney, Wes Light, who decidedly did not share that admiration, later characterized that phenomenon as "the cult of the old-timers."

At first, ... old-timers, tried to understand individual newcomers and they, in turn, tried to become part of the existing the community.

Beginning in the last half of the 1960s, when pioneers began arriving with vastly different backgrounds and reasons for moving to Crested

Butte, a few of the earliest, like Don Bachman, George Sibley, Barbara Kotz, and Susan Anderton respected the mining-era residents who, on an *individual* basis, had cordial and harmonious relationships with the newcomers. As the tourist town pioneer population increased rapidly and became a critical mass, however, *social* conflicts intensified between long-time residents and the pioneers. Intense struggles arose between the newest town immigrants and the residents who preceded them, over a range of life-style and local growth issues. Notably, they existed irrespective of whether the new town immigrants were totally opposed to development or desperately wanted it.

The political campaigns for Crested Butte mayor are illustrative.

In the 1966 election, both candidates for mayor were old-timers: Lyle McNeil and Betty Spehar. McNeil had held elected town positions for almost twenty years. Spehar, born and raised in Crested Butte, was a professor at Western State College and the first woman in Crested Butte ever to run for public office. (She had earlier made an unsuccessful bid for a town trustee seat). In '66 all the candidates for town trustees were life-long residents with the exception of Jerry Sampson, a ski area trailblazer. He and his wife, Tina, owned the Grubstake. A front-page, pre-election, newspaper banner headline urged the *164* registered town electors to, "Vote in Town Election". The same edition had a large display ad supporting a slate of candidates that said:

> For A Progressive, Financially Sound Town of Crested Butte VOTE FOR Lyle McNeill, Mayor. For Trustees: George Dorson, Ladd Fullmer, Richard Hays, Gerald Sampson, Scott Gorsuch, Johnny Walker – Town election—April 5. These men pledged themselves to the Progressive and Financially Sound Town Government which the people of Crested Butte deserve and badly need in this critical period of the growth of our community. They deserve and need your vote next Tuesday. This advertisement sponsored by the Citizens for a Progressive Crested Butte Committee.

Eighty-eight percent of the those eligible voted, and the entire slate won. McNeill defeated Spehar by 13 votes, 79 to 66.

In the 1968 election, two life-long town residents again vied for the mayor's office. This time the incumbent McNeill was challenged by a former miner and the current school custodian, Tony Gallowich. Incumbent trustee candidates included Ladd Fullmer and Jerry Sampson. John Cobai and Jim Cole were incumbents who had been appointed earlier to fill vacated council seats. Additional mining-era candidates included Joe Saya, Rudy Somrak, Jr., and Tony "Whitey" Sporcich; trailblazer Dave Watson and early pioneer Don Bachman also ran. This time the "preferred slate" included a combination of old timers and early new townspeople: McNeill for Mayor, and Don Bachman, Jim Cole, Jerry Sampson, Rudy Somrak, Jr., Whitey Sporcich and Dave Watson for the council positions. Their collective political ad intoned, "For Intelligent and Sober Thought to the Present And [sic] Future of Crested Butte." With the exception of Dave Watson, who lost to Joe Saya, the proposed slate won.

Some inevitable minor tensions existed between old-timers and younger new ski area trailblazers. By contrast, the demographic, social, and political differences between both of these groups and the tourist town pioneers created a massive divide. As the numbers of pioneers increased these divisions intensified, and cultural "fault-lines" emerged. They became cultural clashes that translated into political factions that had vastly different agendas. Their view about growth and development became especially evident. A variety of factions became clear: old-timers vs. pioneers; ski area people vs. townspeople; those with traditional views vs. counter-culturists, etc. Mainly it was people who held "old-western" views versus those with counter-culture values.

As the numbers of pioneers increased these divisions intensified, and cultural "fault line'" emerged. They became cultural clashes that translated into political factions that had vastly different agendas. Their views about growth and development became especially evident. A variety of factions became clear: old-timers vs. pioneers; ski area people vs. townspeople; those with traditional views vs. counter-culturalists; etc....

The first tourist town pioneer editor of the *Chronicle* obliquely acknowledged these clashes in some of his early editorials, and the intensifying nature and diversification of them in his later ones. Only a few months after he began editing the paper, following the 1968 summer debacle inside the Democratic National Convention, with the rioting and mayhem on the streets outside it, Sibley wrote emotionally in an early September 1968 opinion piece headlined, "Democracy in the Streets…":

> One of the hardest things in the world to swallow is passion. Your editor is a young man; my generation is in the jungles of Vietnam against their will and the streets of the city against the police, and my passion is there….the only two questions of importance today – peace and social equity – have already been settled without differences on either side, and no one was even consulted. … My generation, the Negro in the ghetto, and the soldier in the field were unrepresented in this election. … I know who my readers are, I know the communication barrier between my readers and my generation …

Sibley continued:

> Most … readers of this paper are people in what is commonly called the middle to upper-middle class – as bad and imprecise a term as 'hippie' but what are you going to do …. if I can throw off the revolutionary passion of my generation so as to avoid arousing the reactionary passion of yours, perhaps we can talk …

Many years later, Hugh Carson, a self-declared anarchist and draft resistor, echoed Sibley. Carson hid from authorities in plain view in Crested Butte, after participating in the sit-ins at Columbia University in New York City. He spoke insightfully about himself and many other pioneers who were influenced by the social movements of the sixties and early seventies. He said, "Maybe we were so extreme because we saw how police beat up and killed black people in this country and our soldiers murdered innocent people in Vietnam."

The following week, however, specifically alluding to the multiple-year town vs. ski area tensions, Sibley wrote about what he perceived as the somewhat unusually cooperative planning for a forthcoming 4-wheel drive Jeep meet that was intended to bring tourists to the area. He said that two businessmen worked well together on the event, Jerry Sampson, proprietor of the Grubstake, and Rix Rixford, manager of the Crested

Butte Lodge at the ski area. Then, he added, "both men would admit their relationship in the past was not always the best."

The 1970 spring election became a test of the political strength of the growing numbers of early tourist town pioneers. Harold O'Connor, an early pioneer, was a young goldsmith who sold fine, unique jewelry, mainly to tourists. He had been appointed to fill a council vacancy during the prior year. O'Connor challenged Jim Cole, the mayoral candidate who was favored by long-time residents. Cole was well-established; he worked on the county road crew and owned a small gift shop in town. In mid-March a *Chronicle* banner headline announced, "O'Connor vs. Cole for Mayor; 15 Run for Trustees." The sub-headline, "200 Plus Registered for April 7 Election," indicated that there had been a 20% increase in the number of eligible voters compared to the election two years earlier. Virtually all the new registrants were pioneers.

The 1970 spring election became a test of the political strength of the growing numbers of early tourist town pioneers.

O'Connor ran on an eight-point platform that focused on the infant stage of the tourism industry and the "wants" of early pioneers. He called for establishing a sales tax; restoring the town jail for use as a tourist information center; holding town council meetings in the school so more people could attend; expanding the tradition of volunteer town clean up days so it included more than only Elk Avenue and Coal Creek; hiring a new lawyer who lived in town; and using space on the outskirts of town for snowmobile, jeep, and motorcycle events. Addressing the factionalism in town, he also said that he wanted everyone to work together for the town's common good. Cole ran on a five-point program that mainly focused on an infrastructure issue that long time Crested Butte residents wanted: completing a project that would connect all town properties to a sewer system (instead of relying on individual septic tanks); and also getting stable and secure law enforcement, improving the volunteer fire department, seeing that Crested Butte had steady growth, and protecting the town's mining heritage and the environment.

The fifteen candidates in that 1970 election had varying backgrounds and views about what needed to be done.[1] The different platforms and priorities of candidates reflected, in part, the different perspectives of the born and bred people of Crested Butte and the newer residents. Candidates Mark Calve, Jim Wallace and Whitey Sporcich explicitly tried to address the growing feelings of disdain and distrust among the town's main two factions. Commenting on that animus, a *Chronicle* editorial written shortly before the 1970 election, noted:

> I was sitting in violent discussion with a group of people at the Grubstake the other night; .... Once, when half the houses in town stood empty and half the people here today had hardly heard of the town ... it looked as if everyone could be happy ... Now we are many more, and too many of us are extremists. ... One of the uglier aspects underlying the coming town election is the fact that there are candidates running for office on the platform that part of the townspeople have to be run out before the rest of the townspeople can be happy. ... To be ... specific, anyone who says that we have to run the longhairs out of town, or we have to run the snowmobilers out of town ... has absolutely nothing to contribute to the governing of Crested Butte ...

The old-timers and ski-area trailblazers won the 1970 election. Each tourist town pioneer candidate lost by a large margin. From the more than *200* votes that were cast, Cole received 142 votes for mayor compared to O'Connor's 58. Among the elected Trustees, Whitey Sporcich, the Crested Butte old-timer who also was well liked by pioneers, garnered 180 votes, more than any other candidate. Trailblazers

The old-timers and ski area trailblazers won the 1970 election. ... all the candidates favored by newcomers were defeated. That was the last time that would happen.

Elmer Eflin received 130 votes and Doris Walker got 122; Albert Falsetto corraled 92 votes; Crested Butte native John Cobai obtained 87; and Jerry Chiles and Jim Wallace tied for 6th place, both having received 85 votes. The tie for the sixth council seat was decided unceremoniously by a toss of a coin, which Jim Wallace won. With the exception of Wallace, who was also liked equally by life-long residents and pioneers, all the candidates favored by newcomers were defeated. It was the last time that would happen.

After that election, conflicts over a wide range of community issues became more intense. A mid-May 1970 newspaper piece entitled, "Pollution by Irritation" opined, "…this town is becoming the kind of place where various factions sit around just waiting for the members of other factions to do something wrong. …what makes it worse is the apparent willingness of all factions to oblige the others by doing just about everything they can to irritate them." In the face of that factionalism, the 1970 candidacies of the new people in the election, especially those of the early tourist town pioneers like Bachman, Calve and O'Connor, signaled that new town residents were not merely griping and, as became more evident within the following two years, they were becoming politically active.

After that election, … conflicts became more intense. ….."… this town is becoming the kind of place where various factions sit around just waiting for the members of the other factions to do something wrong. … what makes it worse is the apparent willingness of all factions to oblige the others by doing just about everything they can to irritate them."

There was another *Chronicle* editorial written about the growing divide among town residents. It came out just before the annual summer picnic that was held in the town park. Most of those who attended brought carefully prepared home-made dishes for the pot-luck event. The piece implied that the old-timers had old-fashioned values and the pioneers had new ones, and then pleaded that at the forthcoming gathering members of each group should be sensitive to members of the other group, and try to get along. The year after that picnic, significantly, mining-era families began holding their own yearly summer event, to which very few newcomers were ever invited.

Still later that summer, in August 1970, a number of articles and editorials addressed important differences among the town factions. The first was a lengthy feature about a lecture and discussion at the summer Law-Science Academy on "the Physical Effects of Drug Abuse." (The Law-Science Academy held lectures and seminars that bridged the gap between practicing lawyers and doctors and were all open to the public). The paper noted that the lecturer, Dr. Arthur Crollman, and many who came to hear him, approached the topic of drugs from very different perspectives, and those differences reflected the town's divisions. Crollman was concerned

that recreational narcotics were bad for the body; new young people wanted to experiment and enjoy the effects of drug use.

Two weeks later, Sibley tried to explain a recent defeat of a proposed
town sales tax (that he had supported). The loss reflected the tensions
between the pro-growth and no growth pioneers.

> Checking out some local opinions after the sales tax election defeat last
> week, I was surprised at the number of people who had not voted for
> the sales tax because they felt that its passage would too rapidly acceler-
> ate the growth of the town. ... Apparently these people feel that, if we
> get a little work done...we are suddenly going to be inundated by more
> tourists, horrendous big buildings, and all the other things that come
> along with too much growth too fast.

Over time, notably, that is exactly what happened.

In September, yet another editorial appeared concerning the area's
continuing conflict concerning growth. It reported on a fashion show that
was supposed to be a light evening affair. The ski area showed a promotional movie during the event. Some of those attending made it clear they
did not want *any* promotion about Crested Butte. Sibley reported:

> The total effect ... was to increase the misunderstanding between the
> people who are working hard at promoting the attractions of this area in
> the hopes that people will come here, and the people at the other
> extreme who do not care if another person ever takes the left fork at
> Almont again [going to Crested Butte]. ...those of us who feel we have
> a way of life to protect...had better note well and carefully that our
> defenses are not only down, they are non-existent... Can growth be
> controlled at all – or is 'a little growth' like 'a little pregnancy.'

A month later, in October, referring to a county-wide political initiative that targeted tourist town pioneers, Sibley editorialized about a new
food stamp program, and the County's official reaction to it. He commented on Gunnison's decision to ban eligibility for food stamps to people "who are poor by choice." He wrote, "...the resolution amounts to ...a
legal mandate for hippie harassment ... Further, in light of the tension
that has existed in this county this past year...for the commissioners to

stoop at this time to effectively abetting the cause of prejudiced and hateful people is considerable." The relevant section of the resolution that was supported by all three County Commissioners stated:

> NOW THEREFORE BE IT RESOLVED that the County Commissioners Organization of Colorado go on record in making strong recommendation to the United States Department of Agriculture and to the administrative bodies of the food stamp program that these persons be made to comply in good faith with standards of cleanliness and acceptable modes of dress in order to be considered as actually seeking employment....if these persons will not conform ...that they be labeled as 'poor by choice' and barred from participating in the food stamp program.

On December 30, 1970, the *Chronicle* summarized the cultural and political collisions that were intensifying in the community.

> ...into this small and relatively unprepared town have been funneled...all manner of urban burnouts, freaks of every description, real estate speculators, mining speculators, construction workers, tourists looking for a place with no lift lines all day and Aspen night life at night, and a lot of very fine people, all in addition to the people who call Crested Butte home. All of these people seemed to have one thing in common; they were decidedly unhappy to see all the others here too. ...The social conflicts that had been simmering...for the past two years or so were naturally not without their political consequences this year. We elected a mayor and trustees that did not seem to satisfy anybody....As for what the coming year will bring...the town and the ski area will grow.... What seems important...is to grow along with our growth.

What Sibley did not seem to recognize in that editorial, however, was that the fights between the main factions would continue to intensify over the following two years, focusing on several specific community issues. Nor did he foresee that they would result in the tourist town pioneers politically defeating the long-time town residents; and redirecting how town resources would be used.

Chapter 7

The Hot-Button Issues

Beginning in the late 1960s and continuing through the mid-1970s, there were several *specific* issues that long-time residents fought over with the tourist town pioneers. Moreover, these two groups viewed the public policy implications of these issues differently. Several of them highlighted the fault lines and illustrated the different values and interests that motivated each side. At the broadest level, the conflicts were about the power of local government: if it could restrict what someone did with his or her private property, or limit what one could do in his or her own personal life. Zoning, architectural controls, the historical preservation of old structures, and the ability of government to use eminent domain to take an individual's real estate for "the public good," were examples of the struggles over property rights. The clashes over personal issues concerned bar fighting, poaching, pet control, snowmobiling, and recreational drug use.

Beginning in the late 1960s and continuing through the mid-1970s, there were several specific issues that long-term residents fought over with the tourist town pioneers. ... At the broadest level, the conflicts were about the power of local government: if it could restrict what someone did with his or her private property, or limit what one could do in his or her own personal life.

Views about motorized recreational vehicle use, as discussed earlier, divided mining-era residents and trailblazers from the new pioneers. The former wanted snowmobile use allowed anywhere; pioneers wanted to restrict their use. Pioneers did not want the tranquility in town or the areas surrounding it disturbed. Perhaps more important than the noise itself, however, many pioneers felt intimidated by the younger mining-era residents and trailblazers who used them. One of the younger pioneers, Dave

Coney, remembered years later that at his Washington Gulch cabin several miles north of town, he held off snowmobilers at rifle point when they wanted to burn down his cabin. He was also sure that immediately after that confrontation, they set fire to two vacant cabins not far below his, (although he did not actually see them do it).

In January 1969, Bill Frame bought the Inn of Crested Butte at the ski area. He was a former economics major at an Ivy-League School and a budding entrepreneur. He began cross-country skiing and telemarking with a few other pioneers. He and another early pioneer, Marty Krieger, began taking locals to areas outside town to teach them to cross-country ski. In 1970, Frame invited ski instructor Lars Larsen to give cross-country ski lessons to Crested Butte area residents. Several pioneers took the course and quickly embraced the sport. They liked the athleticism of it, and the winter wilderness aesthetic. Seeing a new business opportunity, Frame and Krieger opened The Alpineer, a new boutique in the Company Store that catered to the equipment and clothing needs of "off the beaten trail people."

As both the number of snowmobilers and cross-country skiers grew, increasingly intense tensions arose between them. At the same time competitions in each sport were added to the annual winter events calendar. A snowmobile "safari" was held in January 1969. The course went between Crested Butte and Paonia (an agricultural community about 45 miles away on the other side of nearby Kebler Pass). At the end of that year a "Second Annual Blue Mesa Snowmobile Rally" was publicized. By the following December, in 1970, the *Chronicle* published a front-page editorial that focused on the winter recreation confrontations. It said, "Crested Butte is a winter sports area now. Snowmobiling is a winter sport. So, it only makes sense that Crested Butte must adapt her laws to 1) provide for the use of snowmobiles while 2) preventing the misuse of snowmobiles." A few months later the paper announced that, for the first time, there would be cross-country ski races during the third annual "Flauschink," the celebration that commemorated the end of winter and beginning of spring.

As both the number of snowmobilers and cross-country skiers grew, increasingly intense tensions arose between them.

The Crested Butte town council struggled intensively for a couple of years over snowmobiles. In February 1969, the Trustees passed ordinances that banned their use on the town's main street, and required them to cross it only on its far west side. They also mandated that the machines had to obey all traffic laws that applied to cars in the few areas where they could be used. The council further asked the State Legislature to enact new laws to regulate snowmobile use.

Addressing these issues, a mid-January 1970 newspaper editorial titled, *"The ?"#%#?# Eternal Snow Mobile Hassle"* rhetorically asked:

> Why do so many people locally not like snowmobiles? ...some people love machines and other people hate them. But assuming that obstacle to be insurmountable, there are several more tangible reasons why people do not like the machines. One reason is noise... Another reason is that cross-country skiers feel imposed upon and sometimes intimidated by a line of snowmobiles coming toward them and disrupting the peace and quiet that is one of the main justifications for the hiking out on skis. Another reason, like it or not, lies with the attitude openly exhibited by some snowmobilers toward things that are not really any of their business; if a person is confronted by a man in a snowmobile suit who feels obliged to comment unfavorably on the length of his hair or manner of his dress, that person is probably going to look unfavorably on snowmobiles, and that very thing has happened too frequently here.

That editorial struck a nerve. There were vehement letters to the editor the following week, including one by ski area trailblazer Gene Martin, and another from a new non-profit organization created by pioneers, The Business and Professional Women of Crested Butte. Martin argued that many people, including some younger than 30, thought that snowmobilers were good and further, that the paper's editor "was a one-sided anti-military, anti-school administration, anti-town government, anti-law and order, anti-snowmobile, and even an anti-Christmas person." The women's organization was by then totally independent from the national organization and addressed local issues only. It strongly opposed snowmobile use in town and argued for, "The protection of our children who may not be able to jump fast enough; protection of our elderly citizens who walk to church and to get the mail; consideration of sleeping citizens of our town; consideration of television watchers – especially the elderly; consideration of property owners against trespass and destruction of said property."

Town trustees again acted on snowmobiles in 1970. Illustrating their strong opposition, and their perception that the council represented the views of old-timers and ski area trailblazers, over 30 tourist town pioneers sat in the audience and opposed *any* use of snowmobiles. They argued forcefully that these machines were too noisy and dangerous, as well as opening the town itself to liability. In response to their concerns, the council unanimously banned all snowmobile use in town.

The issue remained unresolved. Two weeks later, about 60 people attended another council meeting where snowmobiles were the main topic. Two early tourist town pioneer town trustees who were appointed to fill council vacancies, Harold O 'Connor and Don Bachman, tried to find a compromise. Not incidentally, both O'Connor and Bachman had recently taken up and enjoyed cross-country skiing. They attempted to accommodate snowmobile owners, but they also wanted their users to meet the state requirement that banned snowmobile use on state and county roads, even as it allowed a municipality to determine how these machines could be used within its own town boundaries. Bachman went even further. He said it might be wise to ban all future events involving motorized vehicles within town limits, including jeep, snowmobile, and motorcycle races, because they polarized the different factions in the community. The *Chronicle* reported on that meeting and the continuing struggles over snowmobiles. In what was an ironic contrast, the front page of the paper featured an idyllic picture of a solitary, peaceful, cross-country skier in an untrammeled wide-open snow field on the outskirts of town, with the caption, "When the world is all yours..." and referred to a story about ski touring inside the paper.

Townspeople undoubtedly felt intensely about snowmobiles. But that paled in comparison to the most emotionally polarizing issue between long-time western-culture oriented, rural, working-class residents and the affluent, big city and suburban reared, tourist town pioneers: pets. The differences were about whether dogs could run free; and, if not, how leash laws would be enforced. House pets were important to pioneers.

Practically all had at least one dog or cat; many had more. Most thought canines should neither have to be registered nor leashed. Long-time area residents disagreed strongly; they wanted strict leash law enforcement. They thought unleashed dogs were a threat to people, cattle, and horses, and that they had become a big problem in recent years. They thought canines should be killed if they harmed or even threatened anyone or anything.

... that paled in comparison to the most emotionally polarizing issue between long-time western-culture oriented, rural, working-class residents, and the affluent, big city and suburban reared tourist town pioneers: pets.

In early 1969, reports and editorials about dogs-at-large began appearing in the paper. They said problems with them were increasing. When a young girl from a long-time town resident's family was bitten in February, pressure from Crested Butte's old-timers increased on the town officials. They wanted them to corral curs that ran loose, and were often unregistered. There were newspaper reports at least monthly about them, and the newspaper reported regularly on council's deliberations and the marshal's activities regarding them. By July 1970, a long time Crested Butte resident, Myrtle Veltri, whose family ranched several miles outside town was quoted, "…if any dog came into her yard again with the owner refusing to get it out, she would 'not only give the dog a load of buckshot, but the owner too, right in the seat of the pants'." Then, to add to the already intense and polarized feelings, that following week Councilman Don Bachman and the town marshal, Norm Pierce, Jr., had to round up loose canines that were chasing horses that belonged to another mining-era resident, Fritz Yaklich. The following month another piece said that dogs needed to be leashed or tied up before the start of the school year. By early September, the Council passed a new law that increased fines for unlicensed pets and appointed Ron Barr to be the town's first dog catcher, an unpaid position. By late winter 1970, in response to ever increasing pressure, Barr announced that he would begin ticketing owners of barking dogs, and those that obstructed entrances to public places.

None of that had much effect on pet control. The following May, in 1971, when the issue arose again, (as seemingly happened regularly during the "*mud*" season as spring was called at that time), there was another contentious town council meeting devoted to canines. By then the council was united in wanting them licensed and leashed. But that was in sharp contrast to the sentiment expressed at the meeting by the mostly tourist town pioneer audience; they wanted less restrictive leash laws. Most did not want their dogs tethered, period. They wanted them to be able to be under "voice control." Eric Ross, one of the town's new alternate life-style residents, presented a petition with 146 signatures opposing the proposed law; fellow pioneers Steve Glazer, Don Bachman, and Don West also spoke in opposition to it. Joyce Cobai, a young Crested Butte mining-era woman, spoke in its favor. After *four* hours of heated discussion on that one issue, Councilman Jim Wallace finally made a motion to table the matter, and asked Ross to propose an alternative ordinance.

With the help of John Levin, the former New York City assistant district attorney and partner in The Grubstake, Ross presented a different leash law the following week. In what was deemed a measured response to each side's concerns, Ross' leash law ultimately was adopted. It banned dogs from running freely, but allowed a well-trained, unleashed, canine to walk in the company of its owner, as long as he or she could prove their pet was voice controlled. At the same meeting the Council approved an allocation of $100.00 per month as a salary for Ron Barr, who thereupon became the town's first *paid* dog-catcher.

That law, however, still did not end the struggle. In fact, it intensified. A few weeks later Barr began ticketing dog owners whose canines were unlicensed or were running loose. However, he could not impound them since there was no "pound" in town, and he did not have a truck to take them to Gunnison's. Town trustees then questioned if he was earning his pay and urged him to enforce the law more stringently. Barr resigned four months later. He said the hassles associated with the job were not worth either the money or the bad vibes from the community. Two other pioneers immediately applied for the position: Chuck Pierce and Tom Glass. The latter had political aspirations, and soon afterwards became a council member and then the town's mayor.

Two Samoyed Huskies belonging to a well-loved trailblazer couple, Walt and Nadine Israel, were shot and maimed by a newly-appointed Crested Butte born and reared town marshal, Norm Pierce, Jr. That was the first of several dog shootings that enraged pioneers, and dramatically highlighted the different ways old timers and new people viewed pets. At about that same time, another dog killing occurred. A young rancher, who was widely thought by tourist town pioneers to be "anti-hippie," admitted shooting the animal. He said it was running freely in a field where his cattle grazed, and he shot it to protect them. Ranching was the economic backbone of Gunnison's economy, and the rural dominated Colorado legislature earlier had enacted state laws that supported killing dogs if they "worried" cattle. The pioneers grudgingly recognized the rancher's arguments and actions but, as a pioneer said forty years later, "it really may have been the ranchers' way of expressing their anxiety about losing their town to new people." For a long time thereafter, pioneers nevertheless felt that shooting pets was unjustified and brutal, and that it demonstrated old-timers were callous and even inhumane.

In fall 1971 and early winter 1972, the issue came to a head: dogs and cats were poisoned and shot frequently, sometimes after they had been tied to a tree or fence. It became almost commonplace. Pictures of the dead pets were featured on the front page of the *Chronicle*, along with letters to the editor from their owners. Cat owner, Kathleen Stupple, a new resident who would later become the first female pioneer elected to the Crested Butte Town Council, wrote a letter that said someone shot a .22 caliber bullet through her cat's right leg. She wrote, "It seems we have a cat-sniper living among us, firing a 22-rifle within the city limits at helpless domestic animals. I wonder if this helps explain the mysterious disappearance of several cats here this fall."

In fall 1971 and early winter1972, the issue came to a head: dogs and cats were poisoned and shot frequently, sometimes after they had been tied to a tree or fence.

Next, a Siberian Husky was shot in the head after being tied to a tree near the town reservoir. Its owner, Lynn Haller, another newcomer, wrote to the newspaper editor, "We have not yet discovered who shot our dog, but many are helping us in the search. Whoever this sick person is, they are on the loose in Crested Butte with their gun, ready to shoot your pet or child or whatever gets in their path." Then, during the first week of 1972, a front-page banner headline blared, "David Leinsdorf's Dog

Mysteriously Shot and Killed." Beneath it was a large picture of his dead German Shepherd lying in front of his house. Ironically, however, it was not a rancher who shot Leinsdorf's pet; it was another tourist town pioneer, Donner Hanson, who identified with the "Old West" cowboy. He admitted killing Leinsdorf's dog at 4:00 a.m. Two weeks later yet another canine in town was shot and killed, this one belonging to another pioneer, Monica Ariowitsch. She brought her dead dog to the Crested Butte Post Office and laid it beside the front door with a sign next to it that said, "Your child is next! Let's restrict firearms in Crested Butte." A picture of her dog lying beside the sign also appeared prominently on the *Chronicle's* front page.

After all these dead animals were discovered the newspaper's editor, Myles Arber, who distinctly did not share "Old West" ways, wrote in an editorial that said killing domestic pets was sick and had to stop. "I personally do not feel safe knowing that a person with the kind of mentality that would allow him to murder domesticated animals is at large .... if this malicious and diseased killing of animals ... does not stop, I am for helping the Town's animal citizenry organize a lobby to pass a leash law for people."

Whether local government should restrict what an individual could do with private property also polarized the town's people. Unlike the majority of old-timers and ski industry trailblazers, most pioneers wanted the town to control what could be done with real property: with zoning, architectural restrictions, mandating the preservation of old town structures and — with appropriate compensation — even the ability to confiscate private land for public use, all of which had been customary in the communities from which they had come.

Unlike the majority of old-timers and ski industry trailblazers, most pioneers wanted the town to control what could be done with real property: with zoning, architectural restrictions, mandating the preservation of old town structures and – with appropriate compensation – even the ability to confiscate private land for public use ...

The idea of planning divided both miners and ranchers from the newest community immigrants. Even before Crested Butte faced the issue within its borders, planning had earlier become an issue at the county level. Jim Wallace remembered many years later, "I chaired the planning committee for the northern end of the County when Gunnison had to be zoned. We dealt with everything outside town." In fall 1967, Gunnison County ranchers opposed a proposed county-wide zoning ordinance they considered dictatorial, and contrary to their Western way of life but, despite their opposition, it became law. It *required* permits for any construction, and those would be issued only after appropriately scaled drawings were submitted to the local authorities. The plans had to pinpoint precisely where a new structure would be located, showing that it conformed to the County's new mandated setbacks from highways. It also required that structures had to be inspected before they could be occupied. To add financial injury to insult, anyone who wanted to build had to pay new fees to cover the costs of implementing that law.

Following the eventual enactment of that contentious zoning regulation, the early Crested Butte tourist town pioneers began a multi-year effort to establish a zoning ordinance within the town boundaries. It was first developed by members of the Crested Butte Society, the non-profit pioneer organization that was formed to promote cultural activities and preserve the town's historical character. Led by a committee headed by Dr. Art Norris, its members thought the town should use its authority to determine what types of edifices could be built, and where. Those were controversial concepts because the traditional western mind-set defined "planning" as a restriction on personal freedoms and considered it socialistic.

That view reflected two seemingly contradictory but nevertheless co-existing ideologies that were a part of the history of the town, the West, and perhaps even the nation itself: a strong belief in personal autonomy and rugged individualism coupled with a high value placed on "community cooperation." This traditional code held that a man's property was his "castle" and whatever happened in or around it was the concern of only those who lived in it. At the same time that person was encouraged, even expected, to volunteer with other like-minded neighbors to build communal facilities such as a community grange, church, or silo (all the while traveling to the site on public roads, to the extent that they existed). That life-style and value system clearly was part of the Western ranching and mining way of life. It was also part of the emerging recreation community ethic, but by then it was called "volunteerism."

Long time town residents who held these traditional values thought an individual should be able to build whatever he wished, wherever he wanted, without prior government approval. They did not think a zoning code should limit that. Despite the multi-year controversy surrounding the issue, eventually the Crested Butte Town Council adopted a zoning code.

Soon after, the new town zoning law was challenged. There were intense conflicts over it that erupted in the summer and fall of 1971 and culminated in winter 1972. First, construction began on a multiplex in the southwest corner of town. It was the earliest blatant violation of the new zoning law. It was a six-unit structure that was stylistically different from the traditional small, wood frame, Victorian style, single family houses

... the new town zoning law was challenged. There were intense conflicts over it that erupted in the summer and fall of 1971 and culminated in winter 1972.

that surrounded it. While it was being built, it was called "Stiltsville" by the tourist town pioneers because its rectangular factory built mobile home units sat atop steel I-beams. Besides that, the developer did not go through the appropriate processes dictated by the new zoning ordinance. He did not obtain prior approval for the design, nor did he get a permit. Most pioneers thought any building larger than the existing small ones detracted from the town's quaintness, were out of character with its historic structures, and were aesthetically unacceptable. Perhaps of even greater significance, they thought "Stiltsville" symbolized accommodation to the budding growth in town, as did larger structures generally. A survey conducted for the town council a year later found that town residents thought the town was "just about the right size," and many opposed apartments specifically.

Another related issue that polarized long-time residents and pioneers was the demolition of the existing old structures, in particular one on the main street of town built and owned by the mining era Kochevar family. It was razed in the summer of 1971. It had been vacant for many years, was extremely dilapidated, and was called "the whorehouse" by tourist town pioneers who thought, incorrectly, that it once had been one. (This derogatory moniker aggravated Trudy Yaklich, a young mining-era woman. Forty-five years later she said that it still irked her when pioneers or recreation community settlers used that terminology to describe the no longer existing old Kochevar structure, "especially when those who should know better, continue using the term and perpetuating the story.")

Pioneers thought the town's old buildings should be reconstructed and preserved as a few others already had, including one on the lot immediately east of Kochevar's decaying edifice. It was renovated by an early pioneer multi-media artist, Dana Atchley. The pioneers thought rehabilitating those old homes would enhance the quaint style of the town and accentuate its historic aura. The survey referenced above found that 95% of the people interviewed wanted the old structures preserved. Besides, as was the case with Kochevar's boarding house, until a structure was rebuilt, it could be used as a "crash pad," crafts workshops, or a "free store." In contrast, long-time residents wanted the old structures demolished. They thought they were potential liabilities for the owners, were "old-fashioned," were reminders of their past hard times and, perhaps most importantly, that "hippies" occupied them. Describing the different perspectives and hard feelings that surrounded the issue, the September 8, 1971

Pen and Ink Drawing of Old Kochevar Buildings. Courtesy of Susan Anderton.

Chronicle's front-page headline said, "House Razing Followed by Slow Burn." The following article said the building "was bulldozed down and burned up Saturday, resulting in a smoldering not only at the site but among some Crested Butte residents. …Mayor Jim Cole said the house was pinpointed as being in violation of the town's health ordinance which requires plumbing and running water for any structure being occupied."

Bob Teitler, one of the new pioneers from New York City, tried unsuccessfully to stop a moving bulldozer after the main structure on the property was demolished. As part of that job, an out-building was also scheduled to be removed. Teitler, who with his young family was renting the house next door that Atchley had recently restored, shouted menacingly at the driver, Bill Lacy, and pointed a loaded rifle at him while he was driving toward it. Almost 45 years later, Teitler recalled that another pioneer, Cordley Coit, was also pointing a semi-automatic rifle at Lacy (which Coit denied). Within a few days after that incident, reflecting a privileged upbringing that was typical of many pioneers, Teitler called his father to get money to buy the newly-leveled business zoned property.

In reaction to the controversy regarding that demolition, the following week's newspaper commented:

> The Crested Butte Board of Trustees was caught with egg on its face last week when a group of citizens showed up at the town meeting to point out city officials violated a town ordinance in the burning of an old house on Elk Avenue. …The building blazed and smoldered for some 72 hours with an on-and-off attendance of the fire hoses, and at one point a nearby resident was ignored when he complained that sparks were falling on and near his home. It isn't the first time that public officials have broken one law in their eagerness to enforce another. Nor is it the first time that communications have bogged down because of lack of empathy on both sides.

After the outpouring of the newest town immigrants' hostility toward "Stiltsville," a variance to the new town zoning law was requested. It sought permission to build a new motel with retail shops right next to it, in the middle of the town's main street. These businesses were to be developed on vacant lots immediately next to the Way Station, an existing restaurant and bar that was popular with Crested Butte's long-time residents. The old-timers wanted the owner, Margaret Dunlap, to build the motel and adjacent shops. They argued that constructing them would initially provide jobs for locals, and then when they were completed, they would provide needed, on-going, service jobs.

More importantly perhaps, ideologically, old-timers still thought government should not be able to tell anyone what he or she could do with his or her property. The overwhelming majority of tourist town pioneers were adamantly against the proposal. They felt constructing a typical mid-twentieth century style motel on the town's main street violated the zoning code and, like "Stiltsville," would detract from the town's Victorian appearance. They thought preserving and enhancing the historical character of the town would attract tourists, and the zoning ordinance should be used to stimulate the town's economy and future development. They believed the "common good" allowed local government to dictate what an individual could do with his or her real estate and, moreover, that local government had the responsibility to determine what it considered the common good to be.

The Way Station owner, moreover, was perceived by many pioneers to be unfriendly and even actively hostile toward them. They thought she disliked and discriminated against them, and provided a haven for those who felt the same way. At the front door of her establishment, she prominently displayed a sign saying, *"No shirt. No shoes. No Service."* Signs like that were often seen in American hotels, restaurants, and other retail businesses during that era, and it indicated an owner's distain for young counter-culture people, those they called "hippies." As a minor point in a long opinion piece that articulated the many reasons opponents wanted the proposal voted down when it came up for a Council vote, the *Chronicle* editor rhetorically asked, "And what kind of tourism will it promote and name will it give the Town if the arbitrary and discriminatory serving policies she employs in her restaurant were to spread and infect her proposed motel and shops?"

Already riled by the "Stiltsville" and "bulldozed/burning building" confrontations, the proposed variance for the Way Station galvanized the new pioneers. Opposition to Dunlap's requested change became a *cause célèbre* among them. It became a continuing topic of street, restaurant, and bar-room conversations. There was increased attendance at town council meetings when the proposal was on the agenda. Editorials and letters to the editor that opposed it were written, including one from a new realtor. A petition opposing it quickly collected over 100 signatures, almost all of them from the town's most recent residents.

At the council meeting where the matter was to be decided, an Ivy-League educated pioneer lawyer, John Taylor, represented a group of property owners who opposed the variance. By that time there were plenty of lawyers in Crested Butte but, significantly, Dunlap was represented by a Gunnison lawyer, Ricky Santarelli. Ultimately, town trustees — John Cobai, Albert Falsetto, and Ray Oehlert, two old-timers and an early ski area trailblazer — voted to grant the variance. Jim Wallace and Doris Walker, both early tourist town pioneers, opposed it. A council member was absent at the meeting when the roll call vote was taken, and because three-fourths of the six council members were needed for the proposal to pass, to the frustration of the majority of those present and voting, the trustees were forced to deny the request.

The front-page newspaper story about that pivotal conflict declared, "Threat to Zoning Code Defeated." The following piece added, "The contest was viewed as crucial for the preservation of the Town's zoning code."

That was one of the earliest demonstrations of the pioneer's political organizing strength. In a commentary praising the decision, the newspaper's editor, Myles Arber, opined that the defeat of the proposed ordinance signified a sense of empowerment and signaled (new) townspeople taking control of their destiny. It urged them to register to vote in the coming 1972 spring election. "The [tourist town pioneers] ... won a significant battle by mustering the arms to vote down this first important challenge to their right to ... decide the course of the development of their town .... That ...may have signaled that Crested Butte has gotten a glimpse of how it might be if it decided to rise to the challenge and defend its concept of itself ...." He added, looking to the near future, "There will be a very important election held here April 4th, and if this momentum is to continue you must participate. Register... and express yourself by voting. If you live here, it is your town. If it is your town, vote for it."

Chapter 8

'Musical' Marshals

L aw enforcement ultimately became the focal point for all the hot button issues and cultural conflicts, and the main political issue in town. Between 1967 and 1974 it was the subject of intense community debate as the population boomed and its character changed. During those seven years, the different town councils appointed ten new marshals.

Law enforcement ultimately became the focal point for all the hot button issues and cultural conflicts, and the main political issue in town. Between 1967 and 1974 it was the subject of intense community debate. ... different town councils appointed ten new marshals.

During that period, the different cultural groups in town fought over which laws were to be enforced, and who did the enforcing. They did not agree about which laws were important, and what personal characteristics they wanted the local lawman to embody. In the years before the 1972 town election, mining-era residents and most ski area trailblazers wanted a traditional "law-and-order" man, who would crack down on recreational drug use when it began to appear. After that election, the new tourist town pioneers wanted someone who reflected their feelings and respected their lifestyles, one who believed in the values of "peace and social justice," and who recognized recreational drug use as part of the local life-style. A couple of years later, as the growth-oriented pioneers and recreation community settlers became more powerful politically, although they too used recreational drugs, they wanted the anti-growth alternate lifestyle and "outlaw" pioneers to leave, and again favored a more traditional law enforcer. The councils' choice of lawmen during that era directly reflected those shifting political priorities.

As early as August 1966, possibly in reaction to the increasing national social unrest and political turmoil, or to some early new locals' and summer transients' life-style choices, there was an indication of the mining-era populations' discomfort with what was happening around them. An unusual, bold type-faced, **"NOTICE"** appeared on the newspaper's front page. It read:

> The Mayor, Trustees, Marshal and police officers, as conservators of the peace, shall have power to arrest, or cause to be arrested, *with or without process* [emphasis added], and take before the Police Magistrate, all persons who in their view shall break or threaten to break the peace, and the Police Magistrate may commit or admit them to bail as the case may require. They shall have the power to arrest or cause to be arrested as aforesaid, all persons who shall be found in the act of violating any ordinance.

Presumably, that "official" notice was based on a prior mining-era town council discussion and vote.

Shortly following that notice the town's part-time marshal, Rudolph Somrak, resigned. He had successfully kept the peace for five years. He was considered a fine local lawman because he approached his job in an informal, low-key, manner. When the ski area began, and new people came, he showed his openness to the industry by saying he wanted Crested Butte to become "the best year-round recreational center in the state."

A successor to Somrak was appointed, but did not last. In June, 1968, the town again tried to hire a local lawman, but the trustees could not agree on his responsibilities, or on the personal qualities they wanted him to have. They formed a special committee to define the job. It consisted of an old-timer who was appointed to the council a few months earlier, Gal Starika, the

In June, 1968, ... trustees could not agree on the [marshal's] responsibilities, or on the personal qualities they wanted him to have.

first female councilmember; Jim Cole, a ski area trailblazer; and a tourist town pioneer, Don Bachman. In the meantime, Somrak was re-appointed to the position as an "interim."

Surprisingly, by February 1969, even though there was high unemployment and underemployment in town, no one had yet applied for the vacant position. A *Chronicle* commentary thanked Somrak for his service noting that he "could talk with an offender's (sic) mothers, fathers, husbands, wives, etc. if there was a problem." Continuing, it said the community was changing, that it no longer was just a small town where a part-time law officer would suffice, and someone was needed who knew the law, criminal procedures, etc.:

> When Gunnison's Assistant Chief of Police John Boxley spoke to the Board of Trustees last Monday, he strongly suggested that the town try to hire a stranger to the town and the town's factional problems – in short, an impartial man not committed to or against the young, the old, the locals, the newcomers, the skiers, the miners, the hairs, the clean-cuts, or what-have-you. In so far as it is humanly possible, a man is needed who is interested in nothing but making a reasonable living enforcing equally on all the law as it is written...

However, Gunnison law enforcement personnel, including Boxley, were not universally held in high regard in Crested Butte. His message was heard differently by various town factions. While old-timers liked what he said, young tourist town pioneers thought Gunnison lawmen were "anti-hippie" and discriminated against them; and that they actually instigated lawlessness. They cited an example from the previous summer: Tony's Tavern, a 3.2 bar frequented by pioneers and Western State College students, hired a band one night and collected a small cover charge to pay for it. Everyone paid the cover willingly except a few members of the WSC football and wrestling teams. They demanded free admission which the owners refused. A crowd formed that was led by an off-duty Gunnison Deputy Sheriff, Rocky Selander. According to the newspaper, rowdies threw beer cans through the front plate glass window and threatened people inside. The crowd turned into a mob and a riot nearly ensued. Tony's owner took out a .38 revolver that he kept behind the bar, and fired it into the air above the horde. Then, lowering the gun so it was pointed at the throng he said he "was not a very good shot". He quieted the rabble, and it disbanded. That incident reinforced pioneers' feelings about Gunnison law enforcement, further alienating them from it.

Articles and editorials on the incident followed. Bachman wrote a long letter to the editor that clearly illustrated the intense community feelings. It ended by addressing the Gunnison County Sheriff directly:

Your deputy Sheriff Cope: one of the County's law enforcement officers. A law enforcement officer intimidating the very citizens he is sworn to protect. I demand that you reply to this letter publicly as you are responsible for the conduct of this man ... and that you take action to see that this man will no longer be in a position of public trust. It is ironic that during the disturbance that the dispatcher called and advised one of my employees that your office would be unable to assist in quelling this mob.

Chronicle editor George Sibley commented that a lawman was needed that knew how to handle mobs, because Crested Butte was a recreation center and rioting was some people's idea of a good time. He implied that similar disruptions had happened in other town bars, and their owners faced situations like the one at Tony's Tavern. He also said that more money for law enforcement was needed to pay for competent police and that the ski area manager, Gus Larkin, offered to con-

... law enforcement was needed that knew how to handle mobs, because Crested Butte was a recreation center and rioting was some people's idea of a good time.

tribute if the local lawman could also be a Gunnison county deputy who would provide service to the ski area. Larkin said similar events occurred there, and when requests for help were made from bars at the area, the Sheriff's office ignored them.

The following week a piece headlined, "Shouting Match at Tony's Says Sheriff," reported that Cope said the bar's window was broken by someone's loud voice, and that he would file charges against Bachman for assault with a deadly weapon. Blaming the victim was familiar to many pioneers. Through their experiences in the Civil Rights, Free Speech, and the Anti-War Movements of the 1960s, they learned that the more harshly a demonstrator was treated by the police, the more likely it would be that he or she would face more serious charges. If a protestor at a public demonstration was beaten by police with a club, for instance, he or she would be more likely to be charged with felonious assault rather than merely disturbing the peace or resisting arrest. The paper also noted "As of press time..., no action has been taken by the Sheriff." There were never any follow-up stories about the matter so, seemingly, the sheriff apparently never took any further action.

A month later, Bachman filed a formal grievance. He filed complaints against, among others, Deputy Sheriff Rocky Selander and Rob McClung, a member of the WSC college football and wrestling teams. (Ironically, McClung was hired as Crested Butte's marshal in 1974 to "clean up the town" by those who wanted more growth and development.) At that time the most recently appointed "interim" law enforcement officer, Norman Pierce, Jr., also filed formal "disturbing the peace" charges against Selander and McClung. Sibley's comments that week compared the abusive police tactics of the county sheriff's officers outside Tony's Tavern, to those used by Chicago police against protesters at the 1968 Democratic National Convention, which led to chaos in the streets.

The clearest difference between the town's two major factions regarding legal matters was about the way drug laws should be enforced. Old-timers thought marijuana, psychedelics, and all other narcotics except alcohol were bad, and laws prohibiting them should be strictly enforced. They agreed with the county assistant police chief when he was quoted in January 1968,

The clearest difference between the town's two major factions regarding legal matters was about the way drug laws should be enforced.

"The dangerous aspects of the 'mind expanding' drugs cannot be overestimated.... Nothing fouls up young people more." In contrast, most pioneers thought drugs were benign, that they were an integral part of their chosen life-style and, most importantly, that laws banning them were obsolete and should be overlooked.

That spring, after an arrest, a case was dismissed against six young "outlaw" pioneers who were charged with manufacturing the drug DMT. According to Dave Coney, allegedly its principal manufacturer, DMT is an LSD-like psychedelic drug. Denver's young executives preferred it because it was an intense, short, high they could enjoy during their lunch hour and then return to work, and still be productive in the afternoon (unlike the popular corporate executives' "three-martini lunch" of the fifties). Following that dismissal, Sibley's editorial addressed local law issues. Entitled, "The DMT Wrap-Up: Keystone Kops in Retrospect," it focused on the recent drug bust and the wanton illegality of procedures county police used when making it. No one ever obtained a proper search warrant, nor was there even a legitimate authority available to serve it if one had existed, like a sheriff, deputy or any other representative of the law. Sibley wrote that he strongly suspected the drug, indeed, was manufactured in the house the officers entered, but that it was more important that the illegally executed police entry was done right. Sibley thought it was too bad charges against the defendants had to be dropped, but he concluded that the judge who insisted that proper procedures had to be followed, was a true patriot and not "a bleeding-heart liberal" as many longtime Crested Butte and Gunnison County residents had said. Moreover, Sibley added that he thought the county lawmen, because they used improper methods to nab their prey, acted like lawless thugs.

Following that turmoil, five people applied for the vacant town marshal position. In May, Peter Colwell, a young man with a background in social services in the Northwest was hired. He was liked immediately by most of the townspeople, especially the new pioneers. After only a week on the job, however, his vehicle rolled over a steep hillside above nearby Lake Nicholson, and he was killed instantly. As a tribute, a new town park was named after him. Two months later another young man was hired, Walter H. Niezguski. He had been a WSC football player who was in and out of Crested Butte before being hired, but he was relieved of his duties within months because "he was too often hard to find in downtown Crested Butte."

Given the difficulty of finding and retaining competent lawmen who were acceptable to the two major factions, as well as the need for the lawmen to cover an area that actually exceeded the town's boundaries in the northern end of the county, the county commissioners budgeted $2,400.00 to supplement a marshal's salary. At the same time Sheriff Cope *rhetorically* agreed to deputize a new town lawman, who could patrol the areas surrounding town, including the ski area. While he was sheriff, however, he never matched his rhetoric with the reality of finding someone he deemed acceptable, and his pledge was never honored.

Given the difficulty of finding and retaining competent lawmen who were acceptable to the two major factions ... the county commissioners budgeted $2,400.00 to supplement a marshal's salary.

With Sheriff Cope's verbal commitment in place, the town trustees hired another marshal, this one from Washington State, Les Edgerton. Six weeks later, the town and the county sheriff were still trying to work out an arrangement so he could represent the Sheriff's office part-time. But in January 1970 Edgerton also resigned saying he wanted to return to Alaska. Actually though, someone discovered he had been convicted for a minor burglary in Wyoming fifteen years earlier, when he was 18 years old. Many townspeople, especially tourist town pioneers, liked him and did not think the previous conviction mattered; some even thought it was an asset. The town council re-hired him, whereupon he continued with his duties. However, the sheriff never approved of him, or authorized the already allocated pay supplement. A few months later, Edgerton resigned for the last time.

Following his resignation, the town trustees immediately hired Russ Reycraft, Jr. on an "interim" basis. He was an early pioneer from the East who owned and managed a small apartment building in town. He was low key in fulfilling his duties, and mainly continued rounding up unlicensed dogs and pursuing other petty crimes. Over half a dozen cars, for example, had gas siphoned from their tanks. He and his deputies caught three Gunnison teenagers pilfering the gas. When that arrest was made, the *Chronicle* noted that, contrary to the belief of many old-timers who thought hippies were the culprits, it had been typical, traditional, Gunnison teenagers, who committed the petty offense.

Because Reycraft was only employed on a temporary basis, a permanent marshal was still needed. A newspaper issue noted that, and an editorial focused on law enforcement and drug use in Crested Butte was written. It intimated that a hard "law and order" approach did not seem to work in Crested Butte, that laws meant to control what a person did to himself or herself were unnecessary, and laws should be enacted and enforced only to protect the community.

Candidates for the coming 1970 town council election began announcing their intentions and formulating their platforms. By then, council candidates were divided into two broad categories: long-time Crested Butte residents and newcomers. New people were further divided between ski area trailblazers and the early pioneers. Given the conflicts over the lawman's job and the frequent turnover of marshals, candidates considered law and order issues a priority.

All council aspirants called for "better law enforcement." Precisely what that meant differed among them. Born and bred Crested Butte residents John Cobai, Albert Falsetto, Tony Gallowich, and Whitey Sporcich said they wanted to "improve town law enforcement and get 'good' law and order." Trailblazers Elmer Eflin, Dave Watson and Jerry Chiles thought that would happen by hiring someone who would "be acceptable to the Gunnison County Sherriff;" and pioneer Don Bachman wanted "stable" law enforcement.

The 1970 election was a clear victory for the old-timers and trailblazers. The new council members immediately set about hiring a permanent local lawman. Trailblazers Elmer Eflin and Doris Walker prepared a job description and a "code of conduct" for the position. Most parts of each document were standard, like stating the expected working hours and conditions, but there were two unusual aspects: the job description explicitly stated that the marshal had to "be in a clean and neat looking uniform…" and "must not indulge in alcoholic beverages even at home, for the days he is on duty" and in a separate section titled, "Narcotics and Dope Traffic" it stated that "Emphasis in this enforcement shall be centered on the supplier, however, no person shall be permitted to use narcotics or dope and shall be handled in a similar manner to violators of the State Liquor Code."

This time the council wanted someone with *prior* training or experience. Out of over 40 applicants, the council was interested in six. Articulating the consensus sentiment of the new council, Elmer Eflin said that they wanted a "traditional lawman" but that they also "…wanted a man whom we hope will have the respect of the people, who will not be 'nitty-picky' or overly technical in enforcement … someone who will be impartial and not biased by the length of hair or style of dress." Despite that caveat, the council hired Don Brandon. He was a 20-year Marine Corp veteran who worked on the Pueblo, Colorado, police force for 11 years. Five of the six trustees voted for him. Jim Wallace, the only early pioneer council member, who earlier had been a part-time deputy, cast the sole dissenting vote.

This time the council wanted someone with prior training or experience. … the council hired … a 20-year Marine Corp veteran who worked on the Pueblo, Colorado police force for 11 years.

After less than six weeks, Brandon made his mark in the community as an unbending, "law and order" man. Because of his severe approach, particularly toward the town's new people, a banner *Crested Butte*

Chronicle headline blared, "TOWN IS LOSING ITS SENSE OF HUMOR". The report that followed said that within the past week he arrested and jailed five pioneers for being drunk and disorderly. He also arrested the owner of Tony's Tavern and, in front of the Post Office, frisked, handcuffed and arrested a young contractor who was taken to Gunnison for questioning because his license plate was found near a mine that had reported things were stolen from it. Not all of the arrested men were longhairs or anti-growth hippies; some supported growth. But, all of them were early town newcomers.

Those arrests united the different pioneer factions. They circulated a petition that quickly collected 90 signatures and called for Marshal Brandon's "immediate dismissal." The petition said he polarized the town even more than it was before he was hired. The following week, he was forced to resign.

After less than six weeks, Brandon .... was forced to resign.

That led to another petition that asked the council to reinstate him. It was signed mainly by the town's mining-era residents and reflected their "law and order" and anti-hippie views:

> We the undersigned ...express to the Mayor, Board of Trustees, and other officials ..., our deep concern and belief that there is a growing element of lawlessness in the town and that effective steps are not being taken to enforce the ordinances of Crested Butte and the laws of this State to protect the dignity, persons, and property of the citizens and visitors to our community. It is the demand of the undersigned that you take strong and immediate action to hire a qualified and effective law enforcement officer, give him the tools and training needed to do his job (first giving consideration to rehiring Brandon), and give him your full support and backing when he does perform his assigned duties.

Because a lot of signatures were gathered and, presumably, to mollify the old-timers, the town trustees were forced to disclose a series of lies he told that made it impossible to credibly re-hire him. Interestingly, those particular lies were never written about in any published reports about the council's decision.

Apparently hoping for another strict lawman who would crack down on counter-culture people, the town council hired a second career military man, Jake Marriot. He also had 23 years of police experience. His view about enforcing laws, however, differed markedly from his predecessor. He preferred "to counsel rather than arrest" and, according to the paper "generally seems to interpret the Marshal's task as being as much a keeper of the peace as an enforcer of order." His tenure, however, lasted only four months, until the end of November, 1970. He submitted

... the town council hired a second career military man. ...He had 23 years of police experience .... He preferred "to counsel rather than arrest" .... His tenure .... lasted only four months .... his resignation letter .... said, "... there are some that intended me to direct the law towards certain persons. ... law is intended for each of us, not for those alone that perhaps dress a little peculiar or let their hair grow longer than others.

his resignation letter and said there were two factions in town, "...there are some that intended me to direct the law towards certain persons.... That would have been impossible for me to do, since all I can see is a people, as a whole .... law is intended for each of us, not for those alone that perhaps dress a little peculiar or let their hair grow longer than others. If we demand respect for our rights, then we are bound to respect the rights of others..."

Marriot felt the law should be enforced fairly, and old-timers were pressuring him to come down hard on hippies. He said, moreover, that they were in Crested Butte to stay and were good people, if one took the time to get to know them as he did, when they volunteered to help renovate the old town jail; and the Trustees and older townspeople better recognize that, and them. Marriot wrote:

> In fact, I am talking about the hippies, long hairs, etc. .... In comparison to these human beings and 'The other People', I have found cooperation and general obedience to the laws. 'The other People' have been more of a problem in my enforcement of the law and to a degree, uncooperative. I refuse to judge a person by his appearance alone.... As a matter of record, I would like...to commend and thank those hippies, long hairs, etc. that helped with and contributed to the renovation of the Crested Butte Jail .... Indeed, there are two factions. There are the good citizens and the 'gripers'. The good citizen affords me...the respect that is much needed .... The 'griper' only creates disharmony.

His letter said he had been in law enforcement work for a long time and was accustomed to people griping about police and giving them grief, as the mining-era residents were doing, but that it was time for him to get out of it. The Trustees did not accept his resignation and asked him to remain. He agreed at first, but one week later, he made his departure final.

Needing a new lawman yet again at what might be considered an inconvenient hiring period, the beginning of the Holiday season, and since the town officials elected in 1970 represented mainly the interests and values of long-time residents and trailblazers, the council's next hire was a "native son," Norm Pierce, Jr., who also was hired on an "interim" basis. Unlike his two predecessors, he was young, inexperienced, and untrained.

> ... since the town officials elected in 1970 represented mainly the interests and values of long-time residents and trailblazers, the council next hire was a "native son," Norm Pierce, Jr., who also was hired on an "interim" basis. Unlike his two predecessors, he was young, inexperienced, and untrained.

Reflecting the continued struggles over the law, and even disregarding the two "interim" appointments, an end of the year *Chronicle* editorial noted, "The social conflicts and political pressures all came together on one of the great matters of national concern – law and order. ...nobody seemed able to decide exactly what was needed in the way of a town Marshal. ...With the resignation early this month of CB's third 1970 Marshal...."

At the first council meeting in 1971, the trustees made Pierce, Jr's appointment permanent. They ignored the advice that Marriot gave in his resignation letter. They said they hired Pierce, Jr. because they thought he did his job "energetically and well since the resignation of Jake Marriot." The council then sent the lawman to the Colorado Law Enforcement Training Academy (CLETA) for basic police training.

A few months later Pierce, Jr. hired a new deputy, Dave Watson. He was already a polarizing figure in Crested Butte because he owned and operated the local snowmobile business, and large numbers of pioneers did not like him. He had been a candidate in the most recent council election and was defeated overwhelmingly. Recognizing that he too had no previous experience, the council also sent Watson to CLETA.

Tourist town pioneers increasingly disliked and distrusted the local law and, not surprisingly, the even more law-and-order oriented county sheriff's office. Importantly, in February 1970, a challenge to the long-time incumbent County Sheriff, George W. Cope, was announced. Claude Porterfield, a former miner and 10-year veteran of the Gunnison City Police Department, announced that he would run against the existing sheriff on the Republican slate. He promised to "give 'fair' but 'impartial' law enforcement in Gunnison County." Notably, four years earlier, Sheriff Cope trounced his Republican opponent by the widest margin in any of the county electoral contests. He had garnered 73% of the 2,228 votes cast. This time, with substantial support from Crested Butte voters, most of whom were traditional, mining-era, hard-working

Tourist town pioneers increasingly disliked and distrusted the local law and ... the even more law-and-order-oriented county sheriff's office. Importantly, in February 1970, a challenge to the long-time incumbent County Sheriff, George W. Cope, was announced. Claude Porterfield, a former miner and 10-year veteran of the Gunnison City Police Department .... promised to "give 'fair' but 'impartial' law enforcement in Gunnison County" .... with substantial support from Crested Butte voters, ... Porterfield soundly defeated incumbent Sheriff Cope. He received 55% of the County-wide vote...

Democrats, plus the town's new pioneers who voted mainly because of their fear and hostility toward the incumbent Sheriff, Porterfield soundly defeated Cope. He received 55% of the county-wide vote: 1,150 to 941.

During the spring and summer of 1971, Marshal Pierce and Deputy Watson dealt with a crime wave of sorts in Crested Butte: burglaries and thefts, street fights, bar melees, underage drinking, trespassing, and nude swimming in nearby Nicholson Lake (although no one ever pressed formal charges for that offense, perhaps because mining-era bachelors used to sit in their pickup trucks with binoculars, enjoying the scenery across the lake where swimmers dried off and sunbathed). Additionally, a phenomenon that later would be labeled "eco-terrorism" by radical environmental activist Edward Abbey began occurring in the area. As the lawmen tried to control these crimes, they encountered increasing hostility.

Noting the growing wave of "eco-terrorism," presumably by pioneers who wanted to stop sub-division growth, especially outside the town's boundaries, the police blotter reported "several billboards south of town had been destroyed *again*" (emphasis added) at what years later became the town's largest subdivision, Crested Butte South. More than forty years later, Henrietta Raines remembered that a sign was cut down in the dark of night two miles south of town that advertised houses for rent in Crested Butte. She and her first husband managed those properties for her father-in-law, Law-Science Academy founder, Dr. Hubert W. Smith.

The police blotter also reported that Crested Butte area rancher/developer, Bill Lacy, pressed charges against four women, presumably tourist town pioneers, who entered his Washington Gulch cabin "to get out of the rain." He found them cooking breakfast. More burglaries were reported in town and at construction sites, both in town and at the area. There also were documented narcotics arrests, and a newspaper reported that Marshal Pierce, Jr. shot, but did not kill, two dogs in town that attacked a goat.

As confrontations between Crested Butte long-time residents and tourist town pioneers became more hostile and frequent, the town attorney, Fritz Russell, asked that Under-Sheriff Harvey Lowell be made a Crested Butte Deputy. That was an attempt to beef up the town marshal's office, and to get the federal money that was allocated to Gunnison County for Crested Butte but had never been released by the county. According to the *Chronicle*, "The reason for this rather strange move – Lowell lives in Gunnison – ...was that the monies ($2,400.00) allocated to the Crested Butte Marshal's office by the County Commissioners could not be received without Lowell's being at least a ...functionary here as well as at the county level."

By 1972, concerns and conflicts over law enforcement grew even more intense. At the beginning of the year, Marshal Pierce, Jr. asked for the resignation of one of his deputies, Frank "Cozy" Cozzetto. Cozzetto, a former miner, was widely liked including, significantly, by tourist town pioneers. The marshal recommended Harvey Cooke as his replacement. Cooke had been reared in Crested Butte. A profile piece headlined, "New Deputy Takes Well to Town" described his background: it said that even as a teenager he was independent, that he served in Vietnam for two years, that he came back to Colorado and worked in nearby mines, and then worked in a Vail hotel as head of its custodial staff.

On a weekend night in early spring, a new 3.2 bar in town, the Saltlick, held a "wet t-shirt" contest. It was overcrowded, with about 700 people who were almost all WSC students and young new townspeople.

The county sheriff, who was watching the activities from outside, wanted to throw a tear gas canister into the crowd, presumably to disperse it. He had to be stopped, by other officers and his friends, as well as local townspeople, including County Judge John Levin. Throwing that canister could easily have led to mayhem.

This exhibition of poor, potentially even deadly, judgment followed an earlier confrontation between some tourist town pioneers and Gunnison county sheriff's officers when a Walt Disney movie, "Snowball Express," was filmed in town. Officers carried riot batons, and one officer wore riot gear and verbally threatened several town pioneers. The more recent Saltlick incident prompted a strongly worded *Chronicle* commentary: The editor railed against law enforcement in Crested Butte, especially by the county sheriff's office and the sheriff's posse. He also implicated Marshal Pierce, Jr., who was hobnobbing with the sheriff's men. The County Deputy Sheriff, Chuck Lowell, told editor Arber when he approached him to ask what was happening in and around the Saltlick, "… If you know what's good for you, you won't mention any of this trouble. My father is already annoyed with something you wrote and if you write about this there'll be Hell to pay."

Shortly after that, pioneer Howie Johns was arrested for resisting and evading the compulsory military draft. As already discussed, there were a significant number of draft resistors in town, and they were respected and well liked. There was a lot of sympathy and empathy for them. Immediately after Johns' arrest, the tires on Pierce's personal car and those "on the town's truck, used for picking up stray dogs and other municipal business, were slashed mysteriously." Accurately or not, the newspaper article continued, "…these wanton acts were meant as…retribution upon all local law enforcement for its supposed role in the arrest of Johns."

A great many tourist town pioneers did not like the marshal's style and his close relationship to the county sheriff's office. A letter to the editor, written in the first person singular but signed by four people, reflected that:

> During the last few months I have been twice required to deal with our Marshal and was both times disappointed. …. it is time for the Marshal to re-evaluate himself and the office. He is a law enforcement officer, not

a judge and is obligated, by accepting this position, to enforce all the laws, whether or not he agrees with them or takes the side of a particular party. Crested Butte is growing and needs effective, unbiased, friendly law enforcement. I hope we see some changes in the near future.

The letter was signed by pioneers Ron Makela, Deborah Danner, Rebecca Pearson and Larry Adams.

■ ■ ■

During the 1972 election campaign, the tourist town pioneers' antipathy toward existing law enforcement was clearly expressed. The pioneers' mayoral candidate and several council hopefuls wanted the marshal to be more responsive to Crested Butte's new people and, for the first time, *independent* from the Gunnison Sheriff. Their views irked old-timers and Marshal Pierce, Jr. However, a newspaper editorial supported that position.

> *During the 1972 election campaign, the tourist town pioneers' antipathy toward existing law enforcement was clearly expressed. The pioneers' mayoral candidate and several council hopefuls wanted the marshal to be more responsive to ... new people and, ... independent ....*

When the new council people won, *before* the newly elected officials took office, after holding the marshal's job for 18 months, Pierce, Jr. resigned. A meeting was held between him, the mayor-elect, and the incoming chairperson of the new police committee. The latter two articulated four guidelines they wanted the marshal to follow:

1) Sever all relations with the County Sheriff's office;
2) Do not carry lethal weapons on duty;
3) Do not wear a "complete" uniform; and
4) Don't show prejudice to people with long hair.

The lawman claimed he was pressured into resigning but, in fact, he was not. Under a banner headline that pronounced, "Pierce Resigns as Town Marshal," the piece included a copy of his resignation letter, along with a letter of rebuttal from the incoming mayor. There was also a long editorial that said two members of the not yet sworn in new council had met with Pierce, and told him they wanted him to *remain* as marshal. It said he really resigned, not because incoming public officials pressured him but because he wanted a newly vacated job in the County Sheriff's Department.

The new pioneer council thought some laws were more important than others. Their predecessors and the broader "law and order"-oriented American public argued that "the law is the law" and all laws should be upheld equally. The new council, however, distinguished between laws they thought were meant to suppress people or inhibit their personal lifestyle choices, and others that had to be enforced to maintain peace in the community. They also thought whichever laws were observed needed to be upheld equally, not against one faction or another. Most council members thought during the mining and ranching heyday, when long-time residents held sway in what early pioneer artist/poet Cordley Coit called the "kolorado kow kulture" era, certain laws were fully enforced against the pioneers, like the drug laws, while others that were common among long-time residents, like driving drunk or poaching, were not.

Following Pierce Jr.'s resignation quite a few candidates applied for the opening. In their first meeting, the new council appointed Kemp Coit as the "interim" marshal. He previously had served as a deputy when Russ Reycraft, Jr., held the position. In the same meeting the council decided to buy out the county's financial interest in the town police vehicle. It had been bought through a Federal Grant that required the county to pay one-fourth, the town to put up another fourth and the Feds to provide the remaining 50%. They also decided to meet with County Sheriff Claude Porterfield and establish a working relationship, a meeting that ended amicably with mutual assurances. The new Crested Butte pioneer council officials affirmed that laws, in fact, would be enforced by the local lawmen, although "gently" and "fairly," and the sheriff said his department would continue to be available to the town, if and when it was needed.

In their first meeting, the new council appointed Kemp Coit as the "interim" marshal .... decided to buy out the county's financial interest in the town police vehicle. .... They also decided to meet with County Sheriff Claude Porterfield and establish a working relationship, a meeting that ended amicably with mutual assurances.

In May 1972, the council sought a permanent marshal and deputy. They gave preference to local applicants who knew the community. About half a dozen people indicated their interest in the job, including a finalist, Lynn Robinson. She had a social science background, as had Coit. The main interview question posed by the police committee was, "What is the difference between 'a law enforcement officer' and a 'peace officer'?" Coit gave what was considered the best response. He differentiated between laws' that infringed on an individual's life-style preference, if he or she did not harm anyone, versus acts that threatened or endangered a community's tranquility or safety, like speeding on streets where children played. That answer, coupled with his performance in the interim position, gave him the edge, and he was appointed. The newspaper also supported Coit. It said he had done a good job in the interim position, that he only provided assistance when necessary, and did not carry a weapon on duty, which reflected his desire to calm community tensions. When he was hired, Coit became Crested Butte's first, *independent,* town marshal.

Significantly, all the applicants for deputy — John Newberry, Rigdon 'Rig' Reese, Roger Dings and Bob Belknap — also had backgrounds in the social sciences as undergraduates. Dings additionally had studied business in grad school, and Reese studied law. Belknap was a Vietnam vet who had prior police experience with the City of Gunnison. During the interviews, both Reese and Belknap distinguished between hard and recreational drugs; and virtually all the interviewed candidates, in one way or another, talked about "informal law enforcement" or what later became widely known as "community policing." Dings, for example, said that he had lived in the community for ten years, knew everyone, and so would never have to use force. Although Belknap lived in Gunnison and was not a Crested Butte local, he was chosen to be the deputy because of his easygoing style, intelligence, experience, and because Coit liked him best, and the council realized the two had to work together as a team.

By July 4, 1972, Coit and his deputies, along with several community volunteers, were ready to maintain the peace during what was expected to be a raucous, wild, and joyful weekend celebration. They did so successfully.

Following Coit's appointment, there were a few last-ditch attempts by the "old-guard" to assert their authority. The strongest was by the

Gunnison law officers who resigned, including Under Sheriff Harvey Lowell, his County dispatcher wife, Joan, and Norman Pierce, Jr. (who, according to the *Chronicle*, was Lowell's protege). They claimed Sheriff Porterfield was ineptly enforcing the law and was cooperating with Coit. They threatened to circulate a petition to recall him. Lowell had charged that the marshal's vehicle reeked of pot, and was otherwise used illicitly by Coit. Porterfield investigated, and concluded the charge could never be verified because, among other reasons, Lowell himself sprayed a deodorizer in the Jeep that eliminated any possible pot odor. Lowell said he had witnesses, but never produced any. Significantly, for months after that, the sheriff was "uncomfortable" with Coit. He would not deputize him as a county law officer, a designation essential for obtaining Federal grant monies. Porterfield maintained his position until mid-August 1972 when he and Crested Butte officials met to discuss the tense relation between county and town lawmen. By the tail end of that summer, communications between the two officers had improved, and Porterfield's concerns abated. A good working relationship was finally established between the two.

Although Coit's appointment was *approved unanimously* by the new tourist town pioneer council, within the first six months of their term factions developed between council people who wanted growth and development, and those who did not. Councilmembers who favored development began dominating decisions, and they were intent on ridding the community of those who opposed growth. They began exerting pressure on Coit to enforce laws more rigorously, particularly on pioneers who lived alternate life styles; those who the growth-oriented pioneers defined as "undesirable." Coit tried to comply; and began coming down harder on the alternate life-style people. Many residents who did not want the town to develop started to leave. They thought Crested Butte had become too conventional and tame and, concomitantly, too expensive.

In 1974, Sheriff Porterfield ran for re-election. His opponent was the former Under Sheriff, Harvey Lowell, who ran as an Independent. Porterfield's platform included stating he respected every individual's rights and had a comfortable working relationship with everyone, and that during his first term he ironed out many difficulties with the former and current Crested Butte mayors, the new police committee, and the townspeople. He won overwhelmingly garnering 2,673 votes (78%). In Crested Butte, which had become the largest county precinct, and where Lowell was widely disliked, the margin was even greater, 90% to 10%.

Kemp Coit had several deputies. Some were unpaid, like Bob Teitler, a former New York IBM salesman, who became the town's tow truck operator. He volunteered because he wanted the authority to stop cars that were speeding on the town's streets, especially Elk Avenue. Another volunteer deputy was Coit's brother, Cordley who, in Coit's words many years later, was deputized because, "I wanted someone to have my back and I knew I could always count on him." Other deputies were paid. One was Joe Blumberg, a trained anthropologist, who managed the delicatessen in the first tourist town pioneer owned town convenience store. He was later forced to resign due to councilmember pressure; he had problems dealing with some pioneers in the bars and was suspected of using psychedelics on duty. Shortly after his "resignation," Blumberg publicly called for the creation of a "Civilian Review Board" to monitor local police amid charges of police heavy handedness, but that proposal was opposed strongly by the pro-growth and development faction, as well as the newspaper editor. It was never accepted politically and was formally quashed by a council vote. Demonstrating his general popularity among the townspeople, and their support for civilian review of police, in the next general town election, Blumberg was elected to the town council.

Joe Rous was another paid deputy. He formerly had been a social worker, and was an insightful and erudite new recreation community settler. Before coming to Crested Butte, he worked with juveniles in the Kentucky Crime Prevention Unit; while also owning a retail "head shop" in Louisville. (Following his tenure as town deputy, he became the lead developer during the earliest phase of the emerging subdivision, Crested Butte South, and also developed two new bars in town). Rous was well liked, especially by those who wanted Coit to be primarily a "peace officer." Although, or perhaps because, Rous got along with most people, especially pioneers, increasingly he too was pressured by those who wanted the town to grow into a full-blown tourist town that catered to the affluent. They wanted him to be more of a "law and order" cop. Rather than compromising his views or the way he did his job, Rous quit.

Rous resigned for several reasons, and he resigned as the deputy county sheriff at the same time. The paper reported, "Rous implied in his comments to the press that he had chosen to leave his job with the Town rather than stay on under circumstances incompatible with his personal values and basic philosophy of what law enforcement is all about." In that week's editorial, suggesting that Rous was no longer suited to the community's needs since he preferred a low-key approach to the job, the development-oriented *Chronicle* editor commented, "Feeling as he does that police work is essentially public relations ..."

In early summer 1973, another act of "ecoterrorism" occurred: in a wetland immediately outside the town, the survey stakes were all pulled out from a county approved, platted, subdivision that Russ Reycraft, Sr. and his Florida based partners wanted to develop. In response, a classified ad was place in the newspaper that offered a $1,000.00 reward for information leading to the apprehension of whoever pulled out the recently implanted survey stakes. It said, "... some misguided individual or group of individuals has gone to the trouble of pulling virtually every stake over the entire area and left us a note saying 'You can thank the People for Ecological Standards Committee'." The ad continued:

> We suspect that persons with the kind of mentality that permits them to exercise this type of behavior will also be immature enough to want to brag about their activities, therefore, we believe there are responsible persons that can identify the perpetrators. .... Russ Reycraft, Sr. will pay $1000 to any bona fide Ecological, Civic or Cultural Group of your choice for the first person who provides the name of the individual or individuals who are responsible...

The perpetrators were never identified, the developers were demoralized, and the proposed development never proceeded.

During that summer, (1973), something of a crime wave hit town. There was a relatively muted reaction to it among the town's tourist town pioneers, perhaps because all crimes seemed to be committed by new people against other newcomers. The paper's editor, who was one of those who wanted "to clean up the town," recognized that. He wrote in October:

.... One of the most precious qualities Crested Butte offers is the relative freedom from fear. To date there was little reason to lock one's door. Unfortunately, ... there has been a veritable crime wave in Crested Butte, with something like over 30 thefts occurring in the past month. ... Large sums of money have been taken from Sanchos Restaurant and the Elk Mountain Lodge. The Tailings has been broken into three times. Money was even taken from a collection box for the relief fund for the Gunnison High School bus disaster [in which teenage students died]. ... Tony Stroh's car was stolen from in front of his house... A new winch was taken from Bob Teitler's tow truck ... Sugar had her purse stolen... We learn of new losses every day. ...What I do not understand is why there is not more anger and disgust over the rash of robberies that has infested the town and ... threatens to alter its nature. ...There is ... an apparent willingness to tolerate 'rip-off artists' who drift in and out. ... There is a time to make a stop to this course, and it is now. ... don't make the town ... uncomfortable for those of us who love it.

That same month, in what would have significant consequences for legal issues in Crested Butte, John Levin was appointed the new judge of the Gunnison County Court. Levin, too, was a development-oriented tourist town pioneer. As judge, he played a major role in "taming" Gunnison and Crested Butte. Well aware that the law enforcement procedures used by Gunnison County lawmen were lax, he insisted that only proper procedures were used, and that laws had to be applied fairly to everyone including, and perhaps especially, to hippies. Levin had a significant impact on redefining the "old-west, good-old-boy" way of dealing with bar fights, drunk driving, poaching, shooting guns in town, and the like. At the same time, he also insisted that proper procedures were followed in drug arrests. Within a month, he had sentenced a bar brawler who had resisted arrest to 60 days in jail, and then he sentenced someone to a year in jail for drunk driving (although he suspended half the sentence provided the offender not drink for a year).

In 1973, in what would have significant consequences for legal issues in Crested Butte, John Levin was appointed the new judge of the Gunnison County Court. Levin, too, was a development-oriented tourist town pioneer. As judge, he played a major role in "taming" Gunnison and Crested Butte.

Although still not identifying eco-terrorism as a form of social protest, the police blotter noted in December that the Crested Butte South Development Corporation's large sign promoting the subdivision seven miles south of town, had been cut down *again*. The blotter reported the sign "… fell prey to unidentified vandals" and simultaneously that "four residents of Crested Butte, three men and a woman were arrested by the Gunnison County Sherriff's Office for supposedly leaving the scene where the sign had fallen."

A few months later, before he resigned, Deputy Joe Rous addressed the changes he saw occurring. In a letter to the editor he described the transition as one from a community that was free from fear to one in the midst of a crime wave:

> … culturally and sociologically our community is experiencing an evo-
> lution that approaches revolution. … Crime statistics are but one index
> of these changes. … the crime rate is equal to or even exceeds the gener-
> ic growth of the community. Crested Butte boasts a heritage of proud,
> strong and responsible people. … too often the piquancy of responsibil-
> ity is precluded by the puerility of the 'Get-It-On' syndrome. And peo-
> ple would take from our community with no thought of giving to it.
> Indeed, it is time to ask some poignant questions. … What can we say
> about five vehicles being stolen from our community during the month
> of December? … What can we say about the store break-ins and the ski
> rip-offs? What can we say about our community's biggest dope problem,
> alcohol, and the fact that most police trouble calls are alcohol related?
> … We must begin to differentiate between the Crested Butte that was,
> and the Crested Butte that is…lest perpetrators continue to exploit our
> nostalgia as naiveté. Gone are the days that merchants could leave
> money overnight in their stores in cigar boxes. Gone are the days when
> we could leave our keys in our ignition. Gone are the days that we could
> leave our valuables unattended! … And while we would not incite our
> citizens to paranoia, we would introduce them to…the difference
> between what is right and what is real.

Six months after pioneers took the reins of government, the town mood and focus began to shift from accepting and supporting "alternate life styles" to increasing tourism and development. As that transition took place, those who wanted growth increasingly influenced local politics and dominated the local discourse. Concomitantly, Marshal Coit fell into disfavor among the growth-oriented pioneer council members and others in the community's business and social leadership. That disfavor came despite, or perhaps due to, being well liked and supported by many pioneers, especially performing and visual artists and craftsmen, alternate life-style proponents, and "outlaws." Dave Coney was one

Six months after pioneers took the reins of government, the town mood and focus began to shift from accepting and supporting "alternate life styles" to increasing tourism and development .... Concomitantly, Marshal Coit fell into disfavor among the growth-oriented pioneer council members ...

such supporter. A popular local icon among the pioneer outlaws, Coney had been arrested earlier on charges of manufacturing psychedelics. He was also a Hot Shot fire fighter, and an early aficionado of back-country skiing; and he hosted wild parties at his Washington Gulch rustic cabin where, especially, the younger outlaw pioneers participated. (Denis Hall, another Coit supporter, described Coney and his place in Crested Butte lore many years later. Hall said, "We were anarchists and he was even further away from the law up in the Gulch.")

Coney remembered Coit's tenure years later and said, "Kemp was neither a sheriff or a marshal; he was a keeper of the peace." He cited as an example a time when the Hot Shot forest fire fighting crew — well known for its "outlaw" members, irreverence, general rowdiness and hard work ethic — came back to town after fighting a fire in the nearby Black Canyon. Coney and another crew member, "Crazy" Dave Ranney, carried a heavy charred log from the bottom to the top of a steep 2,000-2,500-foot ravine, and then loaded it into the back of a van that transported the Hot Shots. When they returned to their favorite watering hole, The Grubstake, they backed the van up to one of its plate glass windows and then heaved the log through it, all to the loud cheers of many Hot Shots who had preceded them inside. Coney noted that when the lawman saw the van backing up to the window and the log being lifted from inside it, he just turned around and walked down the block, away from the unfolding antic, so he would avoid an unnecessary confrontation.

Coit's easy-going style, however, did not sit well with everyone. Those favoring development, as noted above, wanted to rid the town of its wild ways and people, and did so in a number of ways., When two vacancies occurred on the pioneer town council that was elected in 1972, for example, although most applicants for the two positions were either completely against growth or supported only very limited development, the slots were filled by appointees who favored development more than did those whose vacated council seats they filled. Those appointments meant that only one very slow growth proponent remained on the tourist town pioneer council.

By the middle of 1973, the pioneer council's increasing disfavor with Coit's performance began to surface publicly. *Chronicle* editorials about him changed from having been supportive to being strongly critical. By the beginning of that summer, in an effort to reverse the pattern of constantly changing local lawmen and in an attempt to retain Coit, the police committee chairperson urged the council to send Coit to a ten day "human relations" training program conducted by the National Training Laboratory in Bethel, Maine. It did so.

That was a controversial decision. One of its greatest public skeptics was Sandy Hickok, the editor of the town's second newspaper, *The Pilot*. After Coit's return and his adroit handling of a July 4th week-end celebration, she editorialized that although she "snickered" when the idea of human relations training was originally proposed to help Coit "deal with the pressures and diversities which he encounters in his job," after "shadowing" him over the 4th, she saw that he was much better in the way he handled his duties, especially given that Deputy Bob Belknap had resigned. She also said she had a better understanding of the stresses he faced. A month later Coit himself commented on the training saying it "... increased my understanding of others and gave me better tools with which to communicate both of which are essential in my line of work.... All in all it was well worth the time involved."

Marshal Coit's lauded service and renewed popularity did not stop the increasingly growth-oriented councilmen's dissatisfaction with him despite, ironically, him having been officially accepted as a Gunnison County Deputy by Sheriff Porterfield after a one-and-a-half-year delay.

Town pressure on Coit continued, as it did on the police committee chair who recommended the human relations training. That council member, not incidentally, was the last very slow growth-oriented tourist town pioneer council member. Given that, he no longer thought he could influence council or even decisions about the police. He thought he was excluded from important informal conversations and even formal meetings; and that he was constantly outvoted on issues that mattered most to the community. He began missing police committee and council meetings. Without his knowledge the mayor, who increasingly defined him as an oppositionist who was a thorn in his side and against most development, replaced him as the chairperson of the committee with one of the new pro-development council appointees, Ron Rouse.

All the elected council members in April 1974 were pro-growth, the first fully elected "recreation community settler" council. The new council wanted a lawman that would do whatever was needed to attract affluent tourists and make the town comfortable for them. They thought someone who would smooth the rough edges in town by getting rid of the local riffraff required a strong, but hip, "law and order" man.

> *All the elected council members in April 1974 were pro-growth, the first fully elected "recreation community settler" council. The new council wanted a lawman that would do whatever was needed to attract affluent tourists and make the town comfortable for them. ... someone who would smooth out the rough edges in town ... required a strong, but hip, "law and order" man.*

This recreation community settler council held its first meeting in early May. A public review of Coit's performance was scheduled. An editorial before that meeting expressed the opinion that the current council had to re-evaluate Coit and that, further, he would either have to get a lot more council support or step down. In a prior, closed, meeting, however, Mayor Bill Crank summarily fired Coit. That enraged many tourist town pioneers. They did not like the unilateral manner in which Coit was dismissed; and, following his human relations training, they again had liked him personally, and the way he did his job.

Coit asked for and was begrudgingly granted an audience before the full council to discuss his firing. Many years later, Crank remembered that he was increasingly frustrated with Coit because "He didn't enforce any laws. He didn't give parking tickets even when streets needed to be plowed, or cite dog owners who let their dogs run loose. He also didn't do basic paperwork, like filling out daily activity sheets." However, Coit never appeared at the public meeting.

The town postmaster, Russ Reycraft, Jr., who earlier had been an interim town marshal, told Coit not to attend saying, "I and others will handle it." A wide range of about 50 Coit supporters went to that meeting and many spoke on his behalf. John Rule, a local chef and restaurateur, said Coit was doing a "fine job," especially given the unique nature of the townspeople. Sue Dean, an older, more traditional woman who lived in Mt. Crested Butte where her husband was the first town manager, said Coit was doing "a great job." Tom Towler, director of the popular Crested Butte Mountain Theater, said that the townspeople liked Coit and the council should do what their constituents desired, not just what the mayor and his allies wanted. Due to the passionate community protest, the recreation community settler council reinstated Coit, albeit on "probation" and under council supervision.

After the meeting, audience members and other locals, including Coit, gathered in the Grubstake, and joyously toasted him on his reinstatement, and on the implied, but ultimately short-lived, victory for the anti or very slow growth proponents. It was part of a grand "let's keep the town as it is" celebration.

A few months later, Coit was forced to resign. He continued being more of a peace officer than a law enforcement officer. Forty years later, Ron Rouse, who had become the new chairperson of the committee that oversaw the police said, "As I remember it, I had to go to Kemp's house and tell him the council decided to relieve him of his duties." Rouse continued and described

... McClung performed well as deputy. A few months later he was promoted and became the new town marshal; Coit was demoted ...; a few months after that, he was forced to resign.

his reluctance at the time, and the pain he felt being the bearer of bad news, "I went with a very heavy heart. It was a very sad day for both of us." During Coit's probationary period, Deputy Joe Rous resigned. Bill Crank remembered many years later that Coit himself had asked that Rob McClung replace Rous. From the viewpoint of the new settler council, McClung performed well as deputy. A few months later he was promoted and became the new town marshal. He fulfilled the new council's main criterion: while appearing "hip," he could clean up the town and help it get ready to accommodate financially well-off tourists. Coit was demoted and became the town deputy. A few months after that, he was no longer a member of the marshal's department.

McClung was a massive man who held a black belt in one of the martial arts; he was also a former member of the Western State College football and wrestling teams. Not incidentally, the next two deputies he hired, including the dogcatcher, also held martial arts black belts, a significant fact that was included in most newspaper accounts written about the new local law enforcement team. That probably made it easier for them to gain compliance, especially in bars or at boisterous public events, or when confrontations arose over dogs.

The council elected in 1974 thought McClung was more hard-nosed than Coit. They thought that not only would he get rid of the counterculture people, but that he could do it subtlety. Over 40 years later, Bill Crank said he thought that was inaccurate, at least for him. He said, "I had no problems with the hippies. We just wanted *some* law enforcement, someone to at least minimally enforce the law. We hired McClung because he had a good attitude, wanted to be a 'straight arrow' cop – a 180-degree opposite of Coit – and had the physique, could handle trouble, and filed reports. (As already stated, ironically, McClung had been charged earlier as one of those instigating what might easily have become a riot in front of Tony's Tavern. Crank denied knowing about that. He said that occurred before he came to Crested Butte but then added that he did not think that would have dissuaded him from hiring McClung, given his frustrations with Coit).

Myles Arber became increasingly critical of Coit, and argued that he should be fired. In an editorial entitled, "Endorsement of Marshal's Office" Arber said that McClung was helping the town clean up its act and needed support, including from those who supported Coit:

> ... McClung has gone at the job head-on .... the results seem to show that he is overcoming the tribulations of the position and creating a good department. And this despite a good deal of criticism, both personal and professional. ... He is decisive in thought and action, and is armed with enough 'You-know-I-don't-like-to-take-a-lot-of-crap-off-anybody' attitude and the goods to back it up and back down a few wise guys and trouble makers to make things happen around here. ... The

major problem McClung has run into has been his dismissal of former Marshal Kemp Coit.... The differences he and McClung had in style and approach were bound, however, to lead inevitably to a parting of the ways. ...What he [McClung] needs from us, besides time, are support and cooperation.

Two months later, Coit took another marshal's job in a budding tourist town, Virginia City, Montana. A "feel good" piece about Coit thanked him for his service and, more significantly, reflected on how much the town had changed during his tenure:

Crested Butte went through some radical changes while he was Marshal, and those changes demanded constant adjustments, adjustments few people could have made with ease and still maintained their sanity. Coit ... found those difficult to keep making. ... we want to thank him for suffering with this unusual community .... these past five years or so. ... The government of this town has passed into another era and so has the public mood and prevalent behavior. ... the job has changed with it and the man needed to fill it also changed ...

Ultimately, McClung's tenure lasted for a few years. When he finally resigned, he took a similar position in Aspen, Colorado, another tourist town and recreation community that was further along in its development. During his Crested Butte tenure, most residents who did not support growth in the area left town, and the few who remained adapted to the new views of those who favored growth. With that, the lower key, more sensitive approach to law enforcement that the pioneer council wanted, such as not having the Marshal carry a gun or wear a complete uniform, turned out to be short lived. Following Coit's departure the various town councils reverted to what the old-timers and trailblazers wanted from their lawmen all along: stricter law enforcement. The marshal's department steadily became more formal and oriented toward "law and order," although, as in most other tourist towns and recreation communities, it is still comparatively low key compared to big city and suburban police departments. Crested Butte and other tourist towns and recreation communities, notably, are now models for what often is dubbed "community policing."

Chapter 9

Town Politics and Elections: 1972-1974

y 1972, the majority of the Crested Butte town population consisted
of tourist town pioneers. They were polarized economically from the
pro-development ski area residents,
culturally from the mining-era residents
and surrounding ranchers, and among
themselves between those who wanted
development and the anti-growth
forces. During the next two years, the
pioneers who favored development,
together with the newest recreation
community settlers, struggled with

*By 1972, the majority of the Crested
Butte town population consisted of
tourist town pioneers. .... During the
next two years, pioneers who favored
development, together with the newest
recreation community settlers, struggled
with pioneers who wanted the town to
remain unpublicized and undeveloped.*

those pioneers who wanted the town to remain unpublicized and undeveloped. The pro-growth faction used a variety of social, legal, and political
means to rid the area of those they thought held back growth. They began
to prepare the town to become the modern, amenity-laden, cosmopolitan,
community it is today.

Given the increasingly hostile relations between Crested Butte's mining-era residents and the pioneers, the April 1972 town election was historic. Before it, a voter registration drive added 188 electors to the town's
existing 313, a 60% increase. That ini-
tiative began with a meeting of a few
pioneers, including an owner of the
Grubstake, a breakfast waitress, and a
former civil rights community organiz-

*... the April, 1972 town election was his-
toric. Before it, a voter registration
drive added 188 electors to the town's
existing 313, a 60% increase.*

er. A few days later another meeting was held to broaden support for the
effort, and to discuss goals and strategies for the coming election.[1]

Residents who were not registered were identified, and each organizing group member was assigned a number of them to contact. Names of all individuals who received mail in town were also defined, and if they had not already been contacted, they were approached by an organizing group member who asked them to register.

The registration drive was actively supported by virtually all pioneers, sometimes in unorthodox ways. The efforts of Roy "Country" Grice and Bob Teitler are a case in point. While they were working off fines in town for minor offenses they had incurred, they registered about 40 new potential voters. Including the town's transient population, the drive registered almost all the town's newcomers.

On the day of the election, a "get out the vote" effort was initiated, led by David Leinsdorf. Not incidentally, his German Shepherd was one of the dogs killed a few months earlier that had further polarized the new pioneers from the long-time area residents. Leinsdorf checked off a list of those who had already voted, and compared it to the registration roll. In late afternoon, residents who had not yet cast their ballot were identified, and asked to go to the polls to vote.

That voter registration drive and the importance of the coming election was discussed time and again in pioneers' conversations. They were also publicized weekly in the *Chronicle*. Beginning in February, immediately after town pioneers defeated the Way Station's proposed zoning variance, the newspaper repeatedly opined that if new people were going to influence or control the town's future, they needed to register and vote. Continuing

The registration drive and the importance of the coming election was discussed time and again in pioneers' conversations. They were also publicized weekly...in articles and editorials. Large display ads were published that supported the efforts.

through the last issue that preceded the election, voter registration and the pending election was emphasized in articles and editorials. Large display ads were published that supported the efforts. Those were paid for by businesses owned and operated by pioneers, including Montrose Real Estate and the Grubstake. The paper also printed multiple "reminders" in bold typeface that said "DON'T FAIL TO REGISTER FOR VOTING BEFORE MARCH 3."

Pioneers wrote letters to the editor about the coming election. Some letter writers became candidates themselves and then were elected. One candidate's letter to the editor addressed the alienation from electoral politics that many young tourist town pioneers felt, as well as their frequent statements that they would not vote. The letter addressed the powerlessness they felt after what they thought was the debacle at the 1968 Democratic National Convention that ended with the nomination of presidential candidate Hubert Humphrey rather than Eugene McCarthy, and the subsequent election of Richard Nixon. They thought that Democratic contest was stolen by "party bosses." The letter differentiated between the coming Crested Butte election and those at national or statewide levels:

> ... on a local level ... IT MAKES SENSE TO VOTE, because most issues that effect (sic) the way we live ... are determined by the town council. The town council determines whether there are zoning laws, whether there are exceptions made in them so that motels can be built or trailers put up on stilts, whether snowmobiles can zoom through the streets of town, whether dogs can roam the streets, whether town officials can illegally burn old buildings in town, whether law will be enforced fairly or in a discriminatory way; whether there will be architectural guidelines governing new construction, whether there will be adequate water and sewer service in town, whether the town will grow more or less and in what direction. If we elect a decent council, that passes good laws and sees that they are enforced fairly, we can have some measure of self-determination regarding the development of the town.

Alluding to the tensions between the town and the ski area, the letter continued:

> We certainly can't compete with the economic interests of the ski area. ... The only way we can have any control over the way the town develops and grows is by seeing to it that council men and women are elected who will represent our interests .... Otherwise, over the next few years, the town will make it almost impossible for people to live here who want to get it together.

That letter writer became one of the six newly elected council people.

Another successful council candidate, Tom Glass, who earlier had applied to be the town's dog catcher, wrote a letter to the editor after the voter registration drive was completed. His letter addressed specific tourist town issues and interests. Listing what he saw as key, he wrote:

> ... the Town Dump ("Our duty is to find an alternative site immediately"), Streets ("Last spring the Town Council earmarked funds ... to gravel our ... streets ... and no one seems to know what was done with last year's cleanup fund.") Recreation ("What ever happened to the ... ice skating rink? Wouldn't it be nice to have a basketball and tennis court in the Town Park? And a permanent back stop? And an outdoor stage for free lectures, movies and concerts?"), Revenue ("New means of raising revenue must be found. We could impose a bed tax, [and]...a tax on or license for dumping should be enacted."), Architectural Controls ("These are essential, as the irredeemable ugliness of "Stiltsville" attests."), Growth ("We have to prepare for it.").

A personality profile about Bill Crank, the pioneers' candidate for Mayor, was printed in a long front-page newspaper feature. It said he was originally from Ohio, went to college and law school in Kansas where he became a litigation attorney. The piece said he had lived in town for two years and, with his wife Sally, owned and operated the Ore Bucket Lodge. Outlining major issues facing the town and addressing the conflicts between the town's major factions, Crank's platform was summarized. He wanted good water and sewer services; a full-time *independent* town marshal who was not responsible to Gunnison County; a better fire department; broadening and strengthening the town zoning codes; an improved school system; the creation of adequate housing for locals (which he thought might entail forcing absentee landlords to open some of the boarded up houses in town so they could be rented to residents) and the development of a plan to figure out how the town could become financially independent because "we all know the County cannot continue to carry us indefinitely, and we don't want them to, for that is a responsibility we ourselves should shoulder." Crank said he understood that no representative of any one group could govern Crested Butte, and that the effort to get the affairs of the town in order would have to draw, if it were to prove successful, on the energies, dedication, and experience of all the town's human resources:

> I know many of the old-timers are afraid the 'long-hairs' will take over the Town and ruin it, but those fears are groundless. We all came here to live and keep it the kind of place in which we are proud to live. It is not our small differences that are important but the Town, and anyone who is behind the Town will find me working with him.

The Crested Butte Society and The Women's Club, two new organizations that were well respected among ski area trailblazers and the early pioneers, also stressed the importance of registering and voting. For the first time in either of those organizations' existences they decided, along with the *Crested Butte Chronicle*, to sponsor a formal public "candidates' forum" as a public service to town voters. The forum was widely publicized in the newspaper, and in resident's conversations. That highly anticipated event was held in the school gym and was attended by a standing room only crowd of 250-300 people. In front of that audience, two long folding tables separated by a podium, were set out for the candidates. Of the thirteen declared council candidates, all participated except mining-era resident John Cobai. Each candidate made a five-minute opening presentation, and then responded to questions from the audience. Each council candidate was seen by audience members as either an old-timer or newcomer. There was also a mining-era candidate for mayor, Lyle McNeill, who had previously served as an elected official for more than twenty years, first as a council member and then as mayor. By contrast, pioneer mayoral candidate Bill Crank had never before served as a town official.

The forum allowed the electorate to fairly hear the candidates' views on important issues facing the town, even though some pioneer candidates were harassed. One candidate received a phone call asking if it was true that she was not married to the man with whom she was living; another had the air let out of his car's tires during the forum; and the mayoral candidate was accused of associating with hippies whom he knew smoked pot. Nevertheless, that first ever candidates' forum was a success and, notably, set the pattern for every subsequent bi-annual town election.

The overarching issue of the 1972 election was whether the town should grow and, if so, how. Significantly, growth issues, although concerning different specifics, continue to dominate many Crested Butte and Gunnison County elections and legal actions to this day, as they often do in other recreation communities.

The overarching issue ... was whether the town should grow and, if so, how. Significantly, growth issues ... continue to dominate many Crested Butte and Gunnison County elections ...

In 1972, pioneers whose income came from outside the community, whether legal or not, were against growth. Their sources of income did not come from tourism, and the finances they needed to cover the cost of their low-key life-style were met in other ways. Other pioneer groups that did not want the town to develop included students, instructors, artists, and a contingent of "outlaws": drug dealers, draft evaders or resisters, and some other social activists. They did not want the town to be discovered and developed. Anonymity was to be protected. Collectively, anti-growth contingents' views were summarized by a small poster that said, "Crested Butte – Love It by Leaving it the Way You Found It."

George Sibley conceptualized that poster. He meant it as a pun on the epithet commonly shouted derisively at anti-Vietnam War protesters: "America: Love it or Leave It!" He not only coined the phrase but he had small posters printed that he sold. They were widely posted in tourist town pioneer homes and businesses.

Ironically, Sibley highly appreciated and valued the untouched natural environment of the Upper Gunnison Valley; nevertheless, he wanted the town and surrounding area to develop. Perhaps without even knowing it, he was the earliest proponent of "smart" or "controlled' growth. Unlike those who came after him, however, who wanted to cater to the well-off, he wanted to attract a different population. He wanted to grow the local "culture" and "education" industries, and to create what he called a "community of friends" from those who worked in them. He thought locals had to earn a living from tourism, and development was the economic engine for that.

Residents whose businesses, by contrast, depended on tourism — lodges, restaurants, sport shops, contractors and the like – unabashedly

CRESTED
BUTTE

Love it
by
Leaving it
the way you
Found it

E.T.G. © June 1970 Susan H. Anderton George Sibley

Poster courtesy of Susan Anderton and George Sibley.

wanted to see the town grow and prosper as quickly as possible, without restraints. The old-timers also wanted the area to develop, even though most of them were collecting disability insurance, social security, or another form of fixed income, and got by on the town's relatively low cost of living. Although they were apprehensive about the effect new taxes would have on them as the town gained greater prosperity, they wanted to see the town become vibrant again. (All the succeeding town governments recognized mining-era residents' financial limitations, in fact, and exempted them from future locally levied taxes.) Employees in the tourist-oriented businesses included both growth and anti-growth people depending, for example, on their age, marital or family status, how long they lived in town, or why they came.

Within the growth-oriented pioneer faction, there was a "controlled" or "smart" growth group. It also included people from the following wave of new arrivals who came to Crested Butte after the 1972 election, the "recreation community settlers." These included professionals – planners, lawyers, doctors, etc. — and small business owners who started a variety of new enterprises. Their incomes depended on the town growing. Some of them also had sources of income from outside the community. Many of these new settlers, importantly, provided the intellectual underpinning for, and became part of, the new "local power structure" that emerged following the election. They transformed the town from its early "wild west" days and laid the foundation for the more urbane area that appealed to a wider variety of financially-comfortable tourists.

The results of that highly emotional and hotly contested election were dramatic. Pioneers won the mayor's seat and *all* the council seats. Out of 501 registered voters in that election, 383 ballots were cast (76%). The mayoral candidate favored by the old-timers, Lyle McNeill, received 163 votes; Bill Crank, got 220 (53%). Two council candidates received more votes

Pioneers won the mayor's seat and all the council seats. Out of 501 registered voters in that election, 383 ballots were cast (76%).

than Crank. Jim Wallace, received 276, and the only female candidate, Kathleen Ross (nee Stupple), received 227 votes. All the other winning candidates got between 200 and 143 votes.

Mirroring the demographics of the tourist town pioneers, the new council and mayor ranged in age from their early twenties to early thirties, a trend that remains true in Crested Butte and in most other contemporary tourist towns and recreation communities to this day. (Most elected officials are under forty). An early 1973 study was commissioned by the pioneer council that was conducted by a locally formed consulting firm, BKR Associates. Not incidentally, all of its principals played leading roles in the town's "smart" or "controlled" growth faction. The study found that 70% of the town's population was under 30 years old and another 15% were between 30 and 40. Councilmembers' geographical roots and the work they did in town also reflected the full spectrum of the new Crested Butte pioneers and the earliest recreation community settlers. They came from Colorado, Illinois, New York, Connecticut, and Ohio, and two were "army brats" who had moved frequently. With the exception of the lodge-owning mayor, the new town trustees worked at a number of different jobs to make ends meet, as did many other pioneers. In addition to the iron sculptor who was a student, there was a tourist-home owner who also built condos, waited tables and did consulting; an audio-equipment shop owner who worked construction; a ski coach who built and sold pre-fabricated homes; a trust-funder who worked on the ski patrol in winter and in summer worked construction; and a breakfast waitress who was also a homemaker. As an indication of the physicality of most pioneers, and the lack of well-paying jobs in town, four of the six newly elected council people fought forest fires with the Crested Butte Hot Shots in addition to all their other jobs. One, Jim Wallace, was the Hot Shots' original organizer and another, Ron Barr, was one of its esteemed crew leaders for the roughly seven years the Hot Shots existed.

Pioneers effectively wrested political control from the long-time town residents and ended the town's mining town ethic and its open, wild-western tourist town culture. That election became *the* turning point in the formation of what now is today's cosmopolitan, well-developed tourist town and recreation community.

The election signaled the end of rancher and miner ways and values, with their traditionally defined male/female roles, strong work ethic, active church participation, unwavering patriotism, and sense that "might makes right." It was the beginning of instituting peace and social justice values: women's' liberation and equality; sexual freedom; questioning political authority and formal religion; protecting the powerless, including children, animals and the environment; and non-violence. It also signified questioning the significance of work itself, by encouraging people to work less and

The day before the election, the old-timers had a 'hippie' problem; the day after it, hippies had an old-timer problem.

play more. Not only was the election the beginning of the end of the old-timer's way of life, it became the undoing of the early ski area trailblazers' as well since they usually shared or adapted to the Old-West culture. The day before the election, the old-timers had a hippie problem; the day after it, hippies had an old-timer problem.

Before the 1972 election, bar fighting became almost commonplace with the immigration of ski area trailblazers and the earliest pioneers. Trudy Yaklich, a young Crested Butte reared woman who was an important bridge between the old-timers and new people, recalled many years later, "Before new people came, there were no bar fights. We were all one big family, and families don't fight." A plate glass window that was broken often in the Grubstake was actually dubbed the "Wheeler window," because a regular bar brawler, trailblazer Freeman "Trip" Wheeler, frequently threw others through it. Fighting in town was no longer tolerated as a "boys will be boys" activity; it was prosecuted as a serious offense. Drunk driving and poaching, were also redefined. On the other hand, unless someone was overtly flamboyant about the way he or she used recreational drugs, enforcement of drug laws became laxer. "Discretion" became the operational concept in regard to drug use; if individuals were judicious about where they used them, they were not persecuted or prosecuted.

Similar changes were taking place at the County level. Crested Butte resident John Levin was appointed Gunnison County Judge. Although he conspicuously adopted a cowboy hat and boots as his personal mode of dress, he rejected Old-Western ways, and rigorously enforced the laws against bar brawls, driving drunk, poaching, and the like. He also insisted that proper legal procedures always had to be followed, particularly in drug busts.

Many tourist town pioneers, especially the alternate life-style adherents and "outlaws," hoped the 1972 election meant an end to their harassment and, perhaps more importantly, the beginning of a totally open and free anarchist-like community where hippies controlled local government, and counter-culture people could use drugs, experiment sexually, and generally live free in a "hippie utopia." Indeed, that was why many of them voted in that election.

Many tourist town pioneers ... hoped the 1972 election meant ... the beginning of a totally open and free anarchist-like community where 'hippies' controlled local government and counter-culture people could use drugs, experiment sexually, and ... live free in a "hippie utopia." Indeed, that was why many of them voted ...

Shortly after their victory, the new councilmembers went on a day long retreat. Following a gargantuan breakfast at the new mayor's house that featured poached venison steaks, the newly elected officials went to a house near tiny Peanut Lake, just outside town. The retreat's purpose was to discuss the new council's priorities, how they would work together, and on what committees each member would serve. Soon after the meeting began, the youngest council member took out a marijuana cigarette, lit it, and passed it around. With one exception, all the newly elected officials smoked it (and inhaled). The one who did not, said laughingly that he no longer enjoyed pot and preferred other narcotics. The young councilman achieved his goal: smoking that "joint" together effectively nullified using recreational drugs as a political issue in town.

Other councilmember's behavior reinforced that action. Not long after the retreat, for example, in early evening, en route to the local movie house, the new pioneer council's police committee chairperson, along with a recently appointed deputy town marshal and an assistant municipal judge, walked down the town's completely empty main street smoking a joint. Fittingly, they were on their way to see one of the pioneers' favorite films: The Beatles' animated, *Yellow Submarine.*

... the election ... signified that local government would rebuild ... based on an economy that attracted visitors, ... and include peaceful, socially "libertarian" values and ethics.

Clearly, however, the election and the new council members' illegal drug use did not foretell the formation of a hippy haven. Instead, it signified that local government would rebuild the community based on an economy that attracted visitors who would come primarily to play and recreate; and include peaceful, socially "libertarian" values and ethics.

Within the first year-and-a-half of its two-year term the pioneer council's "smart growth" faction became dominant, and increasingly used its power to rid the town of those who did not agree with them. Their perspectives led to policies and projects that simultaneously increased the quality of life for the comfortable, downwardly-mobile-by-choice local residents, and visiting tourists. It created sports and art venues, supported athletic and cultural activities, and maintained the "quaint" physical appearance of the town. Council policies allowed residents and tourists alike wide latitude in exercising their civil liberties and personal life style preferences. The council, in effect, intentionally began to stimulate tourism. It was the political beginning of Crested Butte developing into a prototypical late 20th century new town genre: a recreation exurb that relied on a tourist economy.

Based on the platforms and positions they took at the candidates' forum and in other public settings, the new trustees all seemed to be "slow" growth proponents, although some tilted more toward an "anti-growth" position while others leaned toward more rapid development. That distinction made a significant difference. It redefined the town's social and political dynamic. It was no longer about the mining-era residents and trailblazers versus the pioneers. The new social and political conflicts were between different factions within the pioneer groups. Importantly, they all agreed about individuals' rights; they wanted them exercised freely and fully, and laws enforced gently and fairly for all residents and tourists. Personal freedom issues rarely divided councilmembers; development did.

> ... at the candidates' forum ... the new trustees all seemed to be "slow" growth proponents, although some tilted more toward an "anti-growth" position while others leaned toward more rapid development. That distinction made a significant difference. It redefined the town's social and political dynamic. Importantly, they all agreed about individuals' rights — they wanted them exercised freely and fully. ... Personal freedom issues rarely divided councilmembers; development did.

Councilmembers who opposed growth measures were usually in the minority and were consistently outvoted. The growth in-any-and-every-way-possible-townspeople and councilmembers merged with the smart or controlled growth members. The three factions, in essence, merged into two with all the growth-oriented council people voting to support virtually every individual growth proposal. As would be true in future years in Crested Butte, as well as in other developing recreation exurbs, *over time, the forces favoring growth, with very few exceptions, defeated the forces that opposed it.*

The pioneer council initially addressed long standing community issues, and found new ones that needed attention. In a council meeting soon after they took office, for instance, the new officials focused on law enforcement, water and sewer, the fire department, parking, the town dump, the condition of the streets, dog control, the annual community clean-up, a proposed concrete batch plant, historical sites and architectural control. Extensive agendas were normal for the pioneer council, especially at the beginning of its term. Meetings went on for many hours and, as they wore on, were filled with one-upmanship, word parsing, and intense personal sniping among council people who saw issues differently. Pioneer entrepreneur Steve Glazer commented about those meetings as he encouraged citizens to attend them, "They're the best show in town."

Although the zoning issue was resolved somewhat when an ordinance addressing it was passed by the previous town council, another challenge to it was initiated during the late fall of 1972. Unlike the earlier zoning confrontations concerning "Stiltsville" or "The Way Station," this challenge was not between long-time residents and pioneers. It was between members of the latter group itself, some of whom already had become early "recreation community settlers" who wanted to attract affluent tourists as they perceived Aspen, Vail, and some of the other emerging Colorado tourist towns to be doing. One of them, Steve Glazer, said in a 2013 interview, "I thought growth was inevitable, even though it had downsides. I saw *high end* (emphasis added) tourism as a way to avoid the 'down cycles' in the economy, because there were always wealthy people who could afford vacations."

Tom Glass, the most pro-development tourist town pioneer council member, along with a pro-growth fellow ski patrolman and construction worker, Ed Costie, each filed a formal complaint against the pioneer council member who thought Crested Butte should appeal to and attract artists, students, and working-class tourists because the town was afford-able, and he wanted the town to develop very slowly. This slow growth trustee and his wife rented a small house to families, and larger groups of unrelated vacationers like student church groups, in what the new zoning ordinance categorized as the "business district." It was not clear, however, if a tourist home could legally be rented on a short-term basis as a "per-mitted use" in that district. The complainants asserted it was not a permit-ted use; the defendant said it was. Whether the case should be pursued by the town was left to the determination of pro-growth Mayor Crank, and his friend, the development-oriented town attorney, David Leinsdorf. They decided to prosecute.

In early winter 1972, a front-page story appeared in the paper head-lined, "Blues Project Suit Goes to Court." The report stated, "The com-plaint against ... [the] owner of the Blues Project ... pursued by the town attorney, went to trial today. [The owner] has been charged with a viola-tion of the zoning code by renting out for tourist purposes a house set on a business lot. The trial was very long and the legal jousting complicated and technical." The issue was significant because it was about the type of tourists the town would try to attract, whether they would be compatible with the existing local populace, and what type of development the town would encourage. Reflecting the intense controversy that surrounded the challenge, the newspaper piece continued, "The Town Council will also be considering adoption of a recommendation made to it by the Board of Adjustment to legalize tourist use of the business property when the Council meets January 8."

In late January 1973 the matter was settled. The front-page headline proclaimed, "Blues Project Charges Dropped." The following report said the small business owner and the town had worked out a mutually satis-factory agreement, that the town dropped all charges, and the proprietor agreed to limit rental of the property to single families or no more than five unrelated people. The owner said, "I feel this [settlement] vindicates the position I have taken right off the get-go, which is that I have the right to rent the property on the terms I did all along. The whole thing so far seems now like a fruitless exercise." The agreement resulted from negotia-tions between the town attorney and the lawyer who originally drafted the zoning law, Harrison F. Russell. Several years later the *Chronicle* editor said that case was initiated because the emerging growth oriented local power structure thought the defendant was hypocritical because he was talking "anti-growth," but was pursuing profit by running the Blues Project, and buying other town properties. Forty years after that, a former councilmember who was part of that growth faction, confirmed the editor's view, as he laughingly remembered they brought that action "simply as a gotcha thing."

A few weeks later the councilmember who owned the small tourist home withdrew his attempt to change the zoning ordinance so short-term home rentals could be permitted in the business district. He wanted them allowed in *all* the town's zoned districts, so visitors could find less expensive accommodations than were available in area lodges and hotels. He said that would allow more people to visit Crested Butte, and would stimulate the town's economy.

The Blues Project owner argued that there was an increasingly powerful local group in town that wanted rich people to come to Crested Butte and did not want counter-cultural and working people. The newspaper reported that he said, "It is becoming a 'class question', whereby the Town is developing an 'elitist perspective'." He saw social and economic pressures exerted to force "alternative life-style locals," as well as tourists on limited budgets, out of Crested Butte because of the rapidly increasing cost of living and vacationing in town. The *Chronicle* reported him saying:

> There is a group ... interested in not having 'poor people or working-class people' involved in the Town as tourists or residents, and he feels a need for the Town to diversify .... Zoning which would allow 'tourist dwellings', essentially which would allow rental to more than 5 unrelated persons, would be a 'public service' and would be a step toward providing inexpensive housing for those who otherwise could not afford to come here. [The owner] ... said that before he withdrew his proposal ... he circulated a petition, receiving approximately 120 signatures in favor of the proposal ... and all of the business owners he contacted signed it.

The newspaper piece also said the owner intended to sell his business, and after its sale, re-introduce an amendment that would allow homes to be rented in all districts in town, when he could not be accused of having a conflict of interest.

Shortly after the Blues Project suit was initiated, a second issue surfaced that illustrated the fault lines between those who wanted only limited growth and the pro-development faction. In late October, a municipal airport that could accommodate small aircraft was proposed on a 15-acre parcel of land a few miles south of town. The land was owned by the local, multi-generational, ranching Aubrey Spann family. Eighty percent of its funding was to have been provided by the Federal Government; a 20% match was supposed to come from the town. Importantly, a single individual, Ron Rouse, promised to finance the town's share if he could become the local operator and manager. Both he and the town were represented by the same lawyer, Lynn French. The most pro-development pioneer council member, Tom Glass, and Dan Gallagher who also wanted growth, as well as swing-voter Ron Barr, supported the proposal right away, but all the other town trustees and the mayor voted to set another meeting to consider it further.

At that next meeting, details of the project were presented. They showed, for example, that the runway would be almost 7000 feet long. A petition supporting that development garnered over 150 signatures. With only council member Kathleen Ross, an "anti" growth proponent, in opposition to Rouse's proposal, the measure to proceed passed. However, snags emerged, and opposition mounted. Most importantly, the Spanns refused to sell their land, which meant that for the town to move forward, it would have had to take the Spanns' property under the rule of "eminent domain." The Council again decided to continue pursuing the project and did so by a 5-1 vote with Ross again dissenting.

A guest editorial, written by a tourist town pioneer, Randi Gronningsater, opined that initiating condemnation proceedings so an airport could be built was unnecessary, and immoral. It also said that Lynn French, by representing both the proponent and the Town, had a conflict of interest, and that the town should hire another lawyer. A second letter from Annie McElhinney argued against condemning the Spanns' land. She pointed out that the Spann's had sold or given some of their land earlier when it was for a public good, but that they explicitly said they did not want to sell any of it "for a commercial need for an elite few." She said the proposed airport was not fulfilling a community need, as acquiring a

town dump would because the current one was full; even more importantly, she said, it contradicted the stated values many council members "have
professed in the rights of individuals in our small town ...".

At a succeeding special meeting, the Spanns reaffirmed that they
would not sell their property. That meant the council would have to begin
eminent domain proceedings. A very slow growth-oriented council member who at first supported the proposal changed his position. He introduced a motion *not* to proceed with condemnation, until a current feasibility study was completed. That motion failed on a 4-2 vote; but the issue
became moot. The deadline by which the Federal application needed to
be submitted had passed, and Federal monies were no longer available to
the town. That made it impossible to fund the project.

Since the late 1960s, the early tourist town pioneers had been trying
to figure out what, besides skiing and the little bit of summer outdoor
recreation, might attract tourists. A few fledgling cultural endeavors tried,
like the California Players summertime melodrama offerings or Western
State College's Professor Martin Hatcher's more contemporary theater
offerings, or educational ones like the geological workshops at Cement
Creek and biological research at Gothic, or Dr. Winston Smith's Law-
Science Academy in town but, collectively, these efforts brought less than
a few hundred people to the area. Then the pioneers and a smattering of
ski area trailblazers realized that the "quaint" nature of the entire town and
its history as a mining community could be an attraction. They thought
the physical character of the town itself — its small wood frame houses,
many with Victorian style trim, the old rock schoolhouse and library, and
the wide western streets — needed to be preserved and promoted; and
might appeal to visitors, as it had to them.

Within six months after they were elected the pioneer council enacted two laws that became essential for maintaining and enhancing the
town's charm. First, it created an historic district throughout the town by
a near unanimous vote, with only the Aspen-reared councilmember dissenting. Soon afterwards, the council applied for and received a formal
"Historic District" designation for the entire township. Complementing
that effort, to ensure all building renovations and new construction blended into the existing style and size of already built structures, and would

not overshadow them, the council also enacted a Board of Zoning and Architectural Review, (BOZAR). It required any proposed building in town, whether a modest external repair, complete renovation, or an entirely new structure, to go before it and get its stamp of approval. Those two initiatives initially meant that a limited niche market of cultural aficionados, i.e., those interested in mining or western history, might hear about the town and visit.

Within six months after they were elected the pioneer council enacted two laws that became essential for maintaining and enhancing the town's charm. First, it created an historic district throughout the town .... Complementing that effort, to ensure all building renovations and new construction blended into the existing style and size of already built structures, and would not overshadow them, the council also enacted a Board of Zoning and Architectural Review, (BOZAR).

Significantly, the historic district designation meant the town could qualify for government and non-profit organizations' grants that could be used for various physical improvements, including a new sewer plant and street upgrades, as long as they were used to preserve and restore the town's "original" appearance. Applying for preservation grant monies was one type of outside assistance the new pioneer and later settler councils sought. But it was not the only outside funding they went after. Many of the new Crested Butte pioneers were lawyers or community and political organizers during the sixties and early seventies; they worked on projects funded by government and private non-governmental grants. They knew about various programs that were available, mainly to urban municipalities, for community and economic development. They suspected some of those, or similar ones, could be used for rural development. Since Crested Butte was financially on the brink of disaster and had few sources of revenue (it did not yet have a sales tax), the pioneer council aggressively looked for a wide range of outside funding.

The first new contract laborer hired by the pioneer council was a consultant, Steve Glazer. A few months earlier, he had been an unsuccessful candidate in the 1972 election. He was asked to find and apply for outside monies. Instead of seeking them, however, he spent most of his time assisting the overworked, mining-era town clerk, John Stadjuhar, with bookkeeping duties and taking samples of the town's water supply. The council canceled Glazer's contract. Although council members thought his activities were useful, they had hired him to obtain desperately needed outside funding, which to them was a higher priority. (Forty years later, to honor Glazer's life-long commitment to water issues, the town reservoir from which he originally had taken those water samples, was named after him). Not only did council people think outside monies were essential for town improvements, they also knew they came with administrative overhead monies that could be used for other purposes, including hiring new town staff that, among other things, could relieve Stadjuhar's ever increasing burden.

The pioneer council spent its limited funds differently than prior councils had, which reflected its different priorities. For the first time, it provided funds to non-profit organizations, particularly those involving the arts and recreation. The council gave a small grant to the newly formed Crested Butte Mountain Theater to help mount its first production, "*Dark of the Moon*," and also provided seed funding to organizers of the second Crested Butte Arts and Crafts Festival. Both grants, not incidentally, helped lead to the formation of major town non-profit organizations as Crested Butte transformed itself. The pioneer council also allocated funds for improving the rock-strewn softball field, and later granted monies to develop other athletic venues. Not surprisingly, mining-era residents, who no longer controlled town decision making, did not like or understand those expenditures. The arts and recreation funding was meant to support activities new local residents themselves wanted for their own enjoyment; and that they thought would attract additional recreation-oriented residents and tourists.

The pioneer council spent its limited funds differently than prior councils did, which reflected its different priorities. For the first time, it provided funds to non-profit organizations, particularly those involving the arts and recreation.

Business oriented pioneers and the early settlers wanted to generate greater revenue, especially by attracting tourists with lots of disposable income. They fought hard and continuously for policies that encouraged that. They wanted the streets paved, or at least repaired by having the potholes filled and the streets graveled, a historic district, zoning and architectural controls, additional recreational facilities, better access into town, including developing a nearby airport, and dogs controlled. They thought these measures would lead to the growth they wanted, and discussions about these issues constantly dominated their meetings. Most new pioneer council members supported each issue on a case by case basis.

Wes Light became the second town attorney for the newly elected town council after the first, David Leinsdorf, was elected to the Gunnison Board of County Commissioners. Providing important continuity thereafter, Light also retained his position after the succeeding council was seated in 1974; he then became the first "recreation community settler" council's lawyer. He personified the merging of individual freedom and personal libertarian issues with "smart" or "controlled" growth economics and politics. He talked about himself and his role in Crested Butte's early development in a 2012 interview:

> My personal politics were "counter-cultural": I swam naked in Nicholson Lake and did drugs. I got interested in Town issues and was part of the group that figured out how to wield power within the system, working with the County, Forest Service, Bureau of Land Management, etc. From '73-'76 I was part of the evolution when controlled growth attitudes were 'codified', e.g., adopting architectural controls and home rule. I chaired the Home Rule Commission. We saw ourselves in the lead group of people who wanted to develop within this 'smart growth box.'

Continuing, he referred to an important conference organized by town planner, Myles Rademan. Titled 'The "Developer's Conference," it was designed to attract and inform land owners, developers, contractors, and other interested parties about the newly enacted zoning and building codes, and what they had to do to develop projects. He added, "In fact, that conference led to us realizing that our issues were county-wide, and we needed to get someone on the County Commission. Getting Leinsdorf elected to it ... was an important strategic political move for us."

Both town attorneys, Leinsdorf and Light, in fact, were key members of the new "smart" or "controlled" growth clique. Beginning in the tourist town pioneer council's term of office and continuing through a succession of recreation community settler councils, that faction emerged as the town's new local power structure, and drove the new tourist town and recreation community's development.

Chapter 10

The Emerging Local Power Structure

S oon after the 1972 spring election, schisms surfaced among the new councilmembers. All the winning candidates had *campaigned* on slow growth platforms. After the election, however, two tourist town pioneer council people showed themselves to be essentially against growth, while two others and the mayor revealed themselves really to support development. That mix reflected the different interests within the pioneer population itself.

Soon after the 1972 spring election, schisms surfaced among the new councilmembers. All the winning candidates had campaigned *on slow growth platforms. After the election, however, two ... council people showed themselves to be essentially against growth, while two others and the mayor revealed themselves really to support development.*

Many of the younger, single, earlier pioneers, came to town as counter-culturists to experiment with alternate life styles. Individually and collectively, they tried to "live small." They created new organizations like food cooperatives, alternative elementary schools, and a "free" university, but those organizational efforts had short life-spans and, ultimately, failed.

The first such short-lived attempt was the formation of a non-profit food co-op. It was meant to be an alternative to the local general store, owned by long time mining-era residents, Tony and Eleanor Stephanic. Most pioneers thought Stephanic's basic commodity prices were too high. In the fall of 1970, pioneer entrepreneur Steve Glazer and another young community member, Greg Dalbey, called a meeting to gauge interest in forming a co-op to "help lower the cost of living in Town." One week later the newspaper reported that a new store existed "providing, initially, food, and eventually, any services that are needed, at the lowest possible percentage over costs." Annual membership in the co-op cost only $5.00. Two

weeks after opening, it had 136 members, sold its entire original food supply, and had a $300.00 surplus that was used to re-order provisions.[1] Pat
Shearing was in charge of ordering supplies, and Dave Egan coordinated
volunteers. By the end of the following March, in 1971, the co-op needed more volunteers. It advertised for them saying that even though workers could not be paid, there were many fringe benefits including, "…
catching up on Company Store gossip, which is of as good a quality as any
in town."

Two months later there were 180 paid members. In June membership
was opened to "summer people" and transients. The food co-op held new
board member elections. Notably, three of the original members did not
run again, presumably because of the large time commitment board membership required and what is often referred to in non-profit organizations
as "burnout." Kathleen Stupple, who later became Kathleen Ross, became
a board member. A year later she became the first pioneer woman elected
to the town council. Although membership enrollment had increased significantly, volunteers became increasingly hard to recruit because employment opportunities in town slowly grew. In December 1971, the co-op
folded because, according to Steve Glazer, there was not "enough co-oper-
ation and energy."

Another short-lived attempt at alternative living addressed the educational needs of young families. Pioneers, most of whom themselves had
benefited from first rate educations throughout their lives, wanted the
same high-quality education for their own youngsters, beginning with
pre-school. Although a mining-era woman, Ronnie Ruggera, baby-sat for
up to 10 infants and toddlers and provided hot lunches for them, a *formal* pre-school had never existed in Crested Butte.

In the fall of 1970 Jeanette "Sugar" Glass, a young enterprising pioneer from a plush Connecticut suburb, began the first nursery school. Its
first display ad in the *Chronicle* announced:

Crested Butte —NURSERY— corner of First and Elk. Experienced
Connecticut kindergarten teacher will begin a *progressive* [emphasis
added] pre-school educational program in Crested Butte this fall for
children aged 3-6. Also will operate a skier's child day care center on
weekends and during school vacations this winter. Registration for fall

semester of nursery school will begin in October. For information write: Miss Jeanette Glass, Box 114, Crested Butte, Colorado.

By Thanksgiving, there was a picture of the nursery with its nine registered students in the local newspaper. They were all children of new pioneers. As the town's population grew, enrollment increased, the school flourished and it outgrew its space in the traditional, small, wood frame, mining-era house in which it began.

By summer 1973, the nursery had moved to the first floor of the old Crested Butte elementary school and, simultaneously, it was sold to a second pioneer entrepreneur from the east, Honeydew Murray (who was also part of the six-person New York consortium that bought the Grubstake two years earlier). Murray owned and operated the private nursery school for the next several years before again selling it. That high-quality nursery later became one of the town's important amenities for young recreation community settler families and those that followed them, as they decided to move to Crested Butte.

Many pioneers, in fact, questioned the basic quality of the Gunnison County public-school system. They wondered if their sons and daughters could get a top-flight education in it. Some did not think they could and, importantly, that the teachers in it, almost all of whom were the adult offspring of long-time born and bred Gunnison County residents, were biased against their "hippie" kids. So, they started an alternative non-profit elementary school, "The Real World School."

It was established in the summer of 1973 by several tourist town pioneer parents: Diane Appleby, Diane Kahn, Susan Applegate Robinson, and her husband, educational philosopher and educator, Thatcher Robinson. He was wealthy, the scion of a famous financial industry family that owned Household Finance Company, and he subsidized the school with his personal funds. After getting a Ph.D. from Princeton University in Mathematical Philosophy and then teaching math for a decade at the University of Southern Illinois, he worked in that university's learning laboratories. Shortly thereafter, according to him, he was fired for having been arrested at an anti-Vietnam War protest. He then moved to Crested Butte, which he had visited when he was a child on a summer family vacation.

Robinson thought that conventional schools, even good ones, pre-pared children inadequately and misguidedly by segmenting subjects they studied from each other, and separating their formal education from what they were doing outside the classroom, in what he defined as their "real world." He thought traditional education was too abstract and discon-nected from practical applications.

He wanted a curriculum centered on projects that individual students chose themselves, because they were interested in and important to them. Jan Keyser, was a young *certified* elementary school teacher in upstate New York before she came to Crested Butte. That certification was important to Robinson for purposes of school accreditation. Keyser became the sole paid staff member in The Real World School. Her "pay" was room, board and a ski pass. The school's pioneer planning group[2] met to discuss "the land situation for the provision of a site for the school; the philosophy to be embodied by the school; devotion of the school and participating par-ents to quality over quantity in education; and the emphasis on getting pupils involved in the things that have a reality for them in the real world."

When that educational experiment opened, it had 14 students of varying ages who came from 11 pioneer families. Several of them, not sur-prisingly, were enrolled earlier in "Sugar" Glass's nursery. In an interview forty years later about the school and its emphasis on having students' themselves define projects on which they wanted to work, Janet Carnes (nee, Jan Keyser) said, "Thatcher was very frustrated because the kids couldn't articulate what they wanted to study or what they were interest-ed in and, consequently, they worked on projects Thatcher thought up instead of on projects they dreamt up themselves." The alternative school also frequently used day-long and overnight field trips as part of its regu-lar academic curriculum visiting, for example, orchards, farms, ranches, and hot springs. Parents always accompanied students on these education-al excursions and, notably, smoked pot openly and sometimes used psy-chedelics. Because of Robinson's frustration with the students and his inability to do organizational work, he refused to continue to fund the educational enterprise. After only one year of operation the school folded.

At about the same time, a second kind of alternate education for pre-school and elementary age kids began: a ski program, "The Cyclones." It started because, as one of the early coaches, Phil Hedrick, (a Denver-reared trailblazer and ski instructor) said, "It's every Colorado kid's birthright to ski". The kids skied every Friday, beginning at noon, after the public elementary school closed for the day. Even though, as it was originally conceptualized, that program also folded, it continued in a modified version until, several years later, it was absorbed into the town's community recreation program.

Tourist town pioneers not only wanted "relevant" quality education for their off-spring, they wanted it for themselves. In fall 1973, as part of a national "counter-cultural" trend, a local non-profit "free access college" was organized by Al Appleby and Dick Wells. Appleby's children, not incidentally, were enrolled in The Real World School. Wells worked with the new theater troupe. They proclaimed, "courses would be staffed by resource people with the skills and willingness to teach them." All twenty courses were taught by tourist town pioneers.[3] The effort to create a "free university" also lasted only about a year, as was the duration of the food co-op and The Real World School. Their short-lived organizational life spans were probably because many pioneers were, although idealistic, not aware of, or willing to undertake, the difficult work and challenges associated with creating new organizations, or because their ephemeral interests changed and they moved on to new endeavors in town or elsewhere.

Two of the six pioneer council members who actively supported these counter-cultural efforts, voted against virtually all issues that would lead to growth: attempts to pave streets, control drugs or dogs, or pass sales taxes. One was the second woman ever elected to the town council, Kathleen Ross. (The first had been a community elementary school teacher who was elected two years earlier, Doris Walker). The other anti-growth councilmember owned a small house he rented out to tourists but earned most of his income from professional consulting. Mayor Crank and two Councilmen, Glass and Gallagher, wanted the town to develop more quickly and favored policies and proposed laws intended to foster growth. The other town trustees, Jim Wallace and Ron Barr, supported development on some issues and opposed it on others, depending on the measure that was being considered. Months before differences among the new council people surfaced, the pioneers' collective dreams and aspirations were summarized by *Chronicle* editor, Myles Arber. He speculated,

"… things will begin to look brighter as regards our future, now that it looks like we have a do-something Council."

Differences among the new council members surfaced almost imperceptibly. Well before the end of their two-year term ended, however, those differences were clear. By then, virtually everyone knew where each council person stood in relation to development. In the first council meeting in May 1972, one of the two anti-growth members opposed raising fines for dogs "at large," and a "batch plant" (to make concrete)

> *Differences among the new council-members surfaced almost imperceptibly. Well before the end of their two-year term ended …. everyone knew where each person stood in relation to development.*

that was proposed inside the town boundaries. He had received, presumably, most of his votes from artists, craftspeople, and the pioneer "outlaws." During the ensuing two years, he was defined as the councilman most against growth, and was isolated socially and fought politically by those who wanted development. They later emerged in the ensuing few years to be what sociologists Robert and Helen Lynd defined in their 1920s seminal work, "*Middletown*," as "the local power structure."[4]

During the pioneer council's 1972-1974 two-year term, major initiatives and changes were made and codified, all of which steered the town toward becoming a contemporary tourist town. As that was happening, the council members who did not favor development lost political influence, and the pro-growth mayor and councilmen increasingly dominated politically, and became central players in Crested Butte's emerging local power group. Within weeks after the election, a new marshal was hired. New town laws concerning dog control were passed, including one that allowed dogs to be unleashed if they were under "voice control." (Complete dog control, however, took many years before it finally became effective due to stricter leash laws). The

> *… the very council members who did not favor development lost political influence, and the pro-development mayor and councilmen increasingly dominated politically and became central players in Crested Butte's emerging local power group.*

council passed laws establishing an architectural review committee and a new zoning code, with only one dissenting vote (cast by Ron Barr, one of the two "swing voters" on growth issues). He did not like government being able to tell someone what he or she could do with their property. An architect, Jim Kuziak, a principal in the local consulting firm the town hired to help plan its future, BKR Associates, was appointed chairperson of the influential architectural review committee. In the first few months of the new pioneer council's term, a Historic Preservation and Architectural Control Commission was created. It too was chaired by Kuziak.

By November 1972, the new council decided they wanted a new town attorney, and appointed pioneer David Leinsdorf, a "smart" or "controlled" growth proponent. Shortly thereafter, John Levin was named the judge for Gunnison County. BKR Associates was hired to plan for the town's tourist-oriented future, and to seek outside grant monies. Significantly, each of BKR Associates' principals became part of the emerging local power structure that conceptualized, promulgated, and implemented the smart or controlled growth philosophy. Myles Rademan became Crested Butte's first town planner. Jim Kuziak became chair of the powerful Board of Zoning and Architectural Review, and then, within two years, became Gunnison County's first planning director. After Crested Butte had become a "home rule" municipality two years later, Bruce Baumgartner was hired as the first town manager.

Two pioneer council members did not complete their terms of office; both resigned during their second year. Their resignations allowed the existing growth-oriented town officials a way to gain additional political support. They appointed new town trustees who favored development. Ross was replaced by Judy Naumberg, president of a local group of pioneers that bought The Grubstake from the original pioneer owners. Even though she was identified as part of the "outlaw" and "trust-funder" groups who were against development, her candidacy was supported by virtually all existing councilmen; each one wanted to retain at least one female voice on council. The other new appointee, Ron Rouse, was a growth-oriented businessman who owned and operated the local air taxi service and wanted to develop an airstrip just outside the town. He thought increased tourism was essential.

There had also been other pioneer applicants who wanted to fill the vacant council seats, but they were all seen by the emerging power structure as opposed to development: Bob Brown, Barry Cornman, Ron Makela, and Paul Roggenbuck. Rouse was opposed by a minority on the council but supported by those who wanted growth: the mayor, the ski patrolman/independent businessperson (who would later become the town's mayor), as well as other councilmembers who emphasized the "growth" part of the slow growth concept.

Leinsdorf had been on the Architectural Control Board but resigned when he became town attorney. Council and Architectural Board members thought that a lawyer was needed to replace him. The *Chronicle* editor who, not incidentally, was a law school classmate of Rademan's, was appointed to succeed him. Bob Lyman, another non-practicing lawyer, was named as an alternate.

In 1973 Crested Butte was still primarily a ski town with an almost entirely skiing-based winter economy. Lyman filed a class action law suit on behalf of season pass holders *against* the Crested Butte Mountain Resort, because it wanted to close the resort a week early. Lyman's legal maneuver reflected the tensions between the ski area and tourist town pioneers and was seen by the former as antagonistic. The area wanted to close, not because of a lack of snow which might have been deemed a legitimate reason, but because other than the few local residents that had bought season passes, there were virtually no skiers, and therefore no business. Lyman was represented by David Leinsdorf and Gerry Reese. Reese was another Ivy-League educated lawyer who formed the area's first environmental action group; notably, soon thereafter he was named the City of Gunnison's judge. The suit, following what became a very public ski area versus town confrontation, was settled by a negotiated agreement; it closed some lifts and kept three others operating.

In August 1973, a crucial meeting was held at the home of Art and Bea Norris, both early pioneers. It was called to discuss the absence of planning in Gunnison County, and the 28,000 housing units that Rademan discovered had already been approved for development, but which had not yet gone through the processes the recently enacted county zoning codes required. At that summer's Festival of Arts and Crafts, the Crested Butte Valley Environmental Action Committee had a booth and collected signatures on a petition that declared, "Our aim is to halt unplanned, uncontrolled, unneeded growth." Virtually all those present at the meeting at the Norris' signed the petition; and Rademan, who by then was a Crested Butte town employee, manned the booth at the festival and collected the signatures.

After failing twice, a 2% sales tax was finally passed by Crested Butte voters that summer. It was heavily promoted, especially by the emerging local power group. That passage indicated increasing support for development in town. It also reflected what alternate life-style exponents thought, as they had before the spring election a little more than a year earlier when they voted for candidates whom they believed were anti-growth proponents: their votes and wishes did not matter, and meant nothing to the increasingly powerful pro-development local clique. Consequently, most did not vote in the succeeding '74 election. Out of the only 393 registered electors, about a third actually voted (compared to the over 76% of voters who had cast ballots in 1972). The number of registered voters had decreased substantially during that 16-month period, presumably with many of them having been counter-cultural residents who left town. The sales tax measure passed by a substantial margin (83-56), and immediately began injecting new revenues into the town coffers.

A month later, there was a political response by the remaining anti-growth pioneers to their growing awareness of the consolidation of local business and political interests. It was initiated by Al Appleby, one of the town's new counter-culture residents. Before coming to Crested Butte, he had been a successful west coast entrepreneur. Appleby proposed, "An Act to Require Public Disclosure of Private Interests by Public Officials." It was formally introduced in a town council meeting by the remaining slow-growth council member. Strong objections to Appleby's proposal were raised by the growth-oriented public officials, especially council member Tom Glass and David Leinsdorf. (In 1974, notably, Appleby ran for Mayor as an opposition candidate, and was overwhelmingly defeated).

At about that time a new governmental body was created, the Crested Butte Fire Protection District.[6] Also, at about that time, the Crested Butte Women's Club, whose membership consisted mainly of pioneers and settlers that favored development, elected Jeanne Duval its new President, a-growth-no-matter-what-oriented real estate person.

The "smart" or "controlled," pro-development faction became increasingly focused and sophisticated. Its political need at that time was to differentiate itself from both the "growth, no matter what" people and those who were "no growth, no matter what." BKR called a one-day conference (referenced above) that was to guide future development in the northern end of Gunnison County. According to Rademan, "developers...will be able to find more imaginative and economical ways ... to do their developing ... without having to sacrifice concerns for the environment. ... [and] developing can still be done to offer them a profit ..." He continued:

> This ... conference will endeavor to inform those contemplating development and subdivision projects of the many regulations which must be met, of the most recent techniques in environmental planning, of the economic realities involved in developing and perhaps most importantly, of the need for coordinated and comprehensive cooperation between private developers and governmental officials if this fragile, but rugged area is to remain beautiful.

About a month after that "developer's conference," a proposal surfaced to transform a 320-acre parcel of ranchland property that a local ranching family, the Rozmans, transferred to a legal entity "Crested Butte Properties, Ltd." so they could develop it. It wanted the County to re-zone the parcel so the company could build 2,785 homes, condos, etc. between the ski area and town. Rademan, despite his formal role as the town's staff planner, wrote a long letter to the editor under the headline, "Don't Kill the Goose That Laid the Golden Egg." He asked citizens to attend a meeting to organize opposition to the proposal and outlined the main reasons, many of which provided the rationale for fighting other developments in succeeding years.

He asked a series of rhetorical questions that implicitly provided the rationale for why the Rozmans' project should be turned down:

> Do WE, as a County have any idea of the goals and aspirations of our people? Do we know if ski areas are more important than elk herds or visa versa? Do we know how much water can be withdrawn from our streams and our ground water table before we dry ourselves out, or are forced to dam some of the most beautiful rivers to provide water? Do we have any idea what effect another 1,000, 2,000 or 10,000 people and their automobiles will have on our psyches? Unfortunately, the answer to these, and most other questions that can be asked, is emphatically, NO! Prior to committing our County to irrevocable land use decisions,

I propose that these and other questions must be answered. ...To prematurely allow this or any other major developments to preempt our public interests for private gains is sheer foolishness at this time.

Several other significant events occurred at about the same time. Jim Kuziak resigned as chairperson of the Board of Zoning and Architectural Review. His personal thinking on what was considered "architecturally appropriate" was changing, and he wondered if he should be passing judgment on designs that were proposed by applicants who came before the Board. He was replaced by Joan Adams, a co-owner of the newly refurbished Elk Mountain Lodge, and a part of the emerging local power structure. Other pro-growth Board members at that time included Myles Arber and Wes Light. Gerry Reese was named the City of Gunnison's judge. The chair of the police committee, who by then was the only remaining pioneer councilmember who did not support growth measures, was replaced by the newly appointed councilman, Ron Rouse. Rouse, after unsuccessfully trying to develop an airstrip a few miles south of town, in fact, did develop it a little later. He also became one of the members of the local power structure. Alan Rowitz, who soon would be elected to the town council owned "The Finishing Touch," with his wife Anne. It specialized in floor coverings and interior design, and depended on the area growing. He too became part of the local power clique and was appointed by the council to direct the new, publicly funded, local bus service, the Stage Line. He died, however, soon thereafter. At about that time, a Home Rule Charter Commission was created to study the feasibility of Crested Butte becoming a home rule town which then, by statute, would be independent from the County and any other municipality in it. Those who took out petitions to serve on the commission included Bruce Baumgartner, Ron Hudleson, Tom Glass, Bill Odell, Wes Light, Joe Rous, Bill Hickok, Bill Crank, and Tom Cox; all but Hudleson, Odell, Rous, and Hickok became important members of the town's local power structure.

Beside local government initiatives, important local businesses changed ownership or were newly created, and private voluntary organizations were formed or revamped. Their leadership often overlapped with the growth faction in the pioneer council or, if they did not, they agreed with them politically. After they purchased a small apartment in town, for example, Tom and Sharon Cox bought their second business, a tourist-oriented gift shop, Gifts and Things. Two months later, Tom Cox was appointed to the town's Board of Adjustment. In the next town election, he was elected to the town council and, later, became mayor.

During that period, several new fine-dining restaurants opened, and others were upgraded. New owners bought and updated existing inns such as the Elk Mountain Lodge. New businesses were started to meet the needs of the burgeoning construction industry, including Houston Lumber Company and The Finishing Touch. The Alpineer broadened its focus to include more forms of non-motorized recreation activities including cross-country skiing, backpacking, technical climbing, kayaking etc., and a separate specialty ski store opened, Crested Butte Sports; it catered to the needs of alpine skiers and fly fisher people.

The Crested Butte Society, which formed six years earlier to promote cultural activities in town and honor the town's mining heritage, elected new officers in the spring of 1973. Ralph Clark became its newly elected President. He had retired as a successful lawyer in Ohio and, with his wife Billie, bought, renovated, and donated an important historic railroad depot to the Society. It was used for hosting quasi-public events. and later it provided office space for non-profit community organizations. Sally Crank chaired the Society's "liaison committee" to the Women's Club, Arts' Council, etc.; and Marcia Hegeman who was one of the Society's founders and the wife of the Town Magistrate, became chair of the membership committee. At the same time, a resort and tourism association formed to market the area and provide services to tourists, a forerunner of the later Crested Butte Chamber of Commerce.

All the changes during the 1972-1974 period were, for the most part, hard fought between those who opposed growth and those who supported it. Notably, in the process a local group of "movers and shakers" emerged who did the "heavy lifting" and became the local power structure. Collectively, they laid an ideological foundation that defined "smart" or "controlled" growth as the political rationale for "preserving" the natural environment, while simultaneously creating a new economic industry dependent on it: recreation and tourism.

Chapter 11

Early Reactions to the New Power Structure

When they first took office, it seemed that the pioneer council wanted to protect and maintain their newfound, isolated, environmentally pristine, picturesque, nirvana, by keeping it, for the most part, as it was. That changed as the "smart" or "controlled" growth-oriented local power structure emerged.

There were three crucial responses to the emergence of that local power faction: first, the departure of most of the counter-culture people, the hippies; second, the publication of a second newspaper, the *Crested Butte Pilot*; and third, the incorporation of Mount Crested Butte, a new town at the ski area.

> *There were three crucial reactions to the emergence of that local power structure: first, the departure of most counter-culture people, the hippies; second, the publication of another newspaper, the Crested Butte Pilot; and third, the incorporation of Mount Crested Butte, a new town at the ski area.*

The departure of most alternate life-style adherents and outlaws, as already noted, began within a year following the historic 1972 council election. Even with their exodus, for the "growth-no-matter-what" advocates, the pioneer councils' "controlled" or "smart" development policies were too limiting. They were perceived as being indistinguishable from anti-growth views, and their unique modifying terminology regarding development was seen as simply a smokescreen by those who wanted rapid growth. They thought the town's new laws and policies were restrictive and bureaucratic, and limited their economic potential.

They thought, for example, that the Board of Zoning and Architectural Review's (BOZAR) processes were too slow and, more importantly, limited what they could build. They thought the positions the town took opposing the Rozman and Callaway proposals to develop new projects illustrated that. Some developers and builders, consequently, confined their work to areas in the Gunnison Valley beyond the town's three miles sphere of influence.

About a year after the installation of the tourist town pioneer council and the emergence of the local power clique that supported smart or controlled growth, the *Crested Butte Pilot* began publication. Its earliest issues made clear that the *Chronicle* no longer reflected the sentiments of the *Pilot's* publishers and editor, nor those of mining-era residents, ski area trailblazers, pro-growth tourist town pioneers, or the early recreation community settlers. Moreover, at about the same time, as hostile relations between people on "the hill" and those living in town continued to intensify, Mount Crested Butte was incorporated.

The launch of the *Pilot* and the incorporation of the new town at the ski area were clear expressions of those who wanted the ski area, the town, and the surrounding valley to grow and prosper, without any constraints.

The *Pilot* was started by ski area trailblazer Sandy Hickok, nee Cortner, who had prior newspaper experience at the *Chronicle* when Sibley edited it. Reared in Arizona, she spent her late teens in Crested Butte during summers and on family ski vacations. She identified strongly with Crested Butte mining-era families, especially the young women. She and her early pioneer "growth-no-matter-what" builder husband, who had been a losing candidate in the 1972 town election (because of his views regarding development), thought that, under Arber's editorship, the *Chronicle* did not represent the perspectives of most locals. In the *Pilot's* first issue, Hickok wrote that the paper would reflect the views of *all* the people in Crested Butte that wanted to make a living from tourists, rather than those who came to town to discover new ways of living.

In her first editorial Hickok wrote, "1) [*The Pilot*] is not the word of God passing through the mouth of a mere mortal" and "2) It is the viewpoint of only one of ... 500 persons in Crested Butte." A prominent front-page photo featured a whimsical picture of Crested Butte mining era resident John Somrak on his 1886 long wooden skis (which were originally called "snow shoes"), with a lengthy, heavy, single wooden pole that was used for balance. Other articles in the first issue focused on resort improvements; other newspaper pieces and pictures highlighted new businesses opening in town.[1]

The newly incorporated town of Mount Crested Butte was essentially a quest for autonomy, especially in relation to Gunnison County and the increasingly organized and influential Crested Butte tourist town pioneer council. It was a reaction to the tensions and hostilities that existed between the slowest-possible-growth pioneers plus the smart or controlled proponents versus those who favored rapid, unrestricted development. A petition drive to create Mount Crested Butte as a new home rule town was launched. According to Allen Cox, signatures were collected practically overnight, mainly from old-timers by the former Crested Butte Mayor, Lyle McNeill. Articulating the public relations rationale for the new town, ski area spokesperson Cal Queal, explained, "We need ... our own police protection, our own zoning codes and architectural controls, our own planning, our own parking ordinances. ... we have to control our own future. ... We know some of the people in Town have a feeling that a rivalry exists between the Town and Ski Area. We also know that some differences are necessarily conflicting or that most of the differences cannot be reconciled". He continued, in a way that many pioneers felt was a typical patronizing ski area view of the new townspeople, "We appreciate Town as a highly unusual place with a *very interesting* (emphasis added) assortment of people ..."

■ ■ ■

The ownership groups and editors of the two weekly town newspapers reflected the difference between the rapid and slow growth proponents. As noted earlier, beginning in the summer of 1968, the *Chronicle* stopped being owned and edited by people whose roots were in Texas, Kansas, and Colorado, and who identified with the "old west" culture and supported the ski area development. The paper was turned over to owners and an editor who had big city or suburban origins on the west and east coasts, who came from families with professional and business backgrounds and who had been influenced by the progressive social movements of the 1960's. The first new pioneer *Chronicle* editors opposed some of the old west ways and ski area interests. Arber, especially, used the paper to call for political change at the local level as soon as he bought the paper, and he called for changes that appealed to the new pioneers' youth-culture oriented identity.

When tourist town pioneers won the 1972 council election, Arber owned the paper. Although feelings of alienation began to emerge among older townspeople and trailblazers during Sibley's tenure as owner/editor, they became dramatically more pronounced when Arber took over. Many mining-era residents and early ski area trailblazers thought that newspaper no longer represented their views and interests; or that it was even fair-minded.

Bickering between the two newspaper editors began as soon as the *Pilot* began publication. Differentiating itself from the *Chronicle*, Hickok immediately implied that the existing weekly represented the views of only a minority. A year later she wrote, "... today is the first Birthday of the *Crested Butte Pilot*. ... conceived to bridge ... a gap between the media and its readers." As was often the case during the height of the newspaper years in big cities, in Crested Butte there effectively was a more liberal and a more conservative paper. That could be seen in the format of each paper and, more critically, in the subjects they covered and editorial positions they took.

Although often cloaked in high minded rhetoric like "community interest" or "who speaks for whom," sniping between the papers' editors became increasingly frequent, intense, and personal. Beginning with an April 6, 1973 editorial questioning Arber's appointment to the Architectural Review Board, Hickok wrote:

> ... six town trustees chose Myles Arber to fill the position on the archi-tectural control board .... The Council and the audience present laughed ... a Trustee asked him if he could 'get it together to attend meetings.' ... there were references to the '*Crested Butte Comical*' ... we fail to see how a Council which only a few months ago was concerned that its proposed ordinances were endangered by late and missed publi-cations in the *Chronicle*, can treat so lightly the matter of putting this man on an Architectural Control Board which has the power to affect this town ...

Two-and-a half months later, Hickok attacked again, claiming the editor had a conflict of interest because the *Chronicle* received town monies for the legal ads his paper published when it announced the Architectural Review Board's public hearings.

The town's legal notice advertising amounted to a substantial sum for a small weekly, and the two papers openly competed for it. The intensity of the two papers' fights was based not only on politics and personalities; it also had an economic basis. Beginning when the *Chronicle* was written and published in Gunnison, the Town of Crested Butte routinely published its legal notices in it. That made it "the official newspaper of Crested Butte." George Sibley, the first pioneer editor, wrote in personal correspondence that he "brought the newspaper back to Crested Butte." He said, "Prior to my taking it over ... B&B Printing ... also put out the *Gunnison Globe*. Most of the news in the *Chronicle* ... was recycled *Globe* news, of more interest to Gunnison than CB ... by keeping the masthead alive ... he [Fred Budy of B & B Printing] was able to continue getting the Town of Crested Butte's legal advertising." For a few years after Hickok launched the *Pilot*, that historical practice was hotly contested. For financial viability, each editor needed to publish the town's official notices.

The battle over who published public notices was fought fiercely in council meetings and in both newspapers; and involved the different political factions. Forecasting that there would be competition for the town's legal notices, co-publisher Bill Hickok told the council in early November 1973 that the *Pilot* wanted to submit a competing bid. Without explanation, however, the council delayed the process for six months. Soon afterwards, Arber announced his newspaper's growth, quite probably as a way of laying the groundwork for it to retain the official notices. He crowed, "... The *Chronicle* has grown past the two thousand mark in paid circulation ... It has become a truly county-wide publication and at present enjoys even wider readership in Gunnison than it does locally. It has...grown...from a four-page weekly to an average 20-24 page weekly ..." Sandy Hickok, after the *Pilot's* first full year of publication when she legally could compete for the town notices, challenged his numbers and touted her own paper's growth.

Even though Arber's bid was almost twice that of the *Pilot's*, and the townspeople and elected officials were extremely cost conscious, the council inexplicably awarded its advertising to the *Chronicle*, causing intense community-wide conflict. He had been part of the emerging power clique that championed pro-smart or controlled growth development as were Mayor Crank, Councilmen Glass and Gallagher, and Town Attorney David Leinsdorf. At key decision-making moments in the ensuing few years, they each supported the *Chronicle's* bid for the legal notice contract.

Three letters to the editor summarized the community outrage. The first was written by pioneer entrepreneur Steve Glazer:

> ... The *Chronicle* bid '.21 a line' for the legal notices and the 'Official Town Newspaper' title, while the Pilot came in with a bid of a drastically lower '.12 per line'. Without any discussion a motion was made to accept the Pilot's bid. The motion died. ... I was flabbergasted! Before another motion was brought to the floor I asked why they were ready to accept a higher bid when such a large discrepancy existed. ... The same motion was brought to the floor again, by Ron Rouse and seconded by Tom Glass. A vote was taken and the motion was defeated with the Mayor voting "no" to break the tie. The question was then raised ... if there was any conflict of interests. .... Everyone remained silent except for the red-faced Tom Glass who claimed that his wife's position on the *Chronicle* did not influence his vote. I feel that Jim Cole [whose wife also worked at the *Chronicle*] and/or Tom Glass should have abstained ... By not disqualifying themselves ... they allowed this town to pay almost twice as much money for its legal notices. ... Do we want to see this town run by people whose personal interests interfere with efficient thrifty government? I think the free competitive marketplace should determine who reads what and where they'll read it.

Another letter, written a few weeks later by a new recreation community settler businessman, Bill Haley, was equally irate:

> Shades of Mayor Daley, Chicago, present era and Boss Ed Crumpf, Memphis, Tenn., late '20's, early 30's and Huey P. Long. ... I thought I was relocating to a place where big city politics would be left far behind. ... I refer to the "railroading" of a decision of the Council to pay almost double to put legal notices in a newspaper whose readability, eye appeal and print is far inferior to 'the other newspaper' in Crested Butte. ...

Paying a higher price for poorer quality smacks of petty politics, payola, stupidity, Boss Rule, and/or deals!

Following further controversy, politicking, and legal threats, the Council reaffirmed its original decision. Leinsdorf reasoned that the town was within its rights to award the legal publications to the *Chronicle* and by so doing, it had entered into a binding contract. The dispute continued.

A third letter was written a month later by Marcia Hegeman. She was an early pioneer who helped found the Crested Butte Women's Club and the Crested Butte Society, two prestigious community non-profit organizations that supported growth of the town economy and its focus on tourism. She pointedly expressed the outrage of many residents who were concerned about the Council's decision and town expenditures. In a letter to the president of the Women's Club, with copies to the editors of both papers, she announced her resignation:

> The recent decision of the Mayor and some members of the Town Board of Trustees to spend an additional $3,000.00 of town funds as a result of taking the high bid for legal publications indicates to me that the Town of Crested Butte does not need the financial support of the Crested Butte Women's Club. Notwithstanding this, the Club has decided to pay $700.00 for a sand box and animal play sculpture for the Town Park. ... as long as ... the Women's Club is willing to provide such gifts, the Town will continue spending funds in other ways which will benefit only special interests and not the entire population. ... the Club's funds are being spent irresponsibly ... I can no longer support the...Club. After a five-year association ... this decision is not easily or happily made.

After the Council decision was reaffirmed using Leinsdorf's rationale, a *Pilot* editorial opined what many other townspeople were saying

> ... we must express our supreme disappointment in the Council. ... it appears Crested Butte has its own political machine. ... with the Eastern escapees who have come to town lately bringing big city politics with them and seizing the opportunity to be big frogs in a little town. Its high time we all started to open our eyes and see who really controls this town.

During the next two years competition for the legal notices further intensified, and public fighting between the editors became more personal as the council deliberated about which paper would get them. When the residents who lived "on the hill" in 1973 incorporated Mount Crested Butte, it too needed to publish legal notices, and both papers wanted to be its "official publication."

When the two papers again competed for Crested Butte's legal advertising after the 1974 town general election, many were surprised by the result. Before the bids were actually submitted, a new council member, Vicki Baumgartner, a community school teacher and a member of the local power clique, tried to make a motion about which paper would get the right to publish the official notices. According to the *Pilot:*

> [it} was interrupted by Sandy Hickok's walk to the table to hand in her sealed bid as requested. Myles Arber ... did the same .... **The *Pilot's* bid was ... half of what the town is now paying [bold typeface – sic] ....** Councilman Glass pointed out that the *Pilot* bid would represent a 43 percent savings. ... **Rouse reentered his motion favoring the *Pilot* which was seconded by Glass. A roll call vote resulted in Cobai, Rouse and Somrak voting for, with a pass by Glass. When he was called to vote, he voted no and the tie was broken by another no vote on the part of Mayor Crank resulting in the *Chronicle* being reappointed ... (sic).**

Two "no" votes were cast by Baumgartner and Jim Cole. Notably, Baumgartner, Glass, and Crank were part of the local power clique that wanted growth.

In late 1974 Crested Butte became a home rule town. That granted it autonomy in decision making, which was especially important in relation to the County and other municipalities in it. In January 1975, it held a new election, its first under the new charter. Hickok became one of the twelve candidates to run for the available six Council seats. Despite the *Chronicle's* vehement opposition, she won. Each editor, while hardly acknowledging the financial benefit of the official notices award, continued using the newspapers to attack each other politically and personally.

First, an early March 1975 *Crested Butte Pilot* feature headlined "Mt. C.B. Spends $1,000 to Check Legal Publication Charges" reported:

In the analysis of what was felt to be an exorbitant bill for legal notice publications, the Town of Mt. Crested Butte, since last September has incurred expenses and attorney fees in the amount of $1,047.50. A memorandum, prepared by Town Manager James Dean…explained that Myles Arber of the Crested Butte Chronicle, the town's official newspaper had submitted a bill on Sept. 25 for legal publications from Oct. 18, 1973 through Sept. 5, 1974 in the amount of $13,442.92 …. Feeling that the bill was excessively high, the town … requested the billing … be analyzed by Fred Budy of B & B printers. Budy's computations … shaved $7,311.87 off the bill. … one of the town attorneys also refigured the bill, coming up with a total of $7,361.18 [and] then recommended that the town pay $6,746.12 (sic) … one half of the difference between his and Budy's figures. … Arber then submitted a revised bill reflecting the approximate $4,500 error but including $836.28 in interest at 1% per month since November, 1973. However, the original contract made … no mention of interest. Arber also included an overtime printing charge of $525 and billed the second printing of the zoning ordinance as a first time printing …. Arber requested that Bruce Bye, a former partner in B & B Printers, analyze the bill. Bye's final figure presented … amounted to $4,898.62 showing a Chronicle overcharge of $8,544.30…

A few weeks later the *Chronicle* headline taunted "Cast Ye Not the First Stone, Ms. Hickok" and began:

In another of her frequent diatribes last week against the *Crested Butte Chronicle*, … Councilwoman Sandra Hickok, searching desperately for something to say to support her pretense to be worthy of any intelligent person's attention for more than a few painful seconds, made a feeble attempt to dredge up some dirt regarding the association of the *Chronicle* and the municipal entities for whom the *Chronicle* serves as the official legal publisher. … Ms. Hickok gags publicly every few weeks on the fact that the *Chronicle* won the contracts on the legal publications …. Her claim of seeking to serve the interests of these municipal entities in the name of altruism and public concern is as hollow as almost everything else the girl has said in a public context …. Ms. Hickok has vented her private frustrations at not … getting any… legal notices. … She is still nursing her wounds in public that … the Crested Butte Town

Council said last year, in effect, that to buy cheap is to get cheap, and summarily rejected her bid...

He continued:

Rather than...try to slide through a Council meeting fluttering her eye-lashes to help cloak insipid and unconstructive remarks .... she could be devoting her attentions to something worthwhile .... She detracts great-ly by her mere presence and mode of thought from the strength of a Council, and .... said absolutely nothing worthwhile .... We hope the community will by now have learned the lesson that some basic bottom twitching by Ms. Hickok in public should not mask the more essential fact of the daily inanities we must suffer hearing on things she doesn't have the faintest notion about.

The next week, Hickok responded:

Myles Arber's wiley [sic] red herring toss to the taxpayers of Crested Butte and Mt. Crested Butte in his last ... editorial ... should be high-ly commended by those skilled in the craft of artful dodging. His venom venting and slanderous treatment ... is nothing new. ... However, the question of professionalism and sound business practices remain to be answered: 1) Why was the Town of Mt. Crested Butte overcharged by over $8,500 for its legal notice publications? 2) Why did it take you a month instead of your promised week ... to submit a revised bill ... 3) Why must Crested Butte's Town Clerk ... act as a watchdog to insure that the town is not charged for unauthorized publications? 4) Why do I hear so many complaints from advertisers that a) You quote the adver-tiser a price for an ad and the subsequent bill is higher than the quoted price? b) Unauthorized ads are run until the advertiser loudly complains and even then he is charged for the ad? c) A prospective advertiser is badgered into running an ad because you tell him 'everyone else is'... 5) Why over the past 2 ½ years have so many summer residents and out-of-town subscribers to both our newspapers come into my office and told me that although they have not paid for a subscription to the *Chronicle* for 3-5 years they still receive it? Some have even told me that although they paid for one, two *Chronicles* arrive. ... Admittedly, all the above practices do wonders for circulation figures and cash flow. But no journalist worth his salt would consider you a member of his profession. .... I nicked your ego by starting a newspaper .... I'd suggest to any other fed-up citizens that they continue what I began by striking where it really hurts – in the pocketbook. In the meantime, they should demand an answer to ... those questions.

In the same issue, a letter to the editor from a community cartoonist defended Hickok:

> It was my misfortune to have most recently read, in the Official ... Newspaper of the Town of Crested Butte, one of the best (or worst!) (sic) examples of irresponsible smear journalism I have ever had the occasion to peruse. ... Presumably, Mr. Arber's remarks were intended to be a "defense" .... Mr. Arber chose instead to launch a personal attack on you [Hickok]. ... I took your remarks ... to be a relatively unbiased report of the difficulties encountered in the settling of the *Chronicle* account for the Town legal publications, with there being a considerable discrepancy between the amounts claimed owed by the *Chronicle* and the amounts believed owed by both Towns. ... insofar as tax revenues support the expenditures ... then over-inflated billings are definitely of public concern, and .... whatever damage such a report could have done to Mr. Arber's credibility ... was as nothing when compared to his so immature, emotional, frustratedly (sic) nonsensical attack on your well-being. ... I can no longer condone his unsavory methods. ... I personally would like to see the *Pilot* as the new official newspaper.

Hickok's short term as a public official ended. She won one of the "short" council terms. The three lowest vote getters' in the first Home Rule town election served less than a year. Hickok was a candidate in that election, but lost. The town council morphed once again, making it still more growth oriented.

Former Councilman Tom Glass became the new mayor. He and *all* the new council members favored growth. When the subject of awarding legal notices arose the next time, in July 1976, Glass abstained because his wife was a *Chronicle* photographer (although he did not do so earlier when he was a council member). The mayor also asked Councilman McMillan to abstain because his wife was the *Pilot's* managing editor, and for Ken Hall to do the same because he was living with Hickok's sister. Despite protests from Councilperson Ingham, who wanted the contract to be bid and the bids to be included as part of the Council's consideration, the legal notices were awarded to the *Chronicle*. This time, moreover, the contract was given on an annual basis with *automatic* renewals; someone would have to object prior to the beginning of any given future year before a renewal was not awarded. That maneuver effectively guaranteed that the *Chronicle* got the legal notice contract in perpetuity.

The following week's *Pilot* editorial was short and sweet, as was a letter from a Denver subscriber:

> Crested Butte Taxpayers: you got ripped off. It wasn't a gigantic rip-off. It was a repeat rip-off. Two years ago the Town Council accepted a bid for publishing its legal notices – the highest bid. ... This year the Council didn't even bother to take bids. Its members probably figured that way they wouldn't have to hear the harangue they heard two years ago. They were right.

The Denver letter writer said:

> Regarding your July 16 article on the Council's award of the news contract without bids: .... That kind of arrogance is illustrative of how the Crested Butte Council has been and continues to rip off the taxpaying citizens of Crested Butte. Unless you speak up, the practice will continue unabated. Is that what you want? What other citizens want?

A longer letter to the *Pilot* editor appeared the following week from Gary Christopher, the vociferous, long-time critic of the established local power structure:

> ... Sandy is right, you did get ripped off. ... the taxpayers lost and every person who has to pay all the costs of a legal notice out of his own pocket lost. As ... one of the few citizens ... to witness the episode, I can tell you how it all happened. ...Tommy Glass and Todd McMillan disqualified themselves as their wives were or had been working for one of the papers. Then came an attack on Ken Hall because he was living with Sandy's sister. Wes Light, town attorney stated that the conflict of interest rules were stricter than he previously thought. ... that led Ken Hall to abstain. ... It is ironic that Ken Hall would have to rely on Wes Light's interpretation ... when he, Wes Light, helped write the guidelines in the charter and now advises the Council even though his wife or ex-wife ... sits on the Council and votes. ... With the stage thus set it

was easy for the power group to ram the proposal through giving the *Chronicle* in essence the legal notices forever without even pretending to be democratic about it. … Only John Ingham tried to stop it … trying to convince Tom Cox, Alan Rowitz, and Candy Light that what they were doing was unfair and wrong, but Tom Cox as usual was interested in power and not the democratic process. …. Because of Tom Cox's, Candy Light's and Alan Rowitz's vote, we are being cheated.

In her last comment on the council's decision, Hickok wrote:

A Council member came to me last week apologizing for what may have been a hasty decision to reappoint the *Chronicle* the town paper without taking bids. … he had been told I refused to release circulation figures and that my circulation was only 400. A bit stunned, I explained that circulation figures are a matter of public record and that as of October, 1975 in a postal statement which is required to be filed and published every year, my average press run for the previous year was 1,400 and average paid circulation about 1,000. Then I asked where he had come by his mis-information. It turned out to be none other than my competitor. This Councilman was willing to see if the matter could be reopened … but discovered … that town attorney Wes Light felt a legal contract had been entered into … that could not be broken…

Crested Butte never did award the coveted "official newspaper" designation to the *Pilot*, but two other public entities did. In the paper's third anniversary issue in November 1975, thanking her readers, Hickok wrote, "The *Pilot*'s birth … was easy. Its existence has been … let's just say, we're No. 2 and scrappy fighters. … It is your support that makes this birthday celebration possible. An extra bonus is our recent designation as the official paper for the town of Mt. Crested Butte. We have also, for the past year, been the official publication for the Crested Butte Fire Protection District."

Financial pressure on the *Pilot* continued to mount, and in mid-December 1975, in a front-page piece, Hickok announced a raise in its ad and subscription rates and, in doing so, further disparaged her competition. In an unfortunate, harshly stereotypical, way, she wrote:

... prices, my dear readers and advertisers, must go up. ...our new rates will still be lower than those of our friendly but avaricious competition. ... I may never be able to compete with my Jewish counterpart, but for you ... I have a special DEAL! Subscribe or renew now during this month only at the regular rate. ...

Deeply apologetic, Hickok began the Pilot editorial the following week:

Last Thursday night ... I realized I'd committed a rather serious, but unintentional faux pas. Last week's front story on the ad and subscription rate hike was not intended as an ethnic slur to Myles Arber or anyone else, ... If I really wanted to attack Arber [and we signed a peace pact this fall], I certainly could find a more effective way to do it. ... I am sincerely sorry if I offended anyone and Arber has already been the recipient of my personal apologies.

A little more than a year later Hickok stopped publishing what by then had become the ten-page, *Crested Butte Pilot*, and she sold it. Arber tried to buy it but Hickok would not sell to him. In 2006, using her birth name, Sandra Cortner, she wrote an autobiographical collection of stories and histories of the old-timers and newcomers, "Crested Butte Stories ...Through My Lens." In the chapter describing her newspapering experiences and her final days with the *Pilot* she wrote:

... I put the word out that I wanted to sell ... Myles skulked over late one winter night. Reluctantly, I let him inside. 'I want to buy the *Pilot* and the building,' he announced without preamble. 'Why?' I sat on the other side of the narrow room as far away from him as I could get. 'Simple, to buy out the competition.' He snickered nervously. His high pitched [sic] New York City voice grated on me. I was mildly flattered to hear him finally admit we were competition after years of referring to the *Pilot* as a throwaway gossip sheet. ...My stomach turned over at the thought of selling out to him, of giving up and letting down all the people who had supported the *Pilot* for four years .... 'Forget it.'

Shortly thereafter Hickok sold the paper to two friends who later re-sold it. In the spring of 1985, after several other publishers and editors, Arber bought *The Pilot* and combined it with the *Chronicle*. Once again,

Crested Butte had only one town newspaper, the merged *"Crested Butte Chronicle and Pilot.*

■　■　■

Mining-era residents and ski area trailblazers both wanted the resort to succeed and grow but in the last years of the 1960s the new Crested Butte immigrants began arriving with a different agenda. They were part of the late '60s and early '70s youth culture, what the broader society deemed "drop-outs" or "hippies." They wanted to keep their isolated, uncrowded, inexpensive, ski town "private," and unfettered by the socio-political tensions of the times. By the close of the ski season in April 1971, it became obvious to practically everyone in Gunnison County that relations between the ski area and these new townspeople were strained and painful.

The term "turkey," was widely used by pioneers as a pejorative term meaning "tourist," especially those from Texas who were not wise to the ways of mountain living. It offended both visitors and ski area businesspeople, who depended on skiers for their livelihood. Allen Cox, proprietor of the Nordic Inn was one of the "human bridges" between ski area people and those in town. In a 2014 interview he vividly remembered:

> The people on the hill thought the town was filling up with undesirables – dirty, unwashed, living in miners' shacks with 5-10 people in each, doing drugs, etc. We felt that if tourists went downtown, they wouldn't come back again because they were so unwelcome there. There was an anti-tourist thing going on in town. Tourists were called 'turkeys,' gobbled at, and given the finger. We made our living from tourists, and townspeople didn't like them. They also didn't like the hill people but wanted ski passes. All that helped create the divide.

He added poignantly, "Ranchers weren't great friends of the new Crested Butte people either."

Supporting Cox' recollections, another tourist town pioneer remembered that even children were calling tourists "turkey," and bar brawls occurred when visitors took offense at the epithet and felt the need to defend themselves. By the time Crested Butte Sports, the first boutique alpine ski shop, opened in town at the end of 1972, the term had become ingrained in pioneers' everyday jargon. The ski store's tongue-in-cheek advertisements were based on identifying a town local who did something deemed stupid during the prior week, like getting a car stuck in a snow bank, and labeling him or her "Turkey of the Week." The shop then advertised its new skis and other wares. Paradoxically, by then it was becoming increasingly clear to most townspeople that tourism had become the basis of the new town economy; and newspaper commentaries and a local community-wide verbal education effort was initiated to stop town residents from using the term.

When Arber became editor of the *Chronicle*, he commented on a Walt Disney movie, *Snowball Express,* that was filmed in town. He noted the ski area welcomed the attendant publicity, but that the strong sentiment of some town counter-culturists was that they wanted to avoid any, and to keep the town a secret.

Tensions between the town and "the hill" continued to intensify as the tourist town council initially took positions that opposed growth and development, not only within the town limits, but also at the ski area. They thought *any* development would spoil the environment that they thought attracted tourists.

Myles Rademan of BKR Associates did most of the intellectual work that defined the natural environment, "wild-life and wilderness," as the economic underpinning for the tourism industry. Probably the town's most effective organizer, he first mobilized the town pioneers to actively oppose growth, though rhetorically he used the term "unplanned growth." (He noted forty years later that Saul Alinsky, the Chicago based "dean" of community organizers, was one of his most important intellectual influences in graduate school. From an "Alinskian perspective" that was ironic because Alinsky organized powerless *poor* people of color in urban communities to fight for their rights, while Rademan organized privileged, white, newly-rural, downwardly-mobile-by-choice, mountain hippies).

In June 1973, the results of a BKR Associates study were released. It showed how much the town had grown, from 372 residents in 1970 to 693 in 1973, and that townspeople were either totally against growth anywhere in the area or wanted it limited to town. A substantial majority said they wanted the town to remain the same size as it was. Virtually everyone wanted open space preserved (98%). Ninety-nine per cent favored having strong controls placed on development to preserve the mountain environment. Indicating the "return to the land' consciousness of most tourist town pioneers, almost two-thirds said if they left Crested Butte, they would move to an even smaller town or a rural area.

That survey was used to help mobilize people in town to fight when development issues arose at the county level. Rademan projected, incorrectly though perhaps strategically for organizing purposes, that the town "might see a population of 5,000" by the year 2000 and reported that in the county 28,000 living units had already been approved for development.

Following the release of the study, *Pilot* editor Sandra Hickok wrote that she generally agreed with old-timers and ski area trailblazers that wanted unrestricted development, that she did not see a need for planning at first. But after reading the results of the report she thought, "Our attitude and perhaps that of many other people in town has been one similar to the ostrich who sticks his head in the sand. ... the town is growing and the valley around it will be developed. It is time we started dealing aggressively with that fact...."

In mid-October, as noted previously, the town opposed a proposal by a prominent Gunnison County ranching family to develop 2,785 dwelling units between it and the base area of the resort. The county commissioners voted against the project. That led to further polarization between the town, the ranchers, and the people on the hill.

Another major development, one that the Crested Butte Development Corporation proposed, came before the County Commissioners at about the same time. It was for a 3,600 acre-parcel six-miles south of town. The ski company wanted to develop a second resort that could accommodate 5,700 people, and would have had two chairlifts, a gondola, an eighteen-hole golf course, fishing, rafting, tennis facilities, an equestrian center, a main clubhouse, restaurants, town condominium villages, clustered individual housing units, employee housing, medical and firefighting facilities, road maintenance, and snow removal equipment. It too was opposed by the pioneer town council. Ultimately, the county commissioners also voted against it. That further intensified animosities between the new people in town and the mining-era residents and ranchers.

Not only did the new town residents fight growth proposals, they opposed some of the resort's operating policies. As already noted, a class-action lawsuit was filed against the area because it wanted to close a week early. When the ski area manager, Gus Larkin, announced a settlement of the case he said, "It's been a good season and we don't want it to end on a sour note. ...the plaintiff obviously thinks he was cheated and there may be others who feel the same way. We trust our decision will...dispel any such feelings..." The *Pilot's* commentary illustrated the differences between the trailblazers and pioneers:

> "... when the ski area was first developed, the town of Crested Butte had essentially no income except for the smattering of summer tourists and homeowners. ... The people who came to live in the town with the inception of the ski area depended solely on the tourist for their living. ... Most of us came to ski and ... earn our living from ... the ski area. It's time we stopped looking upon it as a 'big bad brother' and earnestly try to compatibly live with it ..."

The pioneer town government represented the wishes of the anti-growth and controlled growth factions at first, and opposed everything the ski area wanted to do. In reaction, petitions were circulated to create a new "home rule" town at the base of the resort.

Thoughts about incorporating a new town had been simmering for a while. In September 1973, a *Chronicle* banner headline screamed, "Ski Area Planning Incorporation as Town." It said that action was kept relatively secret and, in fact, was thought first to have been conceived by the ski corporation itself. Incorporation as a home-rule community would free the area from County constraints. The piece also implied that there were substantial tensions between the Town and the hill, and explicitly quoted the official resort spokesman, "We ... have to control our own future"

The front page of the *Crested Butte Pilot* had a similar headline: "Ski Area Petitions for Incorporation." The piece named two people as the circulators. Differing from Cox's memory of McNeill circulating the petition among old-timers, it said "Jeff Jacobsen and Steve Lokey, homeowners at the Crested Butte Ski Area and real estate salesmen for the Crested Butte

Development Corporation began circulating a petition … among ski area residents calling for the incorporation of the area as a town, to be called Mt. Crested Butte. … if all is in order, a Court Order shall decree the formation of the town. The whole procedure could take about two months …"

Two weeks later there was another front-page piece on the organizers of the election who urged all eligible electors to vote and support forming the new town. After three more weeks yet another story appeared in the *Pilot* that gave many of the reasons for the proposed new town to incorporate and, implicitly, alluded to many of the town vs. hill conflicts and quoted much of the proposed town incorporators rational:

> … we are not simply a community; rather… a community with our own special interests, our own kinds of people, our own needs and goals – and they often differ from those of other communities. … We have a need and a right to control our destiny as a community. …. There is little logic in continuing to depend on the county or on other municipalities to call the shots for us.

On November 1, 1973, expressing the pioneer and early settler sentiments within Crested Butte, the *Chronicle* again editorialized about the proposed new entity and, implicitly, concerns about growth:

> … we have formulated what we believe to be the major doubts we have about the incorporation issue … 1) Is the Crested Butte Development Corporation, to further consolidate its control over the Ski Area and give added leverage and freedom to the real estate interests it promotes, simply trying to push this incorporation through? Is it pursuing its own financial and political interests with little chance for the other people who will be affected to find out what is going on? … 2) Does the ski area have the right to a name like 'Mount Crested Butte" and if it is so important for its residents to become an entity separate from the Town of Crested Butte why not make the distinction more stark …? 3) Is the incorporation just a ploy so the CBDC will be able to escape County zoning and enable them to slice up the remaining land any which way; cut roads … that will blight the landscape; and erect tall buildings and sub-divide into town-sized lots, thus changing for the worse the environment we all have to live with? 4) Is the move the beginning of a major expansionary move in which the Ski Area will build a jet airport in the Valley, open up a lot of commercial space, annex everything in

sight, and start to slide down the Mountain to the Town, engulfing all in its path? 5) Will corporate status enable the Ski Area to compete with the Town for annexation, political influence in the County, and state and federal funding on terms which, in view of the political connections and economic power of the former, will prove to be little contest? 6) Will the promoters of incorporation find some way to ramrod the issue past the voters and will the resulting town be, in effect, just a "company town" thoroughly controlled by the CBDC?

The following week both newspapers announced the results of the election: out of 89 registered electors, 70% cast ballots; by a vote of 50-12 the residents voted overwhelmingly to incorporate Mount Crested Butte as a home rule town.

Then, in the beginning of 1974, local residents took out nominating petitions and held their first election. Gus Larkin, general manager of the ski area, was elected mayor; Jeff Jacobson and Steve Lokey, both salesmen in the ski area's real estate company, were elected to the town council, as was Allen Cox and Betty Aiken, proprietors of ski area lodges, and Bob McDaniel's and Rix Rixford, all of whom served as the new town's initial trustees. Cox, who served for many years as a council member and then mayor of Mt. Crested Butte, intoned somewhat hesitatingly forty plus years after its incorporation, "Mt. Crested Butte was essentially a company town."

The formal incorporation of Mount Crested Butte established a second autonomous mountain town within a three-mile area. It developed in a contemporary modern mountain style with large hotels, condominiums, and houses. It openly supported development, was more "Republican" in its culture and politics and, at least for the duration of Bo Callaway and Ralph Walton's ownership of the ski area, had a southern orientation in its marketing efforts (compared to the Town of Crested Butte which increasingly had been supporting smart or controlled growth and Victorian style architecture, "Democratic" thinking and politics, and marketed itself to a more eastern and west coast culture.) Although there were still town versus ski area cultural conflicts, they became less intense. Each town wanted growth and prosperity for what was now clear to all: both towns were clearly economically dependent on recreation and tourism.

Chapter 12

Town Politics and Elections: 1974-1976

By the spring 1974 election, the dominant values in the Town of Crested Butte had changed. Most of the remaining pioneers and many others wanted growth. They often couched their rhetoric in "controlled" or "smart" development terms and sometimes even feigned that they wished things would not change. Tom Glass's 1974 opening statement at the candidates' forum illustrated that: "Even though I'd like the town to remain as it is, that's impossible because we can't stop people from coming here so we need to plan for it." Collectively, the winners of that year's election all favored growth. They constituted the first "recreation community settlers" council.

By the spring 1974 election, the dominant values in the Town of Crested Butte had changed. Most of the remaining pioneers and many others wanted growth. ... Collectively, the winners of that year's election ... constituted the first "recreation community settlers" council.

Although the tourist town pioneer council that was elected in 1972 did not include any old-timers or ski area trailblazers, in the 1974 election two born and bred Crested Butte residents, John Cobai and Jim Somrak, and ski area trailblazer Jim Cole, won. Having been completely shut out two years earlier, the mining-era residents and ski area trailblazers strategized for this election. They decided not to vote for six council candidates and only voted for the few they actually wanted. Their strategy worked, and they were again able to gain a voice in council deliberations and decisions. By then, even candidates who lived their entire lives in Crested Butte and held old-West values and who backed the ski area since its inception, politically supported "smart" or "controlled" growth, even though they thought those terms implied government control. They wanted streets paved, more restrictions on dogs, and a crackdown on drug use, so they supported zoning and architectural control. They also wanted Crested Butte to become a "home rule" town which, by then, virtually all voters recognized as another structural initiative that would not only give the town greater autonomy, it would allow Crested Butte to develop faster, even if it was in the Victorian style preferred by the newcomers. Given that the community's leadership wanted home rule, including *all* the council members, in that year's election, a separate ballet proposal to establish a Home Rule Charter Commission passed overwhelmingly (241-22). All but one of the commissioner members subsequently elected to that Commission favored as much development as possible, as quickly as possible.

By the 1974 election, there was hardly any political support for anti or very slow growth proponents. Each candidate who even suggested limiting growth, lost by a large margin. Al Appleby was the anti-growth mayoralty candidate. He ran on a platform calling for town resources to be used for social programs, rather than for pursuing economic development. He argued that the town had misplaced its priorities and said the pioneer council was a "business Council...that couldn't govern the town and ... divorce themselves from their private interests." He received 46 votes compared to the growth-oriented incumbent mayor, Bill Crank, who got 241. Most candidates who lost opposed growth or wanted to limit it. Two even owned businesses: Barry Cornman received only 127 votes; Judy Naumberg, received 99. Both were defined as sharing the views and lifestyles of alternate life-style and outlaw pioneers. Other losing candidates campaigned on platforms that opposed tourist-oriented development. Peggy Roggenbuck, for instance, an actor and playwright who came to town to join the Crested Butte Mountain Theater defined herself as an "independent artist;" she received 79 votes. She clearly differentiated herself from the winning candidates. Roggenbuck said she neither owned a business or real estate, or had any other financial interests; nor did she have rich parents. She called for a "Zero Growth" policy for the town and argued that residents like her were not represented on the council.

By the 1974 election .... Each candidate who even suggested limiting growth, lost by a large margin.

In 1974, comparatively few residents cast votes. Many pioneers who voted in the '72 election did so because they did not want growth, and voted for the candidates they thought shared their views. As Appleby's comments implied, they felt betrayed by the tourist town pioneer council, and thought that their wishes and votes did not matter. Presumably, many pioneers were disillusioned by those officials who were elected in '72, and their refusal to inhibit development and keep the town as it was. Those pioneers again became alienated from the political process as they had been before the previous election. Although the town's population grew to over 700 residents between 1972 and 1974, in the spring 1974 election, only 291 ballots were cast, compared to 383 in the previous one.

In its first meeting after the 1974 election, the first "recreation community settlers council" enacted a stricter dog leash law. The *Chronicle* was again named as the town's official newspaper and awarded its legal notices. Mayor Crank announced to attending audience members who were angry and outspoken because he had unilaterally fired Marshal Coit, that they could all go home if they wished without it bothering him or the new councilmembers. The *Chronicle* editorialized about the new growth-oriented council under the heading, "Sizing up the new Council":

> … certain things are fairly evident …. the majority of the Council represent a very similar socio-economic and political minority in the Town. … These people … seem more like technocrats than ideologues, more like doers than thinkers and talkers …. These people were not elected on the basis of any sweeping social vision. … The group … will offer far more support to the Mayor. … the new Council undoubtedly represents a conservative outlook …

After eight months, John Cobai resigned the council seat he had won. He was replaced by a pro-growth recreation community settler appointee, Todd McMillan. That further solidified the power of the mayor and the smart growth council faction, most of whom by then were core members of the local power structure.

A little later an important vacancy at the County level was filled that helped the emerging town power clique spread its influence more widely, and become even stronger. Bill Crank, was named to the county's planning commission. He had chosen not to run in the first "home rule" electoral contest after having been re-elected mayor in the 1974 election. By the beginning of 1975, he was a *former* Crested Butte mayor, and was named to the county's planning commission. His appointment was pushed by the newest Gunnison County commissioner, David Leinsdorf. A few months later, two new proposals to develop an airstrip near town competed at the county level. Unlike the previous discussions during the pioneer council's term, this debate was, significantly, not about whether to have an airstrip, but where to put it.

One site was favored by the old-timers and a few early trailblazers on property owned by long-time area rancher Tony Verzuh. The other was on another nearby property developed by councilmember Ron Rouse, part of the pro-growth local power group. His proposal was supported by, among others, County Planning Commissioner Crank, Mayor Tom Glass, a spokesperson for the ski area, and by Myles Arber. Reflecting Leinsdorf's influence in the County Commission, the commissioners voted to support Rouse's application.

A few months later the Crested Butte Businessmen's Association elected new officers. They included businessman and newly elected councilman Tom Cox, and successful restaurateur Eric Roemer. Roemer was the first person in town to articulate that promoting summer tourism could increase the revenue of businesses and, because of the town's now existing sales tax, the town's as well. The businessman's association and the Town of Crested Butte jointly awarded a contract to publicize the area to attract summer business to three women, all of whom were part of the emerging local power structure. At about the same time, the long-time Cement Creek and Gunnison based Sweitzer family sold their gas station and convenience store, the Take-Away-Market, to a local consortium of pioneers and settlers. It consisted of Frank Pillsbury, Carl Verplank, Jim and Joan Adams, and Myles Arber. It became the first supermarket in town and, according to the Chronicle editor, was "... one of the largest grossing operations in the community ..."

Within a week following the 1974 election, Myles Rademan organized another community conference. It was sparsely attended compared to earlier ones. That mirrored the low turnout for that year's election, for essentially the same reason: many pioneers did not think their views mattered to the local power group. That year's conference was attended by a few ski area trailblazers, pro-growth tourist town pioneers, and some recreation community settlers. According to Rademan, those present called for the formation of a town "planning commission" so there would be input from diverse community members concerning the direction, policies, and practices of town government. Rademan agreed, but insisted that input be managed, and a structure created to do that, so the advice could be controlled. He said the planning commission should "… be appointed by the Council … *under the advice of BKR Associates* [emphasis added] other experts, and the Council." Ultimately the commission had twenty-eight members, with an executive committee of six. Four of those six were consistently growth oriented.[1]

The town was changing. The process of "rural gentrification" had taken hold. As in the more well recognized urban version, at first young artists, craftspeople and intellectuals, many of whom were alternative culture proponents and political outlaws who were looking for inexpensive and unknown places to live settled there; they were welcomed into a financially depressed area and eventually accepted. Then, as residents found their properties appreciating and that other people wanted to live in that community, another wave of newcomers came that began renovating and rehabilitating properties and re-selling them; and improving the community infrastructure. These people wanted to make a living in the newly revitalized local community. Businesses, including local real estate offices, opened that catered to the new local residents and to their more up-scale tastes. Still later in the process, ever more affluent people began arriving and still more luxurious amenities were provided to residents; by then, the original trailblazers and pioneers in the gentrification process were long gone, with the exception of those who had become local entrepreneurs.

By 1974, in Crested Butte, that transition was noticed by many of the early pioneers, and their dismay and disgust was clear. Cordley Coit, for instance, wrote a long open letter to the editor asking rhetorically if the town really was interested in the arts. Then he answered:

No, vis-à-vis closing the theater, no arts fair, Fear of Arts and Artists, actors, poets, sculptors, potters, dancers, weavers, filmmakers and musicians are all firstly not a wealthy class of people in Colorado that means they do not pay taxes, buy real estate, face it that's what Crested Butte is about. … What I am saying is that the town's face right now is the face of an uncouth barbarian and the only way that face can change is through education and money. Money for let's say a building which could act as a center for both visual and performing arts. A gallery with studios and rehearsal rooms and proper theater admissions and gallery fees …. As a biased observer, an arts complex … would make Crested Butte a better place to live …when any person arrives here they marvel at the prices people get for sub-standard housing. No artists, except the very rich can afford the slums of Crested Butte. And the politicians in Town – they too are real estate people. What do the mayor, the judge, the D.A. and the new Marshal [McClung] do besides sit around and play monopoly? …the town government, which can afford streets, sewers, parks, water systems, planners, police, judges, dogcatchers, inspectors and secretaries but cannot or will not even give the slightest encouragement to the arts. What sort of people does the Town wish to attract? …. without the town doing something, it will stay as it is: small, dirty and dull to the outsider.

As the town council shifted to one where *all* members supported virtually each effort to stimulate tourism and growth, other changes occurred. Town leaders reinforced each other, worked toward the same ends and, as the Lynds observed in their seminal 1929 book *Middletown*, became the town's local power structure by the mid-1970s. A new bank was chartered and incorporated. The Home Rule Charter Commission, not surprisingly, recommended that the town become "home rule" and hire a professional manager. Several new up-scale restaurants opened. New professional offices including medical practices and law firms, architectural, engineering and accounting businesses opened. All those professional businesses depended on the town growing. A leading "hip" real estate brokerage that sold properties mainly to pioneers, Montrose and Associates, whose logo had been a red amanita mushroom, (that some pioneers thought was a hallucinogen), was sold to recreation community settlers Tom Cox and Peter Hagen, both of whom were growth-oriented and part of the local power structure. BKR Associates received additional contracts from the town and became entrenched among the town trustees and the other "leading" townspeople, until each principal partner accepted permanent paid positions with either the town or county government.

During a four-year period, beginning in spring 1972, the relatively small group of like-minded individuals who wanted to develop a tourist town that catered to increasingly well-off visitors, not only controlled the town's public decision making, but also the major business institutions and non-profit organizations. The council hired consultants to formulate and advocate for town and county-wide plans, began a tourism advocacy and support organization, financially supported the newspaper that endorsed its efforts by awarding it the official legal notices, and controlled and redefined law enforcement. The council also replaced the town magistrate and appointed a member of the local power clique to the position. The leading citizens who pushed "smart growth" created Crested Butte's main new community institutions; they "made things happen." Indeed, they laid the very foundation for what is today's modern, amenity laden, up-scale, sophisticated tourist town and recreation community.

During a four-year period, beginning in spring 1972, the relatively small group of like-minded individuals who wanted to develop a tourist town that catered to increasingly well-off visitors, not only controlled the town's public decision making, but also the major business institutions and non-profit organiza- tions. …. They "made things happen." Indeed, they laid the very foundation for what is today's modern, amenity laden, up-scale, sophisticated tourist town and recreation community.

Even as they increasingly determined what happened inside town, the local power group realized random development would occur in the northern Gunnison Valley if they could not influence county thinking and decisions. Recognizing that, they focused on important county-wide issues, beginning with planning, or its lack thereof, and that the county commissioners had no concept about where development should occur, or what type it should be. In May 1974, David Leinsdorf declared his candidacy for a seat on the Gunnison County Commission. He won overwhelmingly. His platform, for the first time in the County's history, included planning, environmental considerations, and a recognition that the county population was changing. In a paid political advertisement, he said he was running:

For initiative and imagination in managing Gunnison's growth; for pre-serving Gunnison's meadowlands and slopes by concentrating develop-ment in existing developed areas; for increased citizen input in public decisions; for increased cooperation between government bodies and districts." Shortly before the election he publicly announced that he was "anxious to get the Board to start taking the initiative in regard to man-aging and directing the County's growth...

When he began his campaign, Leinsdorf resigned as Crested Butte town attorney. The first recreation community settler town council appointed Wes Light as his successor. During his tenure as chair of the Home Rule Commission, Light had become a central figure as Crested Butte pursued growth. He continued being a key player in that pursuit after his appointment. He was part of the "brain trust" that formulated and implemented what they defined as environmentally-oriented develop-ment. After town electors voted for "home rule" in 1974, in the next January 1975 election, each successful candidate called for still more development. It was the *second* "recreation community settler" council.

The new mayor was Tom Glass, who ran unopposed. He had been the most pro-development town council member since he was first elected to the pioneer council in 1972. Further, five of the six new council members elected in the January '75 "home rule" election owned businesses in town; the other was a young cartoonist who also supported "smart" growth.

Sandra Hickok, one of those elected, owned and edited the recently formed second town newspaper, The *Crested Butte Pilot*. She received the fewest votes (113). Joe Blumberg, the former deputy marshal, received the second lowest number and Tom Cox barely received enough votes to win a seat. Because those three received the fewest votes, they had to stand for re-election less than a year later. Alan Rowitz, co-owner of The Finishing Touch and also a real estate salesman, garnered the greatest number of votes (173). The cartoonist, Ken Hall, won almost as many (171), and Dan Gallagher, a local pro-development audio equipment small business owner who was first elected to the pioneer council, got the third highest number. Glass and at least three new council members — Cox, Rowitz, and Gallagher — were key components of the growth-oriented local power structure.

Ten months later, in November 1975, the town held yet another election. The Home Rule Charter specified that after home rule was adopted, three council people who received the greatest numbers of votes would serve full terms; the other three would finish their terms at the end of October, when another election had to be held to fill those vacancies. That meant council members' terms of office would be staggered in succeeding years. Commission members thought the electorate should make the decision about who should be a councilperson if at all possible, and with staggered terms they thought that would be more likely.

In the second 1975 election following the community becoming a home rule town, incumbent Mayor Glass soundly defeated his declared opponent, renegade Norm Johnson (133-17). Johnson was a pioneer "outlaw" who, although he was a high energy, small-particle physicist, could not get a job in his profession because he refused to work on nuclear weapons, was actively anti-military, and against the Vietnam War. He hardly campaigned. When he posed for his candidate photo for the local newspapers, for example, he shielded his face from the camera. He was not seen as a serious candidate by most voters.

Ed Benner, was a more significant losing mayoral aspirant than Johnson. He declared his candidacy late and became a write-in candidate. One of the few avowedly conservative pioneers, he had earlier lost a bid for a town council seat. He defined himself as a representative of the old-timers and the new people with families, those whom he said "had to work 40-hour weeks and were not trust-funders." He also disliked the local power group. Unlike the manner in which other candidates promoted themselves — in restaurants, bars, and at public events — he kept his effort low-key by going door-to-door, talking individually with residents. He surprised many townspeople, especially those in the town's power clique, by getting 77 votes. The winning candidates for the three contested council seats were the incumbent businessman, Tom Cox (148 votes); and two pro-growth newcomers, schoolteacher Candy Light (120 votes), and John Ingham (101 votes) an optician who barely won. Light recalled 40 years later that she was recruited by Myles Rademan who, when she shared her misgivings about being a political novice and told him she did not know much about the issues and was quite shy, he told her that she did not need to worry, "Because you're a teacher in the Crested Butte school and a woman, you won't even have to campaign." Notably, she was also the wife of the current town attorney, Wes Light, and part of the local power structure. Of those who lost, a young miner, Gary Christopher, came in fourth with 97 votes, almost as many votes as Ingham had received. As had Benner, Christopher defined himself as a political conservative, a voice for the old-timers and earliest ski area trailblazers, and against the local powers that he saw as a potent eastern liberal clique.

Because of Benner's surprisingly strong showing, the *Chronicle* interviewed him after the election for a long "personality profile." He discussed why he ran for mayor, and the different town factions, and he pointedly identified the evolving local power group, and his case against it.

> I ... found several [residents] that didn't care for either Glass or Johnson and planned to either cast blank ballots for mayor or just not come out to vote. ... the older residents ... recognized my commitment to this community and my maturity. ... I also hit a lot of conservative younger people when I went around with the voter registration lists ... those trying to hold down a 40-hour job and get themselves a little more stable. They ... spend less time in the bars and more in their work. Plus, they tend to be more family oriented. I guess I am speaking of the miners past or present or of the stable seasonal or year-round employees. ... most old-timers want to see more business coming in and perhaps even a revival of the mining industry. ... The contrast between their old Christian work ethic and the trust-funders and independently wealthy people coming here for a lark and an easy life is still very strong and affects them in ways that are hard to explain.

Responding to a question about younger business people in town Benner answered, "I know some of the younger people want to see more business here but there are also a lot who came to drop out or are on an escape from a bad trip elsewhere. That also accounts for some of the drugs and alcohol that present problems in Town, although I don't see that many drug cases. But I sure see a lot of drunks around on weekends." Regarding the old-timers he responded, "... they feel stepped on by the New Frontier which is making it look like all their ideals and values are out of date. ... They feel no one listens to them .... They are tired of all the dogs running

Poster Calendar. Courtesy of Susan Anderton. Original Artwork by Grower City Council of the Arts. (After repeated efforts, they could not be contacted).

… the dammed green strips on Elk Ave., the Town doing … hydrological work on Coal Creek flood control without … dredging it out in the past dozen or so years, the frivolous expense of tax revenue. Things like that." Regarding planning Benner added, "I don't agree much with BKR and … planners … I see myself as a practical man less concerned with keeping them in work than they are. Rademan … should now be working himself out of a job gradually as things get taken care of." In response to a query about an earlier answer he gave when he spoke about the "County Club set," he added:

> I was referring to a group in town that seems to stick together and all their political ideas seem to generate out of the cocktail party circuit that basically runs the Town Hall. … that whole crowd sticks together and socializes together and parties together and don't let a lot of other ideas in. … I call them the Crankites. It includes the Cranks, the Glasses, the Adams', the Coxes, the Lights, the Rowitz's, the BKR boys, Raymond Loken, the Levins and you too [Arber] to a degree – the cocktail and dinner party set.

What Benner did not seem to sense was the large number of pioneers who felt as he did about the local power clique, and became alienated from them. First, they withdrew politically, particularly from the ballot box. Among those who remained, reflecting their disappointment with the recreation community settler councils' bent for increased development, the decline in voter turnout continued. In that second 1975 home rule election only 235 of the by then 556 registered electors actually voted (42%). Simultaneously and subsequently, increasing numbers of pioneers left town. They moved down valley or left the area entirely.

In its first meeting in December following the second 1975 home rule town election, Dan Gallagher's council seat was declared vacant; he missed three meetings without an excuse and moved out of town. Forty plus years later, confirming the pioneers' suspicions about political shenanigans and collusion among the local power structure members, Gallagher said he ran for a Council seat only because he and his development-oriented allies, especially Glass, did not want Gary Christopher to win. Even though he knew he would be leaving town right after the election, he became a candidate to block Christopher. After he left, Gallagher received a formal letter from Glass that declared his seat vacant for cause. Gallagher laughingly remembered that at the bottom of the formally typed letter, in a handwritten note Glass "intimately" asked, "Where the fuck are you?"

Councilman Ken Hall nominated Christopher to fill Gallagher's vacated seat because he had received so many votes a month earlier. Hall was supported by one of the new councilmen, John Ingham. The council, however, rejected that nomination because Cox and Light opposed him as did Glass, all members of the local power group. Councilman Alan Rowitz was absent from the meeting. The only other applicant was Todd McMillan, another pro-development ski patrolman (as was Glass), and although the council rhetorically had called for other interested community members to apply, McMillan had been anointed. With that, the *third* recreation community settler council was in place.

In a *Chronicle* issue after McMillan's appointment, the first part of a Gary Christopher "personality profile" was published in which he discussed his formative years in Kansas, that he attended Western State College and studied geology, and then began mining in the Crested Butte area. A second installment was published the following week that focused on his political views and values. He distinguished himself from most other newcomers, who he saw as liberals:

> I had a conservative background myself and when I came to Crested Butte. I saw so many Easterners here and saw them as better organized, more ambitious, better educated as a rule, but that they had taken over and brought in lots of the problems they didn't appreciate in the East. ... look at who are in positions of influence in the County: Leinsdorf as County Commissioner, Kuziak as County Planner, Levin as County Judge, etc. [all new "Eastern liberals."] I am not suggesting like Ed Benner did that a conspiracy exists but .... I see common backgrounds and values and a great sameness to the Crank and Glass administrations in Crested Butte Town government. And I am sure they get together in their private homes to discuss how they feel the Town should be run.... social groups seem to run the Town. ... if you are not a member of that social group it is hard to get your ideas across.

In the same interview, in response to Christopher's charges of eastern liberal cliquishness and cronyism, implicitly confirming them, Arber rhetorically asked, "If the Cranks and the Levins and the Adams and the Baumgartners and the Rademans and the Kuziaks and Gerry Reese and the Lights and Rouses and the *Chronicle* and its staff and several others weren't here, neither would their energies be here. Who else would do for this Town all that they have collectively?"

In a sharply worded editorial, moreover, the newspaper defended the Council's decision:

> ... you don't have to be hawk-eyed to see that above and beyond the legal arguments and the rhetoric the Council does not want to appoint him to join them simply because of what they regard as his lack of personal qualifications and credentials. ... constantly criticizing and bad-mouthing the present Council and their employees in the Town Hall. Given that view, it is not too taxing to try and comprehend why they would not choose to work with him ...

Many of the people Arber named in his rhetorical question to Christopher not only made and implemented local policies, they socialized locally and vacationed together, created and led local quasi-government and non-profit organizations, and partnered in new business ventures. They became the "in-crowd," and profited handsomely from their associations. The original bank incorporators, for example, included Bill Crank, Tom Glass Ron Rouse, Tom Cox, and John Levin, Lynn French, Bill Frame, Alan Hegeman, and Steve Glazer. Besides the incorporators, most of the original stockholders were part of the pioneer and settler local power structure.[2]

At about that same time, the Crested Butte Businessman's Association was formed to promote the area. Two of its initial organizers included Cox and Eric Roemer. Architect Jim Kuziak was hired by the County Commissioners to create its master plan. Notably, knowing that in Gunnison County any type of government planning was controversial, especially among the long-time residents, Kuziak's formal job description was purposely left vague. Commissioner David Leinsdorf commented: "I'd rather have a little confusion than a lot of flak." At about that time, reflecting the close relationship among the local power group members, Crank and Leinsdorf formed a private law partnership because, as Crank said forty years later, "We were friends."

Eric Roemer, who along with Lynn Heutchy and Jim Kuziak, developed a successful, up-scale, tourist-oriented, restaurant, Penelope's, applied in early 1976 to renovate an old, dilapidated structure and convert it into another restaurant. He wanted to preserve it by rehabilitating its crumbling false front facade, but to do that he needed a change in the zoning law and he appealed to the town council and BOZAR members for that change. He said that if public officials really wanted to preserve historic architecture, it would have to grant concessions to developers. As one of the leading businessmen in town and part of the locally powerful, his notions were deemed insightful and practical. After minimal deliberation, given the newly created political structures and processes established for building approval, the major, large-scale, changes he requested were easily and quickly granted.

As this development-oriented group of pioneers and recreation community settlers consolidated their power and focused it on attracting affluent tourists and residents, almost all the alternate life style pioneers left the community. The direction in which the town was going was set. Those who wanted development invested heavily in new endeavors and reinvested in existing ones. They anticipated rapid and immediate growth in the coming ski season, based on the increase in tourism over the recent years and what they saw as the increasing propensity in town to support tourist-oriented economic development. In the previous year alone, 1975, although national and area-wide annual revenues dropped, in town they increased by 122 per cent. There seemed to be cause for optimism among local business people.

As this development-oriented group of pioneers and recreation commnity settlers consolidated their power and focused it on attracting affluent tourists and residents, almost all the alternate life style pioneers had left the community. The direction in which the town was going was set.

At the end of 1975 and continuing through the fall of '76, moreover, an intense confrontation emerged over a proposal by the ski company to expand its operations onto nearby Snodgrass Mountain. That fight generated a lot of publicity for the town and the area. Myles Arber, the newspaper owner and editor who had pursued business opportunities in Crested Butte since he first came to town, alleged improprieties by Howard "Bo" Callaway, the chairperson of the Crested Butte Mountain Resort corporation who was also the U.S. Secretary of the Army.

The newspaper accused Callaway of using undue political influence to have a key decision reversed by the United States Forest Service that would allow the ski area to expand onto Snodgrass. That allegation, ultimately, was never proved. However, the subsequent political squabble played out not only locally, re-energizing many of the dormant yet simmering community tensions, but also attracted statewide and national attention. In a spring 1977 interview, the newspaper editor said he thought the publicity about the conflict would greatly benefit the town irrespective of how it finally would be resolved (much as newspaper publisher William R. Hearst in an earlier era thought American involvement in the Spanish-American War would increase his newspaper's circulation).

In December 1975, a *Chronicle's* banner headline stated, "New Forest Service Plan OK's Snodgrass Expansion"; the "sub-headline added, "To be 2nd Ski Mountain". The accompanying report said a Forest Service's East River Land Use Plan had been only preliminary and was released to the public for study. The part of the plan that was likely to cause local controversy was the proposal to make Snodgrass available for winter sports use and available for the ski corporation to develop. The paper reported

> ... after coming out with its preliminary plan opposing expansion to Snodgrass, the several local Forest Service personnel opposed to the preliminary plan were transferred out of Gunnison County. This week the Forest Service came out with a new plan whose provisions proved diametrically opposed to the recommendations of the previous local personnel. No reasons for the 180-degree change in policy were given, although it seems that the policy considerations of the local personnel were countermanded from above. The growth problem is the key issue of the plan, due to the continuing dialogue between those that prefer to see Crested Butte remain a rural community, and those who feel that planned growth could only improve the economy of the area. ... CBDC (Crested Butte Development Corporation) would, naturally, be in favor of the proposed expansion if it could be accommodated comfortably by the county.

Two weeks later the newspaper's editorial called for an explanation about why changes were made to the "East River Plan," a plan that had been developed over an extended time period, and had substantial citizen participation and input. It recommended *not* allowing the ski area to develop the adjacent mountain.

A month later, the county commissioners, who by then included the newly influential Leinsdorf, addressed a letter to the Forest Supervisor of the National Forest, Jimmy Wilkins. The letter asked him to defer finalization and implementation of the proposed East River Planning Unit's draft land use plan that designated Snodgrass as a "winter recreation area" so that major and secondary impacts of the revised decision could be studied further. The request was granted.

That letter, and the consequent delay, angered and mobilized many long-term Gunnison County area people, including ski area residents, ranchers, former miners, and local business people, especially those who lived in the County long before the tourist town pioneers and recreation community settlers arrived. By mid-march 1976, one of those businesspeople, Bill Sweitzer, a Gunnison County denizen for over 30 years and part of the prominent Sweitzer oil company family, wrote an open letter to the Forest Service in *support* of its revised decision:

> ... While we must protect our environment, so must we continue to develop this environment to serve as many citizens as possible. I find it rather amusing to see ... newcomers to Gunnison County that oppose ... development of Gunnison that brought these people here in the first place. They seem to be saying, 'Now that I've found my place, to hell with anyone else.' ... development of the Crested Butte Ski Area will definitely benefit the most people by providing the opportunity to see and use what God has given us with as little harm as possible. With more than 80% of the land in Gunnison County being 'Public Land,' how can anyone fault the development of less than 1% of this land so that more people can enjoy it? This public land is not for the exclusive use of a few, but for the use of all.

By the time Sweitzer's letter was printed, the Crested Butte and Gunnison communities had really become riled up. Arber, the newspaper owner/editor, had stepped on many toes since coming to town and made more than a few local enemies (as had many others who tried to make change). He found himself under attack and had to defend himself. He devoted a series of *Chronicle* pieces focusing, not only on the recent history of the area and the East River Plan, but also about the likelihood that inappropriate influence was exercised by Callaway to have the plan's original recommendations reversed, so the area could develop Snodgrass Mountain. He also wrote about how he pushed to make Callaway's alleged influence peddling a national issue that involved U.S. Senate hearings into undue influence having been exerted by the Secretary who, not incidentally, also had recently been named the national campaign manager for the re-election of incumbent President Gerald R. Ford. (The hearings were conducted by Colorado Democratic Senator Floyd Haskell).

In mid-March, speculating about why he thought the ski company wanted to expand, Arber wrote about what he thought the economic realities were that the ski corporation faced:

> ... to attract new capital and maximize ... their remaining unencumbered assets ... to develop ... Snodgrass Mountain ... it first had to surmount two potential obstacles: clear County zoning and subdivision regulations and ... secure Forest Service permission to run lift lines ... the second of its obstacles. ... They applied to the Forest Service for a permit granting them development rights ... Seemingly, to influence his ability to overcome the second obstacle, on his last day as Secretary of the Army, Callaway held a meeting with the Deputy Under Secretary of the Department of Agriculture, under whose authority the Forest Service operates. He also asked the Under Secretary and the Assistant Chief Forrester of the Forest Service to attend.

Following that meeting, according to Arber, the Under Secretary said, "... I then asked the Forest Service to take a good look at the situation again in view of what Callaway had to say."

In succeeding newspaper issues, articles and editorials highlighted local conflicts that existed for many years between different segments of the Crested Butte community. Since his arrival in town, Arber mistakenly had been defined by many "growth-no-matter-what" residents as an anti-growth person who, when he first came during the pioneer's "heyday," was politically and oftentimes socially, a convenient guise for many growth advocates. But in the years after the 1972 election, many growth-oriented townspeople had "come out" about their views that favored growth. The *Chronicle* editor wrote pointedly in 1976:

> Quality and growth have never been the issue for us. Snodgrass has never been the issue. The editorial policy of the *Chronicle* has never expressed opposition to Snodgrass, never opposed Mountain Lair [another Callaway proposed development that was thwarted earlier by the county commissioners after extensive opposition efforts by pioneers], never opposed the ski area or its expansion, never opposed having an airstrip nearby, never opposed the expansion of Gunnison County Airport or the building of Meridian Lake Development. We backed the paving of Elk Ave. and the passage of an increased sales tax for capital improvements. We have wanted to see the Town Park improved and new services come into Town. People who accuse us of being anti-growth or wanting to limit the economic prosperity of this area would seem to have a very low level of reading comprehension. ... growth is not the issue. ... we are for growth and prosperity ...

In April 1976, on a motion made by David Leinsdorf, the county passed a six-month moratorium on development. It was also announced that the US Senate hearings into the Callaway matter would be televised nationally, thus insuring greater publicity for the area. Those decisions generated even more hostility toward Arber and others in the local power structure who, some thought, had aided and abetted the editor in pursuit of Callaway. Mayor Tom Glass and Judge John Levin, both of whom attended the initial meeting with Sen. Haskell, were especially suspect.

Terry Hamlin, who became Mayor of Mt. Crested Butte, and Archer von Louda, a successful Mt. Crested Butte businesswoman, wrote lengthy letters that attacked Arber for his muckraking about Callaway's alleged dirty dealings. Hamlin said he was raised on a farm in Grand Junction, Colorado, and worked at many jobs in Crested Butte from dishwasher to construction worker to ski patrol director. He astutely observed:

> During those years, the Town of Crested Butte went through an agony/ecstasy period corresponding to national trends: population

transfigurations, freedom movements, drug scenes, growth problems, water, sewer, ski area bankruptcies, mine and mill openings/closings, businesses starting and failing, war, peace, energy shortages, construction, development, economic recessions. This resulted in an influx of a new younger, liberal/radical majority who, by force of numbers and by virtue of their economic independence, became the citizens, the government, the conscience of the town, a town where they could afford to live, buy property, and dabble at business. Their dictating policy became: 'We are here now and this is where we wish to live. We will make of this town a living museum and save it from itself.' .... The permanent citizens of Mt. CB are ... like myself. They work hard, are motivated and occupied with making a living while providing a desirable town and environment, a place where they and their families can exist. ... you devoted almost an entire page of your newspaper to accusations, name-calling, innuendos, claims of political corruption and conflicts of interest, the forming of a municipality to serve a corporation's interests, puppeteering of Mt. CBDC employees. A number of year-round Mt. CB residents do have a vested interest in the success and growth of the ski resort. ... Your residence is CB ... so represent the feelings and thoughts of that majority if you must, though I question that you do. ... reserve your calls for purges of town Councils and municipal governments to that which is your own .... I am one who disagrees vehemently with your editorializing policies, techniques, beliefs, criteria and libelous, slanted journalistic practices.

The editor responded to Hamlin by saying that he had a personal interest in the ski area developing and therefore, unlike himself, he was incapable of seeing the bigger "moral" picture and, thus, he was immoral. The newspaper owner/editor did not admit his own self-interests, however, whether for personal publicity and self-aggrandizement, increased personal profits if the publicity about the area resulted in land and business price increases, increased newspaper circulation, etc.

The second letter, from Archer von Louda, addressed the kerfuffle between Arber and Hamlin directly. She sarcastically wrote:

... it is so refreshing to be able to pick up a newspaper and feel confident, that its contents are factual, unbiased and without ulterior motive. ... Yes, Myles, you instill such a feeling of trust between yourself and your readers. One becomes overwhelmed with the thought that your own behavior is totally selfless—your only concerns being those of fairness, justice and the good of the community. Of course, one advantage to living in such a small community is that everyone gets to know everyone. And those of us who know you and have had the privilege of dealing with you in business, know that you, yourself are the epitome of honesty, morality and strength of character; truly the 'concerned citizen' … If the hearings are to be conducted in Gunnison or Crested Butte, I am sure the resulting publicity and rocketing sales of the local newspaper are again just merely coincidental side effects that have not crossed your mind.

Keeping the fires of controversy burning and generating continued publicity, two weeks later a poignant petition was presented to the Crested Butte Council by a number of long-time area residents. It supported the Forest Service's new position. It said, "… we, as adults raised in this area would like to see skiing extended onto Snodgrass Mountain. …we do feel that careful expansion … is vital to the economic and general welfare of the people in this area."

By this time the statewide and national print and audio-visual publicity had increased. It was widespread and, for the most part, supportive of the *Chronicle* while virtually all the local commentary was against him. Even his pro-growth allies distanced themselves from him, as evidenced by letters to the editor from Mayor Glass, who emphasized that he only met with Haskell once and asked him only three questions; and from Judge Levin who wrote that he too met with Senator Haskell, but not as the county judge, merely as a concerned private citizen. That did not stop Arber. He continued on his quest, and further inflated his sense of self-worth even comparing himself in one speech to Eugene V. Debs, the great civil libertarian, International Workers of the World union leader, and five-time Democratic Socialist presidential candidate.

At the same time, the *Chronicle* editor also pleaded for financial support by claiming that a local boycott of his paper by a few businesses was hurting it. That was ironic because he profited handsomely from his many Crested Butte investments, and fanned the publicity flames that increased area property values by commenting about the historic confrontations in the community:

> All the old divisions … are beginning to show themselves again in the heat of these times. The community is forced to acknowledge splits between the Town and the Mountain, between Crested Butte and Gunnison, between the businessmen and other residents, between young and old, between Easterners and Westerners, between old-timers and newcomers, between pro-growth and anti-growth segments, between liberals and conservatives, between those in favor of corporate control over this end of the valley and those opposed, and most significantly, between people and their neighbors. We acknowledge our part in stirring up a whole lot of dust.

By the end of May 1976, the Senate Snodgrass hearings in Washington ended. The issue seemed to have died down locally. However, legal actions against Arber were initiated that summer by at least three employees of the ski company, two of whom were also Mt. Crested Butte Council members; rallies and fund raisers in support of the newspaper editor were also organized. Those actions were also publicized and covered nationally, a boon to those who thought the publicity would help the area develop quickly. One insightful national press commentator concluded that, in fact, the protagonists on either side of the political brawl could agree on only one thing: all the publicity was good for the area.

The protracted melee generated an enormous amount of press coverage for Crested Butte relative to anything that preceded it. The 1975-76 ski season ended, local businesses had done well and almost everyone looked forward to a banner summer with new events scheduled to attract tourists, plenty of new construction, and greater overall prosperity. In August 1976, for example, it was announced that five new restaurants would soon open.

The sense of community well-being continued through the fall. Along with the crystal-clear streams, yellowing aspen leaves, and crisp autumn air, there was a general community feeling of well-being. In November 1976, Myles Rademan conducted another community assessment, a "Community Update." It showed that major changes had taken place in the community since its earlier survey in '73. Although the research methodology between the two studies differed, (with the second one using a less "representative sample" because it gathered data only from those who actively participated in the day-long community conference about the town's future; thereby collecting information from only those who were most politically and socially active and involved), the comparative results of the two studies were notable. Most significantly, the second study group's average age was older (30+ years compared to 26), and its members were in town longer (5 years compared to 2). Additionally, 70% expected to stay in Crested Butte for at least 5 more years. These were people who were settling in, and their need for economic security was growing. Housing shortages and quality educational opportunities for young people were still seen as major town problems, as were diversified recreation and cultural opportunity, and good jobs. In the second study, most people thought the town was about the right size, which was a 2-3 times greater proportion than when the first survey was conducted, and over one-third wanted the town to grow; only 8.5% thought it was too big.

Rademan convened another meeting that fall, but that one was county-wide. It specifically addressed the recent Snodgrass Mountain controversy, and the intense emotions it raised. At the meeting, Rademan proclaimed that the town government policies had been consistently pro-growth. He did so, despite his continued active participation with environmental action organizations, which wanted to slow growth, and in response to the widespread perception in the county that he and the town council for which he was the staff planner, were anti-growth. Former Mayor Crank explained that his earlier defeat of Al Appleby by a large margin was because Appleby ran on a no-growth policy while he, Crank, supported development (although he greatly overstated the numbers of his political victory, saying the vote was 440-40 compared to the 241-46 it actually was). According to Crank, this showed that Crested Butte townspeople, in fact, wanted growth. Mayor Glass, at that same public meeting (as reported in the *Chronicle* and, presumably, in support of that position) "read from the Land Use Policy Statement drawn up by the [pro-growth Recreation Community Settler] Council" that previous September 1975.

By that time, all the local power players clearly had come out regarding development; they supported it in virtually every possible way. Growth, which four years earlier was opposed by over half the townspeople, mainly tourist town pioneers, now was supported by the majority, most of whom had come to town as recreation community settlers. Since 1973 Rademan had successfully organized annual conferences as a way of taking the "pulse" of the rapidly changing community, and to use those conferences to prepare residents for the next stage of development. This time the 1976 community conference theme reflected the changes that had occurred. It asked rhetorically, "Should Growth Now Be Encouraged?"

Accelerating the pressures to develop and grow, during the winter of 1976-'77, an environmental disaster occurred, at least one for a tourist town based on winter recreation: snow failed to fall. In December, less than 3 inches of snow fell compared to the average 40 inches. Major snowfall did not begin until the end of February, by which time almost all the businesses and those who worked in them had suf-

Accelerating the pressures to transition, develop and grow, during the winter of 1976-'77, an environmental disaster occurred, at least for a tourist town based on winter recreation: snow failed to fall.

fered drastically. It was typical at that time for approximately 40% of annual revenues to be generated during the Holiday Season. For that entire ski season only 61 inches of snow fell. The lack of snow in early winter and the sparse amount thereafter became the town's dominant social, psychological and economic force.

Locals called it, "The Winter of Un." No snow meant fewer tourists, especially compared to local expectations and projections. Many of the new small business-people invested everything they had in their businesses, anticipating a banner year based on the town's recent growth. Although they were undercapitalized, businesses expanded and upgraded their offerings, whether they were ski shops, restaurants, or art galleries. Insufficient capital caused many to fold or change ownership; that intensified the changes in town attitudes toward development that had been occurring during the previous four years. The strain on business owners and, of equal significance, the belt tightening and exodus from the town by those who worked in them, produced another major change in the new population that came to town.

Although ideologically and rhetorically many business owners did not like or want to rely on federal or state assistance, two-thirds responded to a town survey by saying that they would like the town declared an economic disaster area so they could qualify for low-interest government loans. They thought that if government monies were available, they should apply for them. Some business owners, like David Bachman of the Bistro Restaurant and Eric Roemer of Penelope's, moved to urban areas like Denver or San Francisco to work as waiters or to work construction; anything to make some money. Personal relationships also were strained; long time marriages and partnerships split apart. A general malaise swept the usually upbeat area.

Despite the disastrous effects caused by the "Winter of Un," there was one important upside. The lack of snow caused the water in the town reservoir to freeze, as did virtually all of the town's water pipes. Snow cover usually provided insulation for the pipes, and the lack of it caused them to freeze. It affected everyone in town. Crews of young people, mainly the few remaining tourist town pioneers, including a few "outlaws," spent days in sub-zero weather thawing the frozen pipes. The old-timers and pro-development pioneers and settlers recognized and appreciated their heroic efforts, and their usual prejudices toward hippies ebbed for a while. The freeze, in essence, had a silver lining: it caused the steadily increasing confrontations between the pro-growth and remaining anti-growth factions to dissipate, at least temporarily.

Several investors with "deep pockets" who heard about Crested Butte and its current woes came to town in January and February of 1977. They tried to buy business and land "on the cheap." Most existing owners held their ground, however, and waited for better offers. Later that winter and spring, though, several sweetened deals were entered into by local business owners who had just had enough. Those business transactions brought in still another group of recreation community settlers who had even bigger financial investments than were made by those from whom they bought their new businesses. They wanted even more growth and development that would appeal to still more affluent tourists.

The widespread national publicity generated by the political clash with Callaway, et. al., coupled with the ski-town environmental disaster that collectively wreaked havoc on the psyches and finances of local residents, led to another major shift in the town's trajectory. Like a logarithmic curve, the desire for ever more growth rose, propelled by the increasingly affluent settlers who had come to town and invested in it (sometimes unsuccessfully for various reasons), and who wanted to appeal to their well-off counterparts. Wanting growth had become cool.

By the spring and summer of 1977, development was clearly what locals wanted. With the influx of new residents and investors following the "Winter of Un," financial success and a pro-development perspective was the *raison d'être* for their immigration, although living a high-quality life was also important. This trend continued to accelerate in the ensuing years and became ever more evident as land costs, development, and the purchase of existing businesses or starting new ones, or establishing professional offices, continued to rise dramatically.

Unequivocally, the major struggles over the town's direction were finally over. Crested Butte would never again revert to being a mining community nor would it ever be a "hippie haven," although both cultures and life-styles influenced its future direction. The mining town history was incorporated into important town legends and lore and became the focus of a town historical museum, The Crested Butte Mountain Heritage Museum.

Unequivocally, the major struggles over the town's direction were finally over. Crested Butte would never again revert to being a mining community nor would it ever be a "hippie haven," although both cultures and life-styles influenced its future direction.

The hippie's free spirit ethic, tolerance for different lifestyles, "doing your own thing," and "going for it," and living existentially in the "here and now," became an integral part of the recreation community's culture.

As the town's pro-growth movers and shakers had intended, from the election of the "tourist town pioneer" town council in 1972 through the third home rule "recreation community settler" council in 1976, Crested Butte had sown the seeds for the town becoming what it is today: a mature, amenity-laden, new type of town in rural America, based on attracting and servicing upper-middle class and wealthy tourists as the basis of its economy; and one that provides a high quality recreation based life-style and culture for its increasingly prosperous white residents; a recreation exurb.

Epilogue

In 1976, I stopped living full time in Crested Butte. Like so many who had immersed themselves in the community, I went back to the work I had been doing before. My focus broadened, however, from addressing mainly civil rights and anti-poverty community organizing and anti-war activities, to also working with environmentalists, organized labor, family farmers, clergy, and others. Later, as an academician, I taught leadership and management to executives from non-profit organizations, almost all of whom came from social service, environmental, cultural, or advocacy groups. Approaching my work and life differently than I had before I first came to Crested Butte, I became less of a "workaholic," and devoted more time to my family and friends, laughter, and play.

Although our family moved to Denver, for the following decade we still lived in our Crested Butte home during each four-day school holiday or longer, including entire summers. Like many others who experienced the magic of the town, I could never really leave it.

In the mid-eighties, we developed a self-storage business in town that I operated for 25 years, and I remained involved in the community as a business owner. I continued skiing on Crested Butte Mountain for about a decade. For the most part though, for 20-25 years, I did not volunteer *actively* in the community's organizational life, but Diane and I financially supported our favorite non-profit organizations, and spent a lot of time with our friends.

After we sold our Crested Butte house, I lived for extended periods during summers and shorter winter stays in a primitive log cabin without plumbing or electricity, located on Brush Creek behind Crested Butte Mountain. Fifteen years later, that 100-year old cabin burned to the ground. We then bought a small condominium just outside town that overlooked a golf course. I still live in that condo complex during the four warm months of the year, and continue to enjoy the back-country and the area's increasingly sophisticated cultural offerings.

In the beginning of the 21st century, I actively re-engaged: I helped organize and continue to sit on the advisory board of the Crested Butte Public Policy Forum, co-chaired the Crested Butte Wild Mushroom Festival for seven years and, during summers, have hosted a public policy interview program and a jazz show on the local public radio station, KBUT.

Being a part of Crested Butte for so many years has enabled me to see things I might have missed had I not remained involved in the community. As the town and area around it became more developed and gentrified, for example, I noticed that its confrontations became subtler and much more genteel, more like those in the cities, suburbs, and exurbs from which most of the affluent new residents

As the town and area around it became more developed and gentrified ... its confrontations became subtler and much more genteel...

came. Eco-terrorism, for example, is a phenomenon of the past. Business transactions are no longer sealed with a handshake; they are handled by real estate agents. Now, even though Crested Butte residents continue to engage vigorously with local issues, there has been a proliferation of legal actions; lawsuits seem to be a first line of dispute resolution rather than the last one.

Most importantly, the culture wars between alternate life-style adherents and mining-era residents no longer exist. The extreme experimentation and wildness of the tourist town pioneers has abated for the most part, and the new people who come to Crested Butte are likely to be more stable. In the survey of town residents in 1973, 85% of the residents were under forty and most had lived in the town for under 2 years, and they were opposed to almost any development. They were attracted by the sense of community, the environment, and recreation, and they fought growth in the area. In a county survey in 2018, the majority of area residents were substantially older and had lived in the county for between 10 and 40 years. They were still concerned about maintaining community and were still mainly recreation-oriented, but they now welcome "responsible" growth.

Outdoor recreation activities are tamer too. For example, there are currently 750 miles or so of formerly rock-strewn hiking and biking trails surrounding the town that now are paved, graveled, or well groomed. Most of the rocks and tree roots have been removed so they do not hinder hikers or bikers. Similarly, more ski runs on the mountain are groomed, as are many of the back-country areas near town where cross-country skiers play in winter.

Outdoor recreation activities are tamer ... town cultural events have become more formally organized, even institutionalized, and are part of the scene that attracts new residents and tourists.

The multitude of town cultural events have become more formally organized, even institutionalized, and are part of the scene that attracts new residents and tourists. In a July 4th celebration in the second decade of the 21st century, for instance, Beverly Griffith, a retired Texas bank vice-president, who is a summer resident and local philanthropist, danced down the parade route on the town's main street in the traditional bright red colors of the "Red Lady" protectors, protesting a proposed nearby molybdenum mine development that the community has been actively opposing for decades. Forty-five years ago, one of the few mature, well-off, summer residents would never have done that. Individual informal events have become formally organized as well. The old-hippie, drug laden, outdoor weddings held high in the mountains, for example, have become a big business. In Mount Crested Butte weddings are now conducted in an area that was especially developed to host them, and they are lavishly catered affairs. The Club at Crested Butte, a few miles south of town, also hosts high-priced marriage ceremonies and receptions.

In general, however, it seems "the more things change, the more they stay the same." Most significantly and consistently, *over time, the forces of development overcome those that work against it.* People who want to preserve the environment or provide better working and living conditions for locals, ulti-

In general, ... "the more things change, the more they stay the same." Most significantly and consistently, over time, the forces of development overcome those that work against it.

mately lose out to developers and those wanting to stimulate growth and cater to increasingly wealthy visitors. When Crested Butte's "smart" or "controlled" growth group pushed out the "anti" and "slow" growth residents in the early 1970s, it foretold the social and political dynamics that would ensue thereafter.

Over the past half-century, despite short term victories for environmentalists and locals who advocate for affordable housing, in the long run developers have consistently won the battles against those who opposed them. Crested Butte, Mt. Crested Butte and Gunnison County have developed an infrastructure that can accommodate many tens of thousands of residents and tourists, including improved roads, sewer, water and transportation systems. Collectively, they paved and multiplied the size of Crested Butte and the areas surrounding it. As a result, an increasingly wealthy and older residential population can comfortably live and play in the area. Forty-five years ago, decrying any sign of middle-class life-styles, anti or slow growth local residents complained when even a Corvette or Mercedes Benz automobile drove into town, or a new 2000 square foot house was built. That opposition morphed into seeking and welcoming growth and wealth. Still, there are remnants of townspeople who value "living small." A commonly heard complaint among town locals today, especially those who have been in town for a long time, is "The billionaires are now pushing out the millionaires."

... despite short term victories for environmentalists and locals who advocate for affordable housing, in the long run developers have consistently won the battles against those who opposed them.

There have been periods, however, when the pace of growth in Crested Butte slowed. It ebbed when the national economy went through downturns. People tightened their disposable income belts and took fewer vacations. Growth also became sluggish when ski area owners did not invest in the mountain or in making the area more accessible. It suffered when the tourism industry became more competitive and skiers chose resorts that were closer to their residences or had improved amenities on their mountains. The number of "skier days," (i.e. the total number of skiers on a mountain during a single ski season), plummeted at Crested Butte Mountain from a high of over 600,000 to 300,000 plus days; its revenues also shrank. This decline followed the decade when the area stopped its most successful ever promotion, free skiing at the beginning and end of the season; simultaneously, other ski resorts in Colorado offered very competitively priced season ski passes. Furthermore, the ski area and local businesses struggle in years when snowfall is minimal, especially during the holiday season.

There have been periods ... when the pace of growth ... slowed. It ebbed when the national economy went through downturns. Growth became sluggish when ski area owners did not invest in the mountain ... It suffered when the tourism industry became more competitive and skiers chose resorts that were closer to their residences ... the ski area and local businesses struggle in years when snowfall is minimal, especially during the holiday season.

There are clear periods when growth accelerates. In winter recreation exurbs, bountiful snow years increase the local economy because a larger number of vacationers come to the area, and spend money skiing, snowboarding, and otherwise recreating. That further feeds economic optimism and leads to more development. Additionally, a change in the ownership group of a ski company, for example, produces a growth spurt, especially if the new owners have a strong track record in the recreation industry. It leads to investor confidence and new business development. In Crested Butte that occurred when the Callaway's bought the ski company out of bankruptcy; they previously had been in the recreation business in Georgia. When Jack Blanton developed and opened a golf course in the late 1970s and early '80s, it stimulated strong economic growth in the entire upper Gunnison Valley. Decades later, after a sharp decline in skier days, the Callaway's sold the ski corporation to the Mueller family. Because the Mueller's owned a successful ski resort in Vermont and people were confident in their abilities, there was substantial new business development and increased growth throughout the Crested Butte area. In fall 2018, the Vail Resorts conglomerate, a single corporation owning multiple ski resorts nationally and internationally, bought Crested Butte Mountain Resort from the Muellers. Even before the deal closed, during that summer, local realtors reported a significant increase in interest in local real estate, and a concomitant 20-25% increase in the price sellers were asking for their properties.

Paradoxically, growth also accelerates following a major downturn in the national economic cycle because many investors sell their under-capitalized local businesses, and homeowners sell their second or third vacation homes, often at losses. Most recently, that occurred during the first few years following the Great Recession that began in 2008. New investors with "deeper pockets" buy them and, as the economy improves, they continue the process of expanding and refining the local area.

As these processes unfold, importantly, the newer local residents' welcome growth more and more because they have greater financial investments in their businesses and residences. With the continuously escalating prices of practically everything, especially housing, the new town residents need the area to thrive. Meeting the needs of long-time locals, environmentalists, and the area's workforce becomes increasingly difficult.

Town officials are elected by locals. As part of council deliberations, town representatives continuously try to balance the forces of growth with the needs of local residents. In the 1972 campaign, the mayoral candidate and a few council candidates identified the need for more affordable housing for local residents. In the 1980s, local government in Crested Butte began providing space for employee housing. Mobile homes that were earmarked for locals were brought into an industrial-commercial area of town. Later, the town created a lottery so some local people could afford to buy vacant lots and build on them. The town partnered with Habitat for Humanity to build homes for low-income residents and, recently, the town government aided in the construction of a multi-story "deed restricted" apartment designated for town residents. The town provided incentives to homeowners if they fixed up the accessory structures on their property, and rented them on a long-term basis as dwelling units (ADUs), that are usually rented by locals. Notably though, that requirement was challenged by two out of state investors who are part time residents; and the locally elected town officials settled a lawsuit with them by having them pay a relatively small amount to the town so they did not have to rent their accessory dwelling units. In all likelihood, that case will set a precedent so, over time, those

Town officials are elected by locals. ... town representatives continuously try to balance the forces of growth with the needs of local residents.

living spaces will become either short term rental units or be allowed to remain vacant for the owner/investor to use as he or she desires. As has been the case for decades, importantly, in the recent county survey noted above, the lack of workforce and attainable housing was identified as the *most* important issue facing the area.

Town governments have expanded the free public transit system that is often used by local residents. Beginning with the Crested Butte Stage Line in the early 1970s, when it bused people between the town and the ski area, public transportation has expanded steadily. Now, bus service transports riders on a regular and frequent schedule between Gunnison, Crested Butte South, Crested Butte, and Mt. Crested Butte. There have also been on-going cooperative efforts between the Chamber of Commerce, Crested Butte, and Mount Crested Butte, to support local businesses and their workers in the "off-season," by allowing local residents to spend $80.00 on "Butte Bucks" to get $100.00 worth of purchasing power. This "money" can be spent only with local merchants (similar to the "scrip" that had been issued to old-time miners, so they had to buy basic supplies at the "company store").

This increase in development over time has changed the size of Crested Butte and the entire high mountain valley area north and south of it, including Mt. Crested Butte and Crested Butte South, and the developments between those towns. There are now approximately 2,000 permanent residents. It also dramatically increased the size of the local dwelling units. What used to be a "large" miner's home of 1,000 square feet, is now smaller than a house designed and built by local high school students as a school project designated for "affordable housing." Most new homes or remodels, many of which are second and third homes for their owners and often serve as "vacation rental homes" when their owners are away, are usually over 4,000 square feet, and many are much larger.

As the overall area evolved and became more sophisticated with many more activities and offerings of all sorts, the circumstances of the residents changed. Now, there are many more families with schoolchildren. The community's school enrollment has exploded exponentially. The tourist town pioneers' demand for high quality education ultimately resulted in a high-quality public education system (as is the case in most recreation-oriented communities). The school's excellent statewide ranking became a magnet that attracts many resident families, as do the many extra-curricular activities that are offered, and often involve volunteer "instructors" drawn from local community members. Parents typically benefited from high quality educations themselves, and have similar aspirations for their youngsters. (Notably, the parents or grandparents of the locals were the generation that first fled the nation's cities for the all-white suburbs in the 1950s and '60s, based on their articulated rationale of wanting "better education" for their children, compared to the education they thought they could get in racially diverse inner-city schools).

Another group, an increasingly large population of residents that is most visible in summer, is older than those who live in the area year-round, and they are wealthier. Many of them are the second home owners, and are retirees who want to maintain an active lifestyle. Notably, they often volunteer with, and financially support, local educational and cultural organizations.

Crested Butte still has a large group of young people, often single, usually in their twenties and early thirties, who remain the town's most visible population. They usually come from financially-secure family backgrounds and themselves are quite urbane. They are a large part of the workforce in the restaurants, bars, shops, recreation activities, and the like. Others among these young adults own and operate many of the town's small retail businesses.

With the area's growth and the increased maturity and prosperity of its newer residents, additional aspects of Crested Butte's community life grew. These enhance Crested Butte's quality of life for both its residents and visitors. Today, for example, there are many more fine dining restaurants, "boutique" shops, cultural events like the mainly classical month-long music festival, various educational forums, more varied art galleries, and a greatly expanded public radio station. There are well organized and publicized activities throughout the year and virtually each weekend during summer months. They attract constantly increasing numbers of well-off tourists. In the early 1970s, Howard "Bo" Callaway, former President of the Crested Butte Development Corporation, and Eric Roemer, initially of Water Street Associates and Penelope's restaurant, suggested that business in Crested Butte and Mt. Crested Butte could be greater in summer than in winter. As tax revenues substantiate, that is, in fact, the case now.

The greatly expanded community of Crested Butte, which once was solely a ski town, still attracts significantly more than its share of creative, innovative, and adventurous people. As noted earlier, in the mid-seventies, the town was designated an "Historic District," which pioneers thought would increase tourism among a limited number of people who were interested in old-west towns. In 2015, Crested Butte was also designated a "Creative District," which its organizers hope will further increase tourism among a much broader population of cultural aficionados. The "Creatives," as local *Crested Butte News* feature writer Dawne Belloise calls them, continue to start new events, athletic activities, and festivals. In their 1993 "coffee-table" book "*The Edge of Paradise*," writer Sandy Fails and photographer Nathan Bilow identified over twenty sports activities that were part of the town's recreational offerings. Since then, 15-20 more have been created. Now, on practically any given weekend one fun-filled festival or sporting event involves locals and attracts tourists.

> *The greatly expanded community of Crested Butte ... still attracts ... creative, innovative, and adventurous people.*

When Larry Tanning wrote a newspaper series about the history of the Crested Butte Mountain Theater, he said that the wildness of pioneers and settlers in the seventies could never be repeated. Indeed, it was a unique era. Undoubtedly, however, recreational drugs still fuel many current activities, particularly among younger local residents and tourists. Sexual freedom and experimentation still exist, especially for those under 90. Women continue to be strong and independent, excelling in athletics, the arts, and owning and operating a large proportion of local businesses and directing the many

> *... recreational drugs still fuel many current activities, particularly among younger local residents and tourists. Sexual freedom and experimentation still exists, especially for those under 90. Women continue to be strong and independent, excelling in athletics, the arts, and owning and operating a large proportion of local businesses and directing ... non-profit organizations .... People who choose to move into town ... continue to go through life changes, including among those who are more mature. There are still plenty of people trying to live in the "here-and-now" and "go for it,"*

non-profit organizations in the area. People who choose to move into town, often to escape the anonymity of urban and suburban life and to seek the intimacy of a small-town, continue to go through life changes, including among those who are more mature. There are still plenty of people trying to live in the "here-and-now" and "go for it," although perhaps fewer proportionately than in Crested Butte's formative tourist town and recreation community era; they also do so with greater wealth and, perhaps, with greater caution. A cursory reading of the current newspaper's weekly "police blotters" shows that even with a police department that is very much more traditional than it was, and now stylistically is like any exclusive suburban or exurban police force, most police contacts and arrests are in one way or another alcohol related. That was what Joe Rous noted when he resigned his deputy marshal position 45 years ago.

Over the past half century, in many ways, Crested Butte has developed and become substantially more cosmopolitan. Importantly, the town is still evolving and it will develop further. In fall 2018, for example, the town council debated whether to allow franchise retail businesses in town, a proposition opposed by most local restaurants and small boutique shop owners but, undoubtedly, over time they are likely to be welcomed by new voting locals. Most tourist towns and recreation communities in the mountains and near lakes and oceans have grown, and continue to evolve, in similar ways. Originally working-class, tight-knit, small-town rural communities, they have become rural enclaves of temporary escape where affluent people go for recreation, rejuvenation, or to "live the good life."

> ... the town is still evolving. ... Most tourist towns and recreation communities ... have grown, and continue to evolve, in similar ways. Originally working-class, tight-knit, small-town rural communities, they have become "rural enclaves of temporary escape" where upper-middle and upper-class people go for recreation, rejuvenation, or to "live the good life."

266

These communities have become reserves for people who can afford to play in them. Born of the prosperity of the post-WW II era and set amidst magnificent rural land and sea scapes, coupled with modern technology, over the past 60 plus years "destination" tourist towns and recreation communities have become America's "recreation exurbs." Although they are not identified with a particular city, these newly created areas service the re-creation needs of cosmopolitan residents, and the tourists who often travel vast distances to go to them for their individual and family pleasure. Collectively, these now well-groomed modern outdoor recreation areas have truly become America's newest playgrounds.

These communities have become reserves for proplr who can afford to play in them. ... over the past 60 plus years "destination" tourist towns and recreation communities have become America's "recreation exurbs." Although they are not identified with a particular city, these newly created areas service the re-creation needs of cosmopolitan residents, and the tourists who often travel vast distances to go to them for their individual and family pleasure. Collectively, these now well-groomed modern outdoor recreation areas have truly become America's newest playgrounds.

---End---

A Note on Research Methodology, Memory, and Myth

In some ways, I began this study more than 50 years ago even before I became a Crested Butte *local,* when I was first an occasional visitor and then a *"summer person."* I recognized something culturally and politically meaningful was happening, although I could not identify exactly what it was. I knew our nation and, in fact, the whole world, was in the midst of major upheaval. Even though it was rural and isolated, I had no reason to think Crested Butte was exempt from the phenomena. Indeed, to the contrary, it seemed that I was in a unique variation of what was then called the *"youth culture"* that swept the Western world and was critical of and in conflict with "the establishment."

Later, after I moved to Crested Butte and the area was in an early phase of becoming the community it is today, it reminded me of other places in earlier eras about which I had read, or seen myself, in which young, adventurous, creative people gathered and carved new communities within larger existing urban centers, and lived new lifestyles. Examples of these included the pre-WWI art scene of Paris' left bank and the south of France with its collection of artists and writers; the "beatniks" in San Francisco's North Beach and in New York City's Greenwich Village during the 1950s; and the 1960s' "hippies" in New York's East Village and the Haight-Ashbury district of San Francisco. All of these gathering places paved the way for, and were the earliest stages of, what became known as *"gentrification,"* the conversion of previously existing urban communities of poor people into affluent neighborhoods. Although Crested Butte exists in a rural setting it is, nevertheless, another example of that process. It is a typical example of *rural* gentrification.

After I became a full-time resident, I proposed a study to the Russell Sage Foundation, the social science research funding organization, for which I and two other sociologists had just finished a two-year consultation. In my July, 1972 letter of inquiry, I wrote:

> I would like to study the process of social, economic, and political change using the community in which I am living …. Traditionally, Crested Butte has been an isolated mining town …. However, in 1952 the biggest coal mine closed and with it the townspeople faced harder times than they had during the Great Depression. Within five years…the town's population dwindled from approximately 1,300 to 300 people. … In recent times the rapidly expanding recreation industry has formed a new economic base. … Within the past four-and-a-half years … the town's population has tripled … and there is no indication that the 'population explosion' will stop soon. … Included among the new town immigrants are about ten non-practicing lawyers (one of whom was an Assistant District Attorney in Brooklyn … and another who was … project director for the study of banking and big business … conducted by Ralph Nader's Center for Corporate Responsibility); there are two architects, a town planner, a half dozen teachers, three social scientists, two geologists, two journalists, a physician and two nurses, an advertising executive from Madison Avenue, a vice-president specializing in marketing for a major greeting card company, a senior partner in a Boston investment firm, two interior designers, a former staff member of the Illinois Council for the Arts and Humanities, and a host of…businessmen (including several building contractors…). In addition, there is a large group of craftsmen … students and student types. Virtually all the new townspeople earn their living…from the booming recreation industry. … When these new people are imposed on a group of tough, old-time Croatian-Slovians [sic] …there are bound to be profound cultural and political differences …. These differences are likely to create great pressures for change …. In addition … the drama is set within a county … which itself is under-going major changes. … There is a growing tension between the ranching interests (that control the county) and the recreation interests that want to develop …

My proposal was turned down.

A half-year before I proposed that study, I began a detailed diary. It amounted to almost 100 single-spaced, small-font, typewritten pages.

270

More than 40 years later, that diary became a source for this work, along with regular correspondence with one of my personal friends on the East Coast. Four-and-a-half years later, I conducted a "participant observation" field study for a Ph.D. anthropology course on "The Effects of an Environmental Disaster on a Mountain Tourist Town." Locally, since there was almost no snowfall, that winter became known as the "Winter of Un." For that project, I recorded almost 300 pages of notes from my observations, conversations, and formal interviews, mainly with the new town residents who came to Crested Butte after the ski area was established.

Beginning in 2011 and continuing for the ensuing six years, I interviewed people who had been year-round *locals* in Crested Butte during the last half of the 1960s and the 1970s. According to one long-time local, woodcarver Will Tintera, about 100 of them have lived in the Crested Butte area since first arriving. As is the case with most former locals, however, the vast majority moved elsewhere and return to visit occasionally, often during summer. With the exception of one year, I have lived in the Crested Butte area during summers since 1968. Most people I asked to interview, but certainly not all, were gracious in granting my request when they heard I was trying to

... I interviewed people who had been year-round locals in Crested Butte during the last half of the 1960s and the 1970s. ... The 75 or so interviews, lasting two-to-six-hours each, were conducted as open-ended "unstructured" interviews. Although I knew roughly what I wanted to discuss and asked a few specific questions, I wanted our conversations to be guided mainly by the people with whom I spoke. ... These interview/conversations included a wide range of people. ... I asked people to talk in the first person singular.

make sense of and write about what we had done in those years. The 75 or so interviews, lasting two-to-six-hours each, were conducted as open-ended "unstructured" interviews. Although I knew roughly what I wanted to discuss and asked a few specific questions, I wanted our conversations to be guided mainly by the people with whom I spoke. These interview/conversations included a wide range of people. I met with long established Gunnison Valley family ranchers and those who were integral parts of the different factions of what became the new recreation-based community. The latter group, according to one woman I interviewed, was divided into the "empire builders", i.e., those who wanted to get rich from the town's development, those who "just wanted to make a living" and support their families, and the usually transient "good time Joes and Janes." Irrespective of the category into which an individual fell, although I told each one it would take about two hours, once we began almost no one wanted to stop. Some interviews took two and three sessions to complete. Many of them evoked deep-seated or forgotten memories. Several people, within 48 hours of their interview, emailed with additions to, or modifications of, what they had said earlier. Those interviews were especially revealing and helped me elaborate some of my existing concepts, and formulate new ones.

I purposely did not use an audio tape or video recorder. I thought either might inhibit our conversations, especially when we discussed "sensitive" subjects. With the permission of those I interviewed, I took handwritten notes. Then, within 24 hours, I entered them into my computer. I asked people when and why they came to town, where they came from and how they were reared, where they went to school, what they did while they were in town for work, play, and community involvements, what some of the "wild and crazy" things they did were, who their circle of friends were, what conflicts they were involved in personally or sensed in the community and, when and why they left Crested Butte. Because I purposely did not record the interviews, many of the quotations in the text, in fact, are not the precise words that were spoken. They are extremely close to what actually was said, since my notes were transcribed so soon after the interview. They capture the essence of what an "interviewee" said. For the purpose of this work, when the reader sees quotation marks around an *oral* statement, even though it might not be the precise quote as it was originally stated, it should be considered as one. All *written* quotations, by contrast, are taken directly from the actual writings I found in newspapers, magazines, books and other print materials.

I told the people I interviewed that I wanted to use whatever they said, but if something was too "delicate," I would not mention their names or those of any other individual about whom they had spoken. I knew some of what we discussed might be uncomfortable or embarrassing to them or their families, even though our interview/conversation took place decades after an individual's actions or something else we discussed had occurred. I told each person that if he or she did not want me quote something particular, he or she should note that in our discussion so I would be especially aware of it when I wrote up my notes and would not include that individual's name in the text. Reflecting the openness and honesty of the responses to even my most intimate questions, during several conversations or in subsequent emails an individual would say something like, "Please don't quote me about that."

I asked people to talk in the first-person singular. I wanted first-hand experiences and knowledge, not hearsay or gossip. In a few instances, if three or more people spontaneously mentioned something about a particular person with whom they personally had an experience, usually a local public official, and it agreed with what others had said about their personal experiences with that person, I considered that

... if three or more people spontaneously mentioned something about a particular person with whom they personally had an experience, usually a local public official, and it agreed with what others had said about their personal experience with that person, I considered that .... a "social fact"...

more than mere gossip. I saw it as a *"social fact"* and incorporated it into my thinking and analysis. Several people, for example, independently mentioned using drugs with a particular judge whom I did not interview. I considered that to have been more than part of the local rumor mill. Collectively it became a social fact, i.e., some judges used recreational drugs, an indication of the social reality of the times. Ultimately, that may have become part of the local community lore. In a similar vein, one or more person's recollections of events initially might have been based on hearsay, and might not have actually taken place, but by the time several people recalled the event or experience and mentioned it, that demonstrated to me that it too had, in essence, become a "social fact" and part of the town's collective memory, it's lore, and reflected part of the reality about the era.

Typically, once we began talking, my questions stimulated memories and, spontaneously, we often veered off course, even though there really was no fixed course. There was a lot of emotion packed into these conversations. We often laughed heartily and, on a few occasions, individuals wept. Most of our conversations took place 35-45 years after an event or series of events occurred. The formerly 18-35-year-olds were at least in their sixties and seventies during the time of our interviews; memories were fading, and specific events or details about them sometimes were hard to remember. David Kahneman, a Nobel winning behavioral economist, recognized this phenomenon clearly when he observed, "there is always a large gap between how one 'experiences' an event and how one 'remembers' it."[1]

> *specific events or details ... sometimes were hard to remember. David Kahneman, a Nobel winning behavioral economist, recognized this phenomenon clearly ... "there is always a large gap between how one 'experiences' an event and how one 'remembers' it."*

Besides my early Crested Butte diary, my field notes for the anthropology course, and the later interviews, I read *every* word in each available weekly issue of the *Crested Butte Chronicle* (well over 98% of those published) from Thanksgiving 1965 through June 1977, including the articles, editorials, gossip columns, letters to the editor, and the display and classified ads. I did the same with the *Crested Butte Pilot* for the three-years it was published. I read select portions of various issues of the *Mountain Sun*, a newspaper that was published for a short while, and several issues of the *Gunnison Times*. I watched, listened to, and took notes from audio and visual recordings of interviews of the mining-era residents who remained in town after the mines closed. These are archived in the Crested Butte Mountain Heritage Museum. I read my agendas, minutes, and other print handouts that were provided to town council members for the two years I served on the council during the 1972-1974 period. Additionally, I talked and corresponded with some people from that era about a number of specific events and issues, as well as some of my concepts about them as they were being formulated. Finally, I read the few tracts and books written about Crested Butte that were published by town newcomers, which were mainly about the town's mining era, as well as the small number of published works I could find on the post-WW II ski or recreation industry.[2]

Some individuals' recollections contradicted those of others, especially in regard to specific details, or as I remembered a particular event. More importantly, however, there was a lot of overlap. Sometimes personal memories differed with the way something was reported in a local newspaper, or in later published written material. When that happened, especially when individual memories contradicted what was written in the papers, I first questioned if people were telling the truth or if they did not remember details correctly. I thought the written word reigned supreme.

Then, I reminded myself that newspapers also report incorrectly at times, as evidenced by printed "public retractions," even in prestigious publications such as the *New York Times* or *Wall Street Journal*. I then recognized such incorrect reportage happened in

... I became less obsessed about the veracity of any one particular statement and more concerned about it as a social fact and then part of the local lore, and its significance to the social history of the area.

Crested Butte as well, because reporters and editors were often emotionally involved with the issues about which they were writing. I realized the local newspapers, indeed, might have incorrectly reported some important events. Ultimately, I became less obsessed about the veracity of any one particular statement and more concerned about it as an indicator of a social fact, that then might have become part of the local lore, and its significance to the social history of the area.

Consider one Crested Butte "*tourist town pioneer*" in the very early seventies, Ray Gambiski. He had been a former WSC football player and then became a combat Vietnam veteran who suffered emotionally from the things he had seen and done during his military service. He was missing early in one winter. Months later his body was discovered a few miles outside town, as thawing spring snow uncovered it. It was never clear, even after an autopsy, if the cause of death was a tragic accident or suicide. Three separate people said they discovered his body. Each town newspaper covered the story and named different individuals as the one who had made the discovery. The *Chronicle* reported that Sue Appel found the decomposed corpse. The *Pilot* reported that Roger Ross discovered Gambiski's remains. What seems socially most significant about that discovery is not the actual person who found the body, or even his death but, rather, that several people from that era remembered him as a very gentle and troubled man, who used Crested Butte as a place to recover from his tormenting military service as several other vets had, and mentioned his tragic death during our conversations many years later.

Similarly, a man who was young in that era distinctly recalled that a gun was shot into the window of a new motorcycle shop in town. He named two young men as the ones who did the shooting. The store proprietor, Dan McElroy, refuted that version. McElroy said, "It was Norm Pierce, Jr. [the town marshal], who shot up my store. It wouldn't have been _____ because he was so into motorcycles…." What is more important than the specific name of the individual who fired the shot is that in that era shooting guns off inside town limits was not unusual. The particular event had meaning because, although it was originally fodder for local gossip, it then became a social fact; part of the town's collective memory, lore and social history.

I began to sense that very few single events or a particular individual's memory mattered significantly in regard to the community's *social* history. It was more significant that a *collective* memory existed about an event or even a person. It illustrated the community's sense of social reality. Ultimately, it became part of its lore and legend. If an individual detail was disputed but part of a commonly held perception, I saw it as a social fact, something all cultures and sub-cultures share. The particular becomes part of an inventive shared history; something I think of as "collective myth making." Western billionaire businessman Phillip Anschutz noted that phenomena in a book he wrote about 50 people who made major contributions to the West's development. His book recognized that "imagination and actual fact merged to become reality."[3]

The particular becomes part of an inventive shared history; something I think of as 'creative myth making'.

A significant part of a community's lore and social history emerges from individual autobiographies, particularly those of its leaders. They are often transmitted as part of these leaders creating their own personal history or, at least, by the images by which they want to be remembered. This, too, can be a form of myth making, albeit on a personal level. When re-told frequently, they too become part of a community's collective memory, legend and social history. Myles Rademan,

A part of a community's lore and social history emerges from individual autobiographies. … This, too, can be a form of myth making, albeit on a personal level.

for example, the visionary Crested Butte town planner, described the reaction of the old-timers to his planning and organizing efforts. In each of separate conversations he had on the subject during the summer of 2015, Rademan said that one old-timer, rancher Tony Verzuh, often threatened to kill him. He said that he had to sleep with a gun given to him by a town marshal, Rob McClung. In the first presentation, he said he had to sleep with the gun for 5 years; in the second talk he said 7 years, and in the last one he said it was for 8 years. The number of years that Rademan actually had to sleep with a gun within reach is important only to his personal autobiography. What is socially and historically important, though, is that in the early 1970s, as an early settler who was a key player in transforming Crested Butte into a modern tourist town and recreation community, Rademan thought he needed a gun for self-protection from a mining-era old-timer neighbor who, like many others, was threatened by the changes in town that were brought on by the newest immigrants. Rademan's sleeping with a gun is meaningful to the community's lore and its social history as an indication of the social tension and conflicts that existed between the old-timers and the pioneers and settlers. It illustrates the intensity of the confrontations between the different social and political factions, especially between the mining-era residents and those who were part of the local power structure, as the tourist-oriented version of Crested Butte first emerged. That "social fact" was part of Crested Butte's reality at the time, and became part of its lore and social history.

Some of the Crested Butte cultural activities included *intentionally* fabricated local mythologies, such as those surrounding and incorporated into "Flauschink" and, later, "Vinotok" festivities. Both of these events have myths that surround them that presumably were derived from the old-timers

... intentionally fabricated local mythologies ... became part of the town's lore and social history.

Serbian and Croatian culture, and were then modified to include aspects of the newcomer's celebratory life-styles. These fabrications were important to a town economy based on recreation and partying. They too became part of the town's lore and social history.

Flauschink celebrates the end of the long winter and the highly anticipated arrival of spring. It boasts three days of revelry in the bars and restaurants, an outdoor parade and various ski events. Vinotok is a fall activity that celebrates the physical and emotional cleansing of the community, and the people in it. It includes a massive bonfire into which townspeople hurl all the things of which they want to rid themselves. Clearly, these intentional myths are more easily documented through newspapers and other written accounts.

Other town myths, notably, were unintentional and transmitted orally, as lore is traditionally passed on from one generation to the next. For instance, based on the experiences of a few of the earliest pioneers such as George Sibley, Susan Anderton, Allen Cox, and a few others there is a myth that the old-timers were decent, kind, hard-working, fun-loving, people "who were friendly and welcoming" to the new young people who came to town. Myles Rademan, when told about that forty years later, simply said, "I certainly never heard or thought that!" Sibley's oft-repeated statements describing the old-timers as fun-loving people who welcomed newcomers with open arms, and Rademan's story about having to sleep with a gun near his bed, although seemingly conflicting, are indeed both "social facts" that are part of the local mythology that eventually have become part of Crested Butte's cultural lore and social history.

Both intentional and unintentional myths have been important and even useful to the town's sense of community. Together, they have become part of Crested Butte's narrative, continuity, lore and, most importantly, its social history.

Endnotes

Introduction

1. "Old City Life," St. Augustine's Culture and Lifestyle Magazine, Vol. 8, Issue 5, 2014, pp. 11-12.
2. Abe Wagner, "Say It Straight or You'll Show It Crooked," T.A. Communications, 1986.

Preface

1. Lynn and Jan French, Steve and Rachael Allen, Harold and Leena O'Connor, George Sibley, Barbara Kotz, and Don and Adele Bachman.
2. Ron Barr, Mark Calve, and Rod Haller.
3. The old-timers were Fritz Yaklich, Willard Ruggera, Tony Verzuh, and Tony Gallowich; the early new residents included Mike Berry, Ray Gambiski, Dana Atchley and a few others.

Miners, Ranchers and the New Recreationists

1. See, for example, Kenneth Kenniston, "Young Radicals: Notes on Committed Youth," HBJ, College and School Division, 1968; or Richard Flacks, "The Liberated Generation: An Exploration of the Roots of Student Protest," Journal of Social Issues, Vol.23, Issue 3, 1967, pp.52-75.
2. Sandra Cortner, "Crested Butte Stories…Through My Lens," Wild Rose Press, Crested Butte, CO, 2006.
3. George Sibley, Handwritten comments on an earlier draft of this manuscript, printed April 30, 2017.
4. Don Bachman, "The Final Four Years of Tony's Tavern," Mountain Gazette, March 17, 2008 (slightly revised and edited 6/23/08).

The New Wild, Wild West: Drugs, Sex, Sports, and Art

1. The original officers were Adele Bachman, president, who with her husband Don owned Tony's Tavern and also Rags and Old Iron, an art and crafts shop. Hazel Gardiner was vice-president; Cathy Collier, an artist and graphic designer, was secretary; and Bea Norris, proprietress of the new, intimate restaurant, the Fondue House, was treasurer.
2. It was attended by goldsmith Harold O'Connor, weaver Lena O'Connor, seamstress Adele Bachman, photographer Sandy Cortner, wood carver Barbara Kotz, painter Gil Arnold, wrought iron worker Jim Wallace, and artist and graphic designer, Cathy Collier.

Mining-Era Women, Mountain Mamas, and the New Feminism

1. Myrtle M. and Michele Veltri, "The Crested Butte Melting Pot," Crested Butte, Colorado, 1973.

2. Notable examples included Mary Yelenick, a former school teacher, who co-owned the local liquor store; Martha Sporcich, who worked in her family's hardware store and gas station; Eleanor Stephanic who co-owned and operated the town's general store; and Gal Starika who, co-owned a popular family restaurant and bar.

3. Gary Ferguson, "The Great Divide-A Biography of the Rocky Mountains," The Countryman Press, 2006.

4. Other early female pioneer artists and business people included, included Barbara Kotz, a wood-carver who owned 'The Alphabet'; Lena O'Connor, a weaver and printmaker who owned 'Jacob's Coat'; Adele Bachman, owned 'Rags and Old Iron' that sold locally hand-made cloth-ing; Claudia Richards, a seamstress who, following Bachman's shop closing, opened 'The Needle and I'; Sandy Cortner-Hickok published (with her husband) and edited 'The Crested Butte Pilot'; Jan Murdock who first owned a picture framing store and later bought one of the most popular bars in town, 'Kochevar's'; Helene Teitler owned a retail bead shop, 'The God's Eye'; and Louise Streppa owned a photo shop that specialized in sepia toned family photos taken in old west frontier costumes. These women's' businesses were supported mainly by locals who pur-chased their various artworks, and also by a few tourists who shopped while on their vacations.

5. Bea Norris, with owned the first 'fine dining' white tablecloth French restaurant, 'The Fondue House.' She sold it to Gwen Thornton and Stephanie Switzer who renamed it "The Pot of Stew". After a relatively short interlude of male ownership when it became the first Mexican restaurant, Sanchos and, following that, the site of the town's initial Italian restaurant, the "Bacchanale", that same building was again sold and again became a French restaurant, 'Soupcon'. It was owned by Candy Smith who, with her sister Cathy, operated it successfully for several years. Judy Naumberg was the principal owner of The Grubstake Bar and Restaurant; Helene Teitler, after closing her bead store, ran a summertime restaurant, 'Yubba da Grubba'.

6. Jan (Freckles) Chatlain, Susie Fisher, Carol Wheeler, Lyn Faulkner, Sue Shoup, Leslie Diamond, Vickie Black, and Candy Hanson.

The Never-Ending Party

1. "'We' included Jeff Halford, Michael Helland, Greg Dalbey, Susie Fisher, Sue Navy, Craig Hall, Jim Gebhart, Rudy Damjanovich, Coney, Annie Karfakis, Brian and Carol Dale, Crazy Dave, Myles and Mickey Mulcahy, Denis Hall, Jack Marcial and some others."

2. "The Committee for the Fourth of July wants to thank … Jim Wallace, Steve Carson, Denny McNeil, Howie Johns, …Diane Kahn, Kate Sibley, Sidney Beckwith, Dave McKinney and other members of the CCPFC [Coal Creek Pig Farm Cooperative, a Western State College anarchist 'anti-organization' organization founded so each member could be 'president', and therefore could cast a ballot in the college's student government, and cause it to oppose the War in Vietnam] who put in time…"

3. Morgan Queal, decorations; Brenda Behrens and Cathy Wertz, trophies; Nadine Israel, timers; Cal Queal, judging the Gelande; Steve Allen, setting up the Gelande; Sandy Hickok, buttons; Art Norris, the parade; The Tailings (owned by Chuck Wirtz), the kite-flying contest; Martha Walton, the church service; Rachael Allen, the funny races; and Trip Wheeler, the motorcycle races.

4. Local exhibitors included: Susan Anderton, Frances Austin, Sandy Badenhoop, Dot Brown, Aimee Colmery, Sandy Cortner, Greg Dalbey, Homer Fenton, John Harding, Barbara Kotz, Gene Martin, Bob Prather, Wendy Prodan, Morgan Queal, Terry Stokes, and Jim Wallace. Out-of-state exhibitors included four artists, three of whom had previous connections with Crested Butte: Monte Hoke and Marsha McCreight, both of Oklahoma City, OK, Nina De Montmollin from Albuquerque, NM and Wilfred Duehren of Milwaukee, WI. The Gunnison exhibitors included Western State College art professor Pat Julio, Diane C. Neal and Shelly Hannon. The other exhibitors came from elsewhere, in Colorado: Robert M. Chapman came from Mineral Hot Springs; John Rothfuss was from Evergreen; Susan Dorris, Carole Waller, and Dorothy C. Harvey were from Breckenridge, and Bernard Heideman lived in Hotchkiss.

5. They were Denny McNeil, Barbara Sibley, Billy "Hee Hee" Folger, Fred Taylor and Jim "Zoo" Cazier.

6. George Sibley, "The Trouble with Money," The Crested Butte Magazine, 1992-'93 winter edition.

7. Steve Church, Carol Shannaberger, Barry Cornman, Brendan McHugh, and Homer Fenton.

8. Adele Bachman, "General Program Notes," Crested Butte Mountain Theater, 2011.

9. Jim Peters, Holly Hunter, Rebecca Terranova, Terry Turner, Dick Wells, Phyllis Baginski, Connie Dawson, Sonia Berthong and others.

Culture Conflict in Crested Butte

1. Plato, "The Republic," (Translated by Benjamin Jowett) Dover Publications, 2000. Also, for example, the classic sociological work by Lewis Coser, "The Functions of Social Conflict," New York: The Free Press, 1956.

2. Kelsey Wirth, "Reflections on a Western Town – An Oral History of Crested Butte," Oh-Be-Joyful Press, 2005.

3. Carroll Morgenson and Gene Martin, two early trailblazers; Rudy Verzuh, the town's postmaster; Helen Morgenson, a long term resident and retired school teacher; Willard Ruggera, the Crested Butte former town manager and a local contractor; Jim Cole, a trailblazer Town Council member; Walt Israel, an early trailblazer businessman and the accountant for the Colorado Rural Electric Association; Barbara Kotz, a pioneer wood sculptress, and Art Norris, the Western State College professor who was also an early town pioneer.

Town Politics and Elections: 1966-1971

1. Mark Calve, a former Western State College student who recently started a house painting business wanted all the people in town to 'work together' and to better the town's financial position. Don Bachman wanted the council to plan for growth, expand municipal services, better zoning, stable law enforcement, additional water sources, the creation of a city park, and the completion of the sewer system. John Cobai, a lifelong Crested Butte resident, wanted 'good law enforcement and a good judge', to finish the sewer system, and get the streets in better shape. Elmer Eflin, who owned new apartments wanted the sewer system completed, a town Marshall that was acceptable to the County Sheriff, additional sources of town revenues, regulations regarding snowmobile use, dog packs controlled, and the town rezoned. Albert Falsetto, who spent most of his life in Crested Butte, wanted the sewer system completed, law enforcement improved, and the town's economic base broadened. Tony Gallowich was a lifelong resident of Crested Butte. His priorities included graveling the streets and getting good law enforcement.

Tony "Whitey" Sporcich was another Crested Butte mining-era resident. He wanted the town streets repaired, dogs controlled, and the police department improved. He also said the divisions in town were a serious problem for the community, and was the only old-timer to appeal to all residents "to work together, whether as an old-timer or a newcomer, a liberal or a conservative, a right or left winger …". Doris Walker was a teacher in the community school. Her priorities included improving the town's streets and sidewalks, and the 'welfare' of the community and its citizens. Jim Wallace, a Western State College art student who sometimes served as a town Deputy Marshall, was another early tourist town pioneer. His priorities included rezoning and "the unification of our town." Dave Watson, was a native of Western Colorado. His priorities included finishing the sewer system, paving streets, and getting better law enforcement. Jerry Chiles moved to Crested Butte a year-and-a -half year before the election. He thought law and order and having a permanent Marshall were priorities for the Town. Owen O'Fallon was a Gunnison County resident for most of his life. He wanted the council to pass a good rezoning and architectural control ordinance, and for the town to find new revenues, and make sure the anticipated growth that was expected would benefit everyone.

Town Politics and Elections: 1972-1974
1. It included Bill and Sally Crank, John Benjamin, Steve Glazer, Bob Teitler, Dan Gallagher, Kathleen Stupple, and David Leinsdorf.

The Emerging Local Power Structure
1. The first Board of Directors included Glazer and Dalbey, plus Don Bachman, Jeff Shenkel, Dave Egan, Nummy Dennis, and Dyan Abston, all tourist town pioneers.
2. The Real World School planning group included Helene Teitler, Jim Adams, Jan Keyser, Eric and Kathleen Ross (nee Stupple), Diane Kahn, Adele Bachman, Alan and Marcia Hegeman, Diane Appleby, and Susan Applegate Robinson.
3. They included: Mental Illness, Myth or Reality, taught by a recently arrived clinical psychologist, Margret Bridgeford; Calligraphy: the Art of Beautiful Writing with Susan Applegate instructing; Performance Persona-Greek for an Actor, Dick Wells; Creative Movement, Dick Wells; Off-loom Weaving, Beverly Weiler; Individual Pottery; Beverly Weiler; Chinese Cooking, Patrick Hickey; House-plant Care, Patrick Hickey; Beginning Guitar, Bart Massey; Collective Vegetarian Cooking, Claudia Richards; Mime Workshop, Holly Longbotham; Silk Screening, Pat Dawson; Ski Touring, Gerry Reese; Stagecraft, Diane Kahn; Tae Kwon Do Korean Karate, Myles Rademan. Additional courses also were offered, including electronics, children's theater, carpentry, massage, astrology, photography, geology, pool, yoga, and auto mechanics.
4. Robert and Helen Lynd, "Middletown," Mariner Books, 1982.
5. In addition to Norris, those attending included Jim Kuziak; Myles Rademan; Ralph Clark, President of the Crested Butte Society and a member of the Upper Gunnison Water Board; Butch Clark, his son, who was asked to be the 'planning liaison' and who later became the volunteer interim county planning coordinator. Also attending were Gerry Reese, Myles Arber and Allen Cox, who owned the Nordic Inn and was one of the original members of the Crested Butte Resort Association.
6. The original board members included Ralph Clark; Gus Larkin, General Manager of the ski area; Dave Duval, one of the few conservative new pioneer town residents who wanted the most rapid growth possible and who started a real estate office, Ptarmigan Associates; and

Russ Reycraft, Jr., the former town marshal and the current postmaster. Another board member, John Liebson, organized that effort and was appointed the District's first Fire Chief.

Early Reactions to the New Power Structure

1. The Alpineer in Bill Frame's new Bullion King Building; the East River Café (which was under new management) in Steve Smith's recently refurbished Saltlick Building; and Gene Martin's Water Wheel (which, after a hiatus, re-opened under new management).

Town Politics and Elections: 1974-1976

1. Alan Rowitz; Dick Montrose of Montrose Real Estate; Peter Hagen of Cox and Hagen, the partnership that bought Montrose's company; and *Ed Benner,* the town's only surveyor.

2. They were mainly area businesspeople: sport shop owner Leo Klinker, Allen Cox, lumber yard owner Charlie Brown, Judy Naumberg, Irwin Lodge developer Dan Thurman, builder Bill Hickok, cable company co-founder Gary Gorbett, Penelope's Lynn Heutchey, the Elk Mountain Lodge's Jim and Joanie Adams, and Dick Sweitzer whose family owned the local oil business and Take-Away market and gas station, and Myles Arber.

A Note on Research Methodology, Memory and Myth

1. David Kahneman, "Thinking, Fast and Slow," Farrar, Strauss and Giroux, 2011.

2. Hal Clifford, "Downhill Slide: Why the Corporate Ski Industry is Bad for Skiing, Ski Towns, and the Environment," Sierra Club Books, 2002.

3. Philip F. Anschutz, "Out Where the West Begins," Cloud Camp Press, 2015.

Timeline

1952 — Colorado Fuel and Iron (CF & I) mine closes.

1958 — Law-Science Academy opens. California Players begin performing in Crested Butte.

1961 — Crested Butte ski area opens.

1964 — Snow mobile competitions start in area.

1965 — B&B Printers in Gunnison starts publishing the Crested Butte Chronicle. Fred Budy is the editor.

1966 — Spring town election and an all old-timer slate are elected; 164 residents eligible to vote. Sheriff Cope elected County Sheriff. Earliest tourist town pioneers begin arriving in town.

1967 — Crested Butte High School closes at end of school year. Old-timer Rudolph Somrak resigns as part-time town marshal; town seeks full-time replacement. Crested Butte Society incorporated.

1966-'68 — Anti- "hippie" and "drug use" articles and editorials appear in Crested Butte Chronicle.

1968 — 4-wheel jeep rally held in summer. Business and Professional Women of Crested Butte formed. Crested Butte Lodge Association formed. Mob forms and near-riot occurs in front of Tony' s Tavern. George Sibley becomes editor of the Chronicle.

1969 — Pioneers take up cross-country skiing, telemarking and other 'quiet' sports. Trustees ban snowmobile use on main street. First Flauschink organized. Pioneers organize July 4th for the first time. Peter Colwell hired as town marshal (but dies in car rollover one week later); Walter H Nezguski succeeds Colwell but is fired. In fall, Les Edgerton is hired as Marshall; only lasts a few months.

1970 — First dog catcher appointed. Russ Reycraft, Jr. becomes 'interim' marshal. With 200 eligible voters, old-timers and ski area trailblazers defeat pioneer candidates and win all offices. Don Brandon hired as permanent marshal; then forced to resign. Harold Mariott replaces Brandon; then voluntarily resigns. Food co-op opens. First moto-cross races held in area. Large influx of new pioneers arrives in Crested Butte. First pre-school started. Claude Porterfield defeats Sheriff Cope in November election and becomes the County Sheriff. Norm Pierce, Jr. appointed 'interim' town marshal.

1971 — Pierce, Jr. appointed permanent marshal. Crested Butte Resort Association formed. Food Co-op closed. First Summer Arts and Crafts Festival held. In summer, Myles Arber becomes editor and publisher of the Chronicle. Pioneer's pets killed. Challenges to town zoning requirements and building demolitions occur, polarizing old-timers and pioneers.

1972 — Spring voter registration drive (501 registered voters). Candidate Forum sponsored by Crested Butte Society, Women's Club, and Chronicle. Spring town election: 'pioneers' win *all* public offices. Pierce, Jr. resigns as marshal. Kemp Coit appointed as interim marshal. Crested Butte Mountain Theater produces first play. Aerial Weekend started. Leinsdorf appointed Town Attorney. Legal action against Blues Project initiated. The 'smart' or 'controlled' growth local power structure emerges. Local airport proposed, and fails. Historic District created. Board of Zoning and Architectural Review (BOZAR) created. Crested Butte Pilot begins publication.

1973 — In January, pioneer council contracts with BKR Associates. Blues Project suit settled. Resort and Tourism Association formed. Town of Mt. Crested Butte incorporated. Summer Festival of the Arts and Crafts discontinued. Summer meeting of environmentalists to address County planning issues, and formation of first environmental action group. Town 2% sales tax passes. Pioneer council opposes two large proposed developments in County (Rozman's and Callaway/Walton's). 'Crime wave' in Crested Butte. Fire Protection District formed. Conference for Developers held. Real World School formed. "Cyclones" ski program started. Free Access University organized. John Levin appointed County Judge. Leinsdorf campaigns for Gunnison Board of County Commissioners.

1974 — Growth-oriented pioneers and 2 old-timers (Cobai and Somrak) win all council seats; become the first 'recreation community settler' council. 'Home Rule Commission' established. Kemp Coit fired and Rob McClung replaces him as town marshal. Leinsdorf elected to Gunnison County Commissioners. Sherriff Claude Porterfield wins re-election overwhelmingly.

1975 — First Al Johnson Memorial Telemark Ski Race held. 'Klunker' bikes come to town. First home rule election held and second recreation community settler council elected. Third settler council elected. Conflict over Snodgrass Mt. expansion (Callaway vs. Arber) begins.

1976 — Water Street Associates proposes and receives zoning concessions from the town to restore the dilapidated Slogar Bar and Restaurant. The Snodgrass Mountain expansion conflicts are settled. Elk Avenue paved. Bi-Centennial 4th of July parade includes a float of painted naked women. Summer Festival of the Arts and Crafts reinstated as The Arts Festival. The first Pearl Pass Bike Tour takes place. The "Should Growth Now Be Encouraged" community conference was held. The 'Winter of Un' began and continued through spring of 1977.

Index